PAP   95¢

THE SENSUOUS GADGETEER

BRINGING TOOLS AND MATERIALS TO LIFE

BY BILL ABLER

RUNNING PRESS

1973

Published by Running Press
38 South Nineteenth Street
Philadelphia, Pennsylvania 19103

Printed in the United States of America

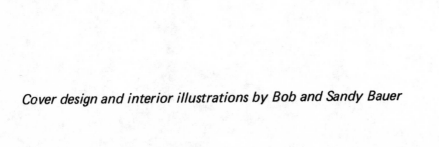

Cover design and interior illustrations by Bob and Sandy Bauer

To Castle Freeman and Alice and to my friends who pitched in at various times: Dr. Joseph Calvin, who saved my life twice; Sam Savage who showed me, among other things, the art of the paper airplane; Mr. Edgar W. Bailey; Dr. Benjamin Weems; Dr. James B. Neville; my friends who saw me through graduate school—Rob and Chris Evers, Akira and Noriko Fujita, Davis and Patty Gammon, Jim Knowles, Ray and Sandy Sauer, Steve and Linda Sears, Terry and Ginny Soules, Hon-chiu and Pauline Wong; Mr. Bob Engman, who gave me a job when I needed one; Roger and Kelly Chaffee; and, Annette Clampitte.

EDITORS NOTE

The Sensuous Gadgeteer is not an ordinary how-to-book. It was written as a continuous stream of ideas in the form of a conversation from one gadgeteer to another. The true gadgeteer will want to plunge in immediately trusting the author as his guide. Those who feel uncomfortable without a sign post showing what is ahead will be comforted by the excellent index.

INTRODUCTION

The Sensuous Gadgeteer is a guide to tools, materials and procedures that are within the reach of a small basement shop. The beginner and amateur (and low-budget) tinkerer, artist or scientist will find here plenty of information to see him through almost any project he can undertake, whether simple or complex. Because *The Sensuous Gadgeteer* begins with simple tools and materials (hammer, nails, wood, file, drill, saw, wrench) the beginner can use it as an introduction to manual techniques. He will find step-by-step instructions leading him through the motions for using these and other basic tools and materials.

After familiarizing you with basics, *The Sensuous Gadgeteer* describes the use of abrasives, adhesives (solder, glues), plastics (plexiglas, epoxy) and finally molds and casting. The last chapter concerns efficiency and effectiveness in the use of manual techniques. An appendix of basic devices, a bibliography and an index are included.

The description for each tool and material is presented with concrete examples (the section on sheet metal describes how to make a ring) so that when you work through the example to learn the procedures you will have a completed piece of work. But this is not a how-to book presenting instructions for the completion of a few projects; instead it gives you skill and insight into tools and materials so that you can plan and complete your own projects. The home tinkerer who wants to build a gadget to close his bedroom window before he gets up in the morning, the artist who wants to build a mold, or the scientist who wants to build a specialized gas burner will all find here not specific instructions, but plenty of information to guide the project to completion.

You will get precisely as much out of *The Sensuous Gadgeteer* as you put into it. Because the emphasis of the book is on understanding rather than on specific projects, read each section through before going over it with tools in hand. The only way to learn the procedures is to actually do all the projects. As you work through them your understanding and competence will grow. The only secret to doing good, reliable work with your hands is to give each step all the planning, care and attention it requires.

I am a professional scientist (a neurolinguist) and I build my own equipment. At just about 30 years of age I have been a basement gadgeteer for 25 years, and *The Sensuous Gadgeteer* contains almost everything I have learned about gadgets in that time, organized so that anyone can read it with understanding. My aim is to bring you down to the edge of the knife as it severs the wood fibers, and down inside the mold with the hot wax and metal, so that you participate so intimately in the interactions between tools and materials that you will always be able to make what you want, when you know what you want to make.

A guide for amateurs by one of them.

APOLOGY FOR GADGETEERING

Everyone can make things. Not everyone can be great at making things, but everyone can be good. All that is needed is to begin with simple things and then to put them together. In order to make good things (by things I mean sculpture, apparatus, and gadgets) you must *want* to make good things. The finished product is only the garbage of the work. It is the making of it that must be enjoyed. Then the excellent product will take care of itself.

Don't worry if you never made things before. Remember that Ben Franklin was a pretty fair violinist, and he prescribed this formula for learning: "Begin young, as I did, at age fifty-five. Practice regularly, as I do, while waiting for other people to keep appointments, and you are sure to succeed."

One last word. Making of gadgets and machines is a skill indispensable in art and science. Every sculpter is a gadgeteer, and many scientists have been gadgeteers, among them Newton (the reflecting telescope), Galileo (the refracting lens telescope), and Archimedes (the toothed wheel). I would even say that the genius of these men was a measure not of their IQ but of their feel for the way objects and materials behave, and a measure of the delight they took in exercising that feeling.

EXHORTATION TO EXCELLENCE

The purpose of this guide is to equip you to make what you want, when you know what you want to make. If you have a finished product in mind, this course will equip you to get it. Appropriately the first part of the guide concerns plans. In both sculpture and science the best plan is the simplest one, namely the one that gets the desired result in the fewest possible moves, and therefore with the least distraction or waste. In sculpture this means eliminating parts that do not directly contribute to the emotional effect of the work. This avoids confusing the audience. In laboratory apparatus this means using the fewest possible moving parts. This reduces the opportunities for breakage. These generalizations are Occam's Razor, and they are a superior guide in the choosing of one plan over another.

I am not an expert. My abilities are only adequate to my needs. Read the book and practice the instructions with joy— you will not be an expert, but your abilities will be adequate to your needs.

The book begins with simple things and tells you how to take care of the tools, so that you never have to be afraid of breaking anything. The guide will lead into design techniques, mass-production procedures, and inspection methods.

When you build a thing, do it once and do it right. You will not be going back later to rebuild things you "threw together" to see if they worked. Do a good job the first time.

Overbuild everything, because all machines are subjected to more stress than they were originally intended to take e.g., if plastics will do, use brass.

In all prototype machines make everything adjustable and make nothing permanent. You never know what you will want to change later.

For each tool and material, cultivate a feeling for what the tool is doing inside the work. Eventually you will reach a level of experience where, when you have an action or process in mind, you will automatically sense what device will perform that action, and you will know how to build that device so that it will work effectively without breaking. The path to that level leads through intimate and almost sensuous knowledge of the way materials behave and interact. You must be at the blade of the knife as it severs the wood fibers in order to know how the wood will behave. You must feel the flow of heat in conductors and in insulators, and be inside the mold with the wax and the metal. When you learn to identify with the materials and objects, you will manipulate them as naturally as you manipulate your own hands.

PLANS

Good plans yield good devices. Good plans often require good drawings. The hidden danger in using paper for formulating plans is that the flat paper obscures the use that can be made of the third dimension. Do your inventing in your head, or by playing with models, and do the drawing later. Use 3-dimension drawings. Get a compass, a clear plastic ruler, a 45-45-90 clear plastic triangle, a clear plastic French curve, some #2 pencils and a big eraser, and practice the drawings. Draw and trace alternately. If you have a drawing containing some lines you want, and you add a line you don't want, erase the unwanted line. When the paper begins to get messy, trace the parts you like onto fresh paper and continue. You can use architectural tracing paper. When you have a finished drawing, trace it in India ink onto heavy paper by working on a pane of glass with a light underneath.

Use a ruler with a raised edge so that the ink won't get between the paper and the ruler, and spread out by capillarity.

DRAWINGS

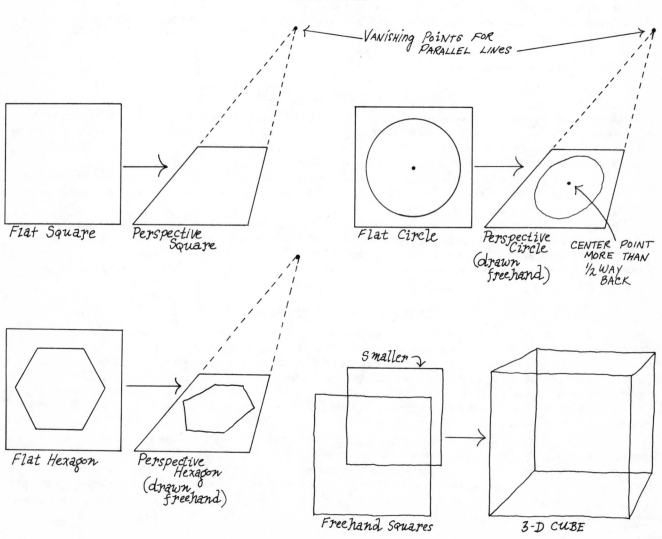

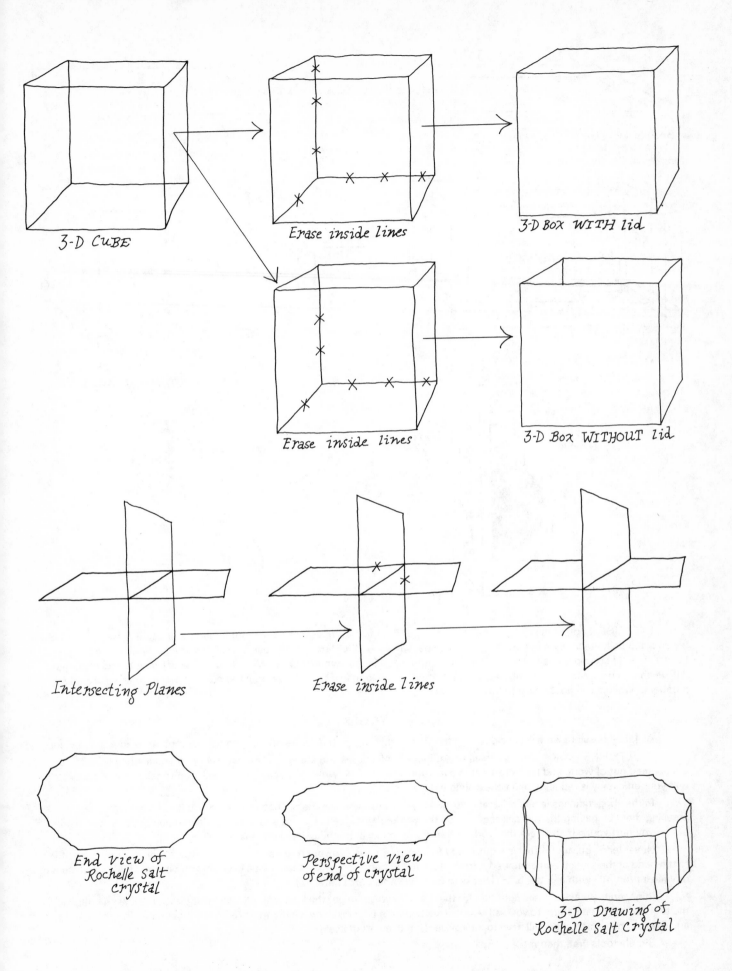

3-D CUBE

Erase inside lines

3-D BOX WITH lid

Erase inside lines

3-D BOX WITHOUT lid

Intersecting Planes

Erase inside lines

End View of
Rochelle Salt
crystal

Perspective View
of end of crystal

3-D Drawing of
Rochelle Salt Crystal

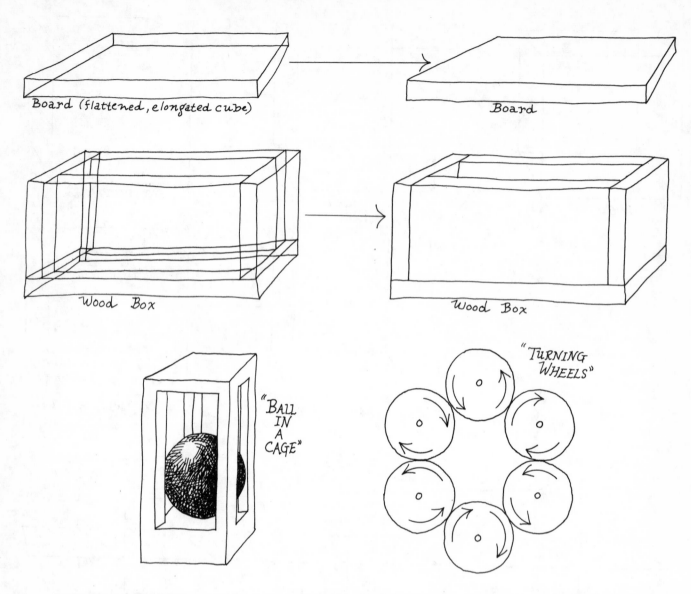

Board (flattened, elongated cube)

Board

Wood Box

Wood Box

"BALL IN A CAGE"

"TURNING WHEELS"

EXERCISE: Look at the picture of a ball in a cage. Put the picture aside and without looking at it again draw a picture of a ball in a cage. The technique of tracing will be indispensable.   EXAMPLE of the use of drawing in figuring things out: If you have a circle of six cog wheels, will they be able to turn, each on its own axis? ANSWER: look at the drawing above. Yes, they will be able to turn. Any even number of wheels arranged in a loop will be able to turn if the number is four or more. An odd number of wheels will not be able to turn.

TOOLS

As far as possible we will consider tools before considering materials. Before picking up any tool remember the obvious.

SAFETY FIRST. Never allow yourself to get injured. All injuries are stupid and embarrassing. If you injure yourself you put yourself out of work, and temporarily stop everyone else working with you because they will stop to take care of you. After that your efficiency is reduced until your wound heals.

In the shop, tidiness is part of safety. Put tools away after you use them. That way you avoid losing them, and you avoid breaking them by having them knock together on the workbench. Clean up chips and shavings. When you get tired quit work before you hurt yourself, or wreck the work, or before you make something you didn't want.

Never lend your tools. That is a quick way to lose your tools and your friends. If you do borrow a tool, return it promptly to the hand of the person you borrowed it from. Return it in better condition than it was in when you borrowed it. If you lose it replace it promptly with a better one. (Thanks in part to *Whole Earth Catalog*.)

In general, always use the right tool for the job. This way you get the best job with the least effort, the least damage to the tool and the least danger to yourself. A small shop cannot possibly have all the tools to do the jobs that will come up once, and the user of a small shop will have to improvise. That is an art in itself.

Simple tools first, then more complex ones.

CLAW HAMMERS

The claw hammer is for driving nails and pulling nails, and for nothing else. If a claw hammer strikes steel or rock the head may chip, shooting dangerous steel splinters into the air. Or the head may dent. A dented hammer will ricochet off of nails and hit your fingers.

The best hammer is a heavy one. A heavy hammer has a large face that will most easily hit the nail. A heavy hammer will not easily be bounced out of its course (and onto your fingers) if it hits the nail awry. When you hold a nail to hammer it in, hold the nail just below the head, and not down near the wood. That way if you miss the nail, or if the nail folds up, the hammer will knock your fingers out of the way before it hits the wood. If your fingers are already next to the wood when the hammer arrives . . . disaster!

In case you do hit your finger and the blister under the nail fills up with blood, use a tiny drill or sharp knife point to drill a hole in the nail, and suck the blood out. Renew the hole every morning and evening until no more blood comes. This will save the injured nail until a new one grows underneath. Even if the nail falls off, a new one will grow underneath, so don't worry. The healing takes about twelve weeks.

When you hit a nail with a hammer, keep your eye on the nail and hit hard. Press the nail into the wood with your fingers to set the point so that it will not skip aside when the hammer hits. Press the nail into the wood as you hit. First tap the nail to start it, and after that hit the nail HARD. Hitting a nail hard reduces the chances that it will bend and fold up. Hitting the nail hard reduces the chances of injuring the work because the nail will accelerate too quickly to drag the work along with it. If a nail is hit softly the friction bond between the wood and the nail will not be broken, so that the nail will pull the wood with it and break the wood. A slowly moving hammer will easily be deflected (onto your fingers) when it hits the nail.

Some materials like plastic and masonite are impossible to nail because they split when the nail enters them. When you want to nail these materials down to wood, drill holes in the material where the nails will go, set the material in place, and nail it down. (See the section on drilling.)

Avoid driving nails parallel to the grain of the wood, especially small sticks of wood, and avoid driving nails parallel to the surfaces of plywood. (See the section on wood and plywood.) Not only will this split the wood, but it will yield the weakest nailed joint. Nails hold in the wood because the wood fibers grip the nail, and if the nail travels parallel to the fibers they have no leverage to grip it. If you have to drive a nail parallel to the grain you may want to use glue to strengthen the joint. Practice driving nails of all sizes. Hit them hard and see if you can drive them in with three or four strokes. A good nailer can sink a large nail into a beam suspended from a single chain attached in the middle, and sink it with three strokes.

Finishing nails are the ones with the tiny heads. Their advantage is that they look pretty in cabinets and window sills.

To pull a nail with a claw hammer set the claws under the head and roll the handle back up to vertical. When the nail is part way out of the wood, put a block under the hammer.

If you hammer in nails perpindicular to the surface of the wood, you will hit your knuckles trying to get a direct shot at the nail (Try it). Get a clear shot at the nail and save your knuckles, by putting the nail in at an angle.

KNIVES

The knife is the basic tool. Chisels, scissors, planes, saws, even files and sandpaper are knives. Understand the knife and you will understand all these tools. Own a good knife and use it for cutting only, i.e., don't use it for a screwdriver or an awl or a lever. Know how to take care of it. A knife can be either a tool or a weapon; we are concerned here only with tools. When you go out to buy a knife you will encounter a bewildering variety of them in hardware stores and cutlery shops. They all look pretty, so don't be like the little kid who likes the taste of the green gumdrops but eats the red ones because they look pretty. You can get a folding knife (a jackknife) or a fixed-blade knife. Both are good, but the knife with the fixed blade will not fold up by accident and cut you. Your choice. Except for hacking your way through the jungles of the Amazon, or for cutting bread and vegetables, you will seldom need a knife with a blade as long as two inches (written 2''; two feet is written 2'). A fixed-blade knife with a blade that short is hard to buy. I bought one once about 1957, the handle broke about 1965, and I lost the blade before I got around to making a new handle. It is now 1972 and I have looked in hardware stores and catalogs from Maine to California and have never found another fixed-blade knife that small. So I made one for myself out of a car spring and a piece of ebony wood for the handle. The blade is 1 13/16'' long. If you are just starting out you won't have tastes as stubborn as that but I don't think you will ever have much use for a knife with a blade any longer than two inches, because when a blade gets too long you can't control it.

The shape of the blade is also important.
Probably the strongest blade is the symmetrical taper
because the point is strengthened by a thick backbone of steel behind it.
However the symmetry of the blade gives the eye no information as to
which side is the cutting edge and which side is the back,
so that you are guaranteed, once every five years or so,
to mistake the cutting edge for the back and press your thumb against it. It only takes a second, and then it is too late.
Get a knife with a scimitar blade. My own knife has a blade like this:

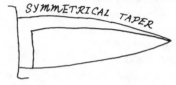

The back is rounded, not squared,
so that I can press my finger or thumb against it
without getting blisters.
The cutting edge is curved so that it will present itself even
to concave surfaces. The backbone of the knife is thick, for strength,
and the sides of the blade taper slowly and uniformly to the cutting edge.
This shape is very useful for making things as we will see in the next section on sharpening knives.

YOUR KNIFE

Get a small knife and learn how to sharpen and use it. Stainless steel blades won't rust, but they are too hard to sharpen in any reasonable length of time, and for some reason they don't stay sharp long in use. Carbon steel is better. If you get a jackknife (NOT a switchblade) make sure the blades don't wobble too much, and that the blades were forged or machined. Blades punched out of sheet metal will often crack in use, and then . . .disaster! Spend the money now out of your pocket instead of paying later out of your hide.

Get a knife with a handle that does not feel like it is ready to fall off. If the handle is too smooth it will give you blisters.

STONES AND SHARPENING

When you buy your knife buy sharpening stones with it, a coarse and a fine stone (or a combination coarse-fine stone), and a hard Arkansas oilstone. The coarse stone is for rough sharpening your knife (taking off steel) and for getting nicks out of it. The fine stone is for sharpening the knife to a useable sharpness. The Arkansas oilstone (cut from novaculite rock) is for polishing the knife. Much of the dulling of knives is caused by rust which starts when water collects in the scratches left in the knife metal by the sharpening stone. If you polish the cutting edge with the Arkansas stone you will not give water a place to collect. Soak your stones thoroughly in oil when you buy them, and put a few drops of light oil or Three-in-One oil on them every time you use them. The oil keeps the stone from clogging. When the knife travels over the stone it grinds the stone to mud, while ribbons of metal are stripped off the knife. The oil floats away the mud and the metal ribbons. Without the oil the mud and metal will soon coat the stone with a smooth surface that is not abrasive, and the stone will be ruined. Synthetic corundum (Al^2O^3) stones are excellent if you can find one. I think that big medical supply houses sell them for sharpening scalpels, but you might have to be a big customer to order from them. They are good because they are harder than other stones, and will quickly give a good edge to your knife without themselves getting worn down. You can also get big stones in substantial wooden cases. These are professional equipment. Get one if you expect to be using it every other day for the next ten years. An outstanding fine stone is the washita oilstone, if you can find one. The *Whole Earth Catalog* says, ''You can't buy quality: You have to grow into it.'' This goes for knives and stones and everything else in life. When you buy a knife or a stone get the cheapest GOOD one you can afford, and USE it. If you need a better one or a more specialized one later, you will know.

SHARPENING KNIVES

In sharpening a knife remember that the knife cuts only when the sharp edge contacts the work. Thus:

Knife shaving

WORK

When a knife gets dull—this is what happens:

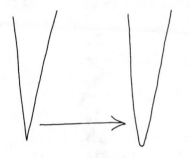

When the knife is sharpened again—this is what happens:

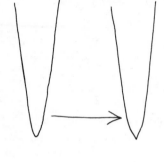

The knife then cuts again, but after it has been dulled and sharpened a few times it comes to look like this

When the knife is in this condition it might not contact the work.

cutting edge does not contact work

knife

WORK

The knife will still be good for vertical slices, but it will be no good for the carving of surfaces. And carving of surfaces is the essential action in cutting materials with a knife. The knife must be restored to its original wedge shape. Get out your kitchen knives and practice.

Oil up your coarse or fine stone (whichever is needed) and place it on a table with newspapers under it. Hold the knife against the stone with the cutting edge touching the stone at an angle of about thirty degrees. Some people sharpen their knives to an even keener angle (twenty-five degrees or less) but then the blade is thin and it will require more skill to use it without denting or cracking the edge. Holding the blade steady at this angle, push the cutting edge across the stone as if to cut the surface of the stone. As you push the knife, sweep it over the stone so that each part of the cutting edge contacts the abrasive surface. Hold the angle steady. Practice so that as each part of the curved cutting edge contacts the stone it is moving in a direction perpendicular to the edge at the point of contact.

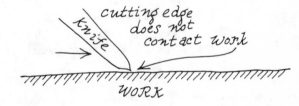

knife

STONE

STONE

knife

Just ONE sweep on each side at a time

Now turn the knife over and repeat the same motion for the other side. Keep flipping the knife over and working it this way until it is sharp. If the knife has been honed down to a good edge (such as the one shown in the first picture of a sharp knife) recently, it will take a new edge right away. If it has been used and re-sharpened several times recently, it will not sharpen up so fast, and will need a thorough grinding on the coarse stone to restore the old shape and edge. In this way, the sharpenings will move in cycles—first a thorough grinding, then touch-ups, then some sharpening, and eventually another thorough grinding. After you have some practice with sharpening knives you will know the knife is sharp by the sound of the steel on the stone. Many people test for sharpness by flicking a finger across the cutting edge. If the edge feels to have a "bite to it," then the blade is sharp. Many people test a knife for sharpness by drawing the blade across the edge of a sheet of paper held up in the air. If the knife cuts the paper, it is sharp. Some people call a knife sharp only when it will shave the hair off their forearm. All are correct.

Draw the blade across your thumbnail. If it feels smooth it is smooth.

To get the blade sharp enough to shave with, sharpen it on your Arkansas stone (using oil) until the blade is as sharp as it will get on that stone. Then strop the blade on a piece of leather. Stropping a knife on leather removes little wires of metal that cling to the edge after sharpening, and it even polishes down some of the scratch marks left in the metal by the stone. When stropping a knife, move the blade away from the edge so as not to cut the leather. You can strop a knife on paper if you don't have any leather.

Keep your knife sharp. You will not get cut on a sharp knife because the sharp edge enters the work and grips it. You will get cut on a dull knife because it will lose its grip on the work and slip out of control. Razor-sharp may be too sharp for some purposes, but because you have to work hard to get a knife razor-sharp, don't worry about it at first.

Hollow grinding a blade is cutting a concave surface in a blade.
Razors and kitchen knives are hollow ground. Hollow grinding can be done only on a grinding wheel, so if you have only flat sharpening stones you can't get hollow grinding. Hollow ground blades have the property of taking a very sharp edge (because they are very thin) and of being easy to re-sharpen for that reason. Hollow ground knives are also fragile, for the same reason, and are best for cutting meat, vegetables, and hair, not wood and plastic. If you want to hollow grind your knife edges, it can be done on a big, slow-sharpening wheel. (NOT one of the fast, coarse, small shop-grinding wheels.) Turn the wheel and hold the knife against it.

When you finish using a coarser stone wipe the knife with a rag to avoid carrying the coarse grit to the finer stone. Wrap the rag around the BACK of the knife to avoid cutting the rag and possibly your hand.

When the knife is sharp, carve something with it. A strenuous but rewarding exercise is to carve out of a single block of wood the ball in the cage that you drew earlier. To do this will require some knowledge of wood and woods.

WOOD AND WOODS

The sculptor Robert Engman says, "The best use of wood is the tree," because in the form of a tree the qualities of the wood are put to use in the most efficient way, and all the properties of the wood are used. Wood conducts sap, and it bears weight. It resists attacks by insects and fungi. When we cut down a tree to take advantage of its weight-bearing properties (and its beauty) we must keep it healthy by replacing with oil the sap that is no longer available to it.

The living part of the tree is a cylinder of living tissue just below the bark and the tree grows as this tissue dies at its inner surface and cells multiply at its outer surface. Thus the major part of the weight of any tree is dead tissue—the wood. Wood is composed of fibers than run parallel to the axis of the tree. Because the growth of the tree runs in annual cycles, the wood fibers do not grow at a uniform rate throughout the year, and the wood shows annual growth rings. These rings (or annuli) which we see at the end of a cut log or branch are really cylinders of fibers that run the length of the wood, and in a cut piece of wood they are called the grain.

Two major traumas occur in the grain when the tree is cut down and sawed into blocks or timbers or boards. First, trees seldom grow absolutely vertical, so that the wood grows under the stress of the weight of the tree. When the tree is cut, its weight no longer rests on the grain, and the grain itself becomes stressed. Second, when the tree is cut into boards or blocks the cylindrical balance of fiber stresses is further disturbed. When water lubricates the wood so that the fibers can move past each other, this stressing results in warping if the wood is soft or thin, and in cracking if the wood is hard or thick.

People have found ways to work with wood in spite of its tendency to warp and crack. The first method is to age the wood, let it crack and warp, and then use the places that are not cracked and warped. For example the wood in some musical instruments is pear wood or ebony that had been aged twenty-five years or more. The instrument manufacturer builds his instrument between the cracks. Of course by cutting the wood he further disturbs the balance in the grain, and a new clarinet may crack during the first six months of use. If it survives the first six months it will be good for years. The best way to prevent cracking in very hard wood such as teak and ebony is to replace in them the oils that begin to be lost when the tree is cut.

Another method used to prevent warping in boards such as guitar necks is to balance the warping forces in one piece of wood against the warping forces in another. This is done by cutting the board lengthwise parallel to the grain, and folding down the two cut pieces so that the nearly identical grains on the two sides of the saw cut are showing back-to-back on top. The two pieces are then glued together.

A further extension of this method, and one of the great inventions of all time, is plywood. Plywood is made from wood sheets (plies) glued together.

To make plywood the manufacturer places the axis of a straight pine tree on the spindles of a huge lathe, and holds a long knife against the turning tree. The knife peels the tree into a continuous sheet of parallel fibers. The sheets are then glued together with the fibers traveling in different directions. The resulting board won't warp or bend. Plywood is commercially available in 4 x 8 foot sheets in 1/4, 1/2, 3/4, and 1" thicknesses, in marine grade, outdoor grade, indoor grade and utility grade. Utility grade plywood has knotholes on the outside. It is not pretty and is sometimes called unfinished.

When selecting a piece of wood for carving, select one that you either want to carve or to own. Different trees produce different woods as solutions to the problems of survival in different climates and habitats. In some places competition for light is important. In some places defense against insects is important. Here is a very short list of woods, enough to get you started, with some information about each.

NOTE: softwoods and hardwoods come from evergreen and deciduous trees respectively. The words soft and hard have nothing to do with the softness or hardness of the woods.

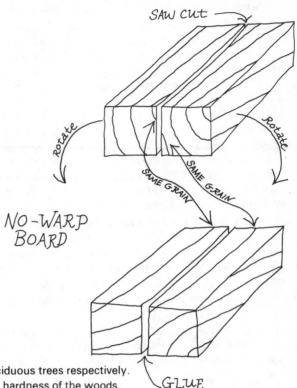

NORTH AMERICAN WOODS

PINE—The wood of the construction industry. Plywood is made from pine. House timbers (the famous 2" x 4" and 4" x 8", which are cut in fourteen-foot lengths) are pine. If you go to a lumberyard and insist on getting ordinary wood you will get pine. Pine, a softwood, is good for structural building such as houses and bookcases, but is too soft for the best carving. When the knife pushes against pine the fibers are too soft to stand up, and they mash together into a mat that is as difficult to cut as a telephone book. The masts of sailing ships were pine trees, and some old trees in New England, marked for mast poles in pre-Revolutionary times, still show the King's mark on their trunks.

CEDAR—A softwood, cedar is so hard that it can be polished like a gem and worn in a ring. Cedarwood is stuffed with aromatic oils, apparently as a defense against insects, and it is these oils which protect clothes from moths in cedar chests and closets. Cedarwood is red and yellow.

OAK—Oak is a hard, open-grained hardwood. Its hardness apparently gives it strength against the wind, but its open grain makes it too rough for small carvings. It is excellent for large carvings and furniture. Oak is white. A freshly-cut oak tree smells like green Spanish olives in brine.

MAPLE—A hard, clear-grained hardwood. Maple is good for furniture but the wood is so clear that it gives uninteresting carvings.

WALNUT—A hardwood. Walnut can be purple or brown, hard or soft, fine-grained or coarse-grained. It is good for furniture, and a hard, close-grained piece would make a fine carving.

TROPICAL WOODS

ROSEWOOD—Beautiful brown-and-tan striped wood. Most commonly seen in the USA as the handles of stainless steel kitchen knives. Popular as a veneer on tables in modern Scandinavin furniture, rosewood is soft but beautiful, and it would make good carvings.

TEAK—From India. "Elephants a-pilin' teak" "Road to Mandalay" by R. Kipling. Teak is used for the decks of ships. Teak takes up minerals into the wood, probably as a defense against chewing insects, and the wood will strike fire against your power saw, and dull it like a butter knife before long. Teak is a pleasure to carve because the fibers stand up to the blade and allow themselves to be cut one at a time. Teak is so oily that its sawdust can be packed into little clods, and the greasiness gives it the water repellency to serve not only as a ship's deck, but as a jam spoon or butter knife. After carving and sanding teak, oil it with the oil from your face. Teak ranges in color from tan-and-black stripes to solid honey. Some pieces are more close-grained than others, and the close-grained pieces are the most water repellent.

MAHOGANY—Mahogany is soft but water resistant and is used in ship building. Mahogany has characteristic rows of white spots running perpendicular to the grain, and these make the wood look almost like skin. Mahogany can be either white or red. The white is used for Japanese motorcycle crates, but only about one percent of that is strong enough for carving.

EBONY—The wood of clarinets. The ebony log is black on the inside and yellow on the outside, and the black wood is harder. The wood is so dense and heavy that the tree must have grown under terrific stress, and it must be cut and carved gradually, over a period of weeks, to give it time to relax. It needs to be oiled. Otherwise it will crack. Ebony is tough and will take wear and use, but it is slightly brittle and may crack if shocked. Like teak, ebony takes up minerals into the wood, and a freshly cut sliver of ebony sparkles in the grooves of the grain. Ebony sawdust violently attacks the eyes and nose. Ebony brings $3.85 a pound in specialty lumber houses.

LIGNUM VITAE—The Lifeline Tree, the hardest wood in the world. It is fibrous and the fibers can be red, green, yellow, black and brown. Lignum vitae sawdust is green. Apparently as a defense against insects, the wood is terribly greasy, and if you touch a freshly broken piece you will get the thick, sticky grease on your hands. Until the advent of Teflon, the bearings of large ships' propellers were lignum vitae, and many a World War II heavy ship had to ride it out in a harbor waiting for the delivery of a log of lignum vitae wood. Sometimes lignum vitae is used for bushings to hold guitar pegs; the grease in the wood guarantees that the pegs will turn without sticking. The wood is so hard that it would be hell to carve, but it would make excellent buttons or belt buckles or hair pins.

For your first carving select a block of wood not bigger than 2 1/2″ x 2 1/2″ x 5″. I recommend good pine or cheap mahogany for a first piece of work, and after that you can decide when to try walnut, teak and rosewood. Because the world's suppy of precious tropical woods such as ebony is being used up but is not being replenished, please use some scrap wood such as pine for your first efforts (and mistakes) and use precious woods only for special projects.

When you work a piece of wood the most important feature you will deal with is the grain. If you cooperate with the grain it is your best friend. If you fight the grain it is your worst enemy. A newly cut piece of wood will look like this:

As you cut the wood you will cooperate with the wood grain if you press the fibers together with the knife. You will fight the grain if you pry the fibers apart with the knife, as this will rip up large sections of wood beyond your control.

When working with a knife, what you want most of all is control. That is why a short knife is better than a long one—you can control it. Never do things with the knife that are likely to send it out of control. For example don't rest the blade on the surface of a block of wood and then push the knife in the direction of its axis, without bracing your thumb against the side of the block and rationing the motion with your thumb. If uncontrolled pressure is applied the block will tip or the knife will slip, and the knife will go out of control. If you are holding the wood with your other hand the knife will slice your index finger to the bone. Never cut toward yourself.

Much effective carving can be accomplished by shaving off material with the knife. Slice after slice, thin slices. Set a convenient part of the blade into the place to be cut, and rotate the blade against a convenient pivot point somewhere else on the cutting edge. In a hollow part of the work the pivot point can be the place where the back of the knife meets the work. You can control the knife by squeezing it along with thumb pressure on the back.

You now know enough about carving wood to do some pretty competent cutting. The knowledge needs some practice to apply consistently. Wood will tolerate being cut perpendicular to the grain. Wood can be cut, chiseled, planed and filed with the grain or across the grain, and it can be sanded with the grain.

It is one thing to know how to carve wood and quite another to know how to carve the objects you want out of wood or any other material. This is a question of knowledge, not of strength, skill or experience. INSTRUCTIONS: In order to carve the object you want out of any block of material, place the block of material in front of you and envision the object you want floating inside of it. When you can clearly see the object you want, pick up your tools and cut away everything else. This method works and it is the only one that does. Don't allow any other method to even cross your mind.

The more rigidly geometrical your object is, the easier it will be to carve.

When carving an object, work it around and around on all sides, keeping the whole piece of work at the same level of completion everywhere, never letting any part get ahead of the others. If one part gets too far ahead of the others, the piece will never get back together again.

When you have finished a wood carving and you want to smooth it, sand it first with medium, then with fine, then with finest sandpaper. If the wood is very hard it might take sanding with crocus cloth. Pine can be painted, stained, varnished or shellacked. Fine woods can be varnished, and the finest woods should be oiled or waxed with linseed oil, human face oil, Butcher's wax or lemon oil.

THE HACKSAW AND THE TUNGSTEN CARBIDE WIRE SAW

These two cutting blades go together because they both fit on the same frame and because they both cut hard materials. The hacksaw is a thin metal blade mounted on a back. The hacksaw cuts lead, copper and copper alloys, and soft iron and steel. The knack to using the hacksaw consists of knowing how to keep the blade moving straight. No wobbling. This comes with practice. When the blade wobbles it binds in the groove it has cut, and it either catches or breaks.

Hold the work to be cut in a vise or on a convenient surface, and start the cut by resting the blade on the work, steadying it with your free thumb, and drawing it toward you slowly. This will nick the surface of the work and give the saw a guide place to start cutting.

The saw does its cutting when it is moving away from you and the sharp points of the teeth are entering the material to be cut. The speed of cutting depends on the pressure applied to the saw, not on the speed of the saw, so work slowly and evenly, and bear down on the power stroke. You may want to hold both ends of the saw, but this requires some practice to keep the saw from wobbling. Put a little cutting oil on the blade. This will carry away metal chips and will keep the work cool.

HACK SAW

Direction of Power Stroke

Handle   Frame or Back

Touch the saw teeth every so often to see if they are still sharp. When they get dull, change the blade. Different hacksaws change blades in different ways, so find out when you buy your saw how to change its blades. The most common hacksaws change blades by turning a wingnut that loosens a square bolt that holds the blade. Some newer saws loosen the square bolt by turning a lever.

If you think that the hacksaw blade has grown dull too soon to suit you (say, after cutting 1/8" of material) get a tungsten carbide wire saw. There are several on the market, and most are good. Stay away from the ones with the washers on the ends to hold the wire saw to the saw frame because the washers have a way of breaking off prematurely. The disadvantage of the carbide saw is that it is three times thicker than the hacksaw blade, and you have to grind three times as much steel to powder before you have your cut. However the carbide saw will cut car springs, stainless steel, bricks, rocks, tiles and bottles— just like a billy goat. Keep your carbide saw cool, and your lungs free of dust, by oiling the blade with cutting oil when you use it. The carbide saw will cut a straight line.

For small delicate work it is sometimes handy to sit in a chair, rest the hacksaw handle on the seat between your legs with the blade facing away from you, and lean the back of the saw against your chest. Hold the work in your fingers and draw it carefully against the blade.

Except for unusual jobs, use hacksaw blades with medium teeth. The hacksaw is handy for cutting very hard tropical woods. The cutting edge is dull when it begins to feel the least bit slippery to the touch.

BALL PEEN HAMMER

Peen is a verb that means to round a thing down by hammering on it. The ball peen hammer is for rounding down and shaping soft metals. The ball is the rounded end of the ball peen hammer.

Use the ball peen hammer for working copper, brass, lead, aluminum, silver, soft iron and sheet steel.

One of the virtues in a finished piece of metal work is its smooth surface, so when you buy a new ball peen hammer polish the hammering surfaces until you can see your face in them. Then they will not put marks in the work. Metal work with marks in it not only looks and feels cheap, but corrodes and wears quickly.

Ball

BALL PEEN HAMMER

Polish the hammer surfaces by rubbing them on oiled emery cloth held in the palm of your hand or the tips of your fingers. Start with medium grade emery cloth, then fine grade, then finish the polishing with oiled crocus cloth, the finest emery cloth made. These are available at your local hardware store. When you use the abrasive cloth, rip off squares about 2" x 2" and use these. You get the job done, and conserve sandpaper.

A good exercise in using the ball peen hammer is making rivets. While the ball peen hammer is used for all soft metal work, its full potential is fulfilled in the making of rivets.

The principle that the ball peen hammer works on is that metals, under sufficient pressure, will flow like clay. When the pressure is released, they become hard again. So when you are working metal with the hammer, imagine that you are pushing clay with the hammer. Strike the hammer firmly against the work and hold it against the work after is has struck. Do not let the hammer bounce off the work. That way you will take advantage of the clay-like qualitites of the metal.

Using a hacksaw, cut off a 1" slug of iron from a medium sized nail and peen a rivet head into one end. Hold the slug vertical in a metal-working vise and leave about 3/16" protruding above the jaws. Beat on the iron with the hammer, straight down at first to swell the end, and then around and around to dome off the end of the rivet. If the rivet shaft becomes bent, straighten it by laying it on an anvil or piece of hard wood and pound down the high places. File off any slivers.

Be careful never to hit the anvil with the hammer. This will dent both and ruin both permanently.

If you buy a hammer head new, or if you have a hammer with a broken handle, you will want to replace the handle. Removing the old handle from the head is never easy. Some people burn it out with fire (this weakens the metal head) and some cut it out with a knife. Buy or make a hickory wood handle to fit the hammer head. The shaft of the handle should run parallel to the grain of the wood and the lines of the grain at the ends of the handle should run up and down—just like a baseball bat. The force of the hammer will flex the grain, not cut across it at right angles and break the handle. The handle must be smooth to prevent blisters. Fit the end of the handle snugly into the head, trimming the handle until it fits. Using a saw cut a thin split into the handle where the head fits. Commercial hammer handles come already split. Make a wooden wedge and drive this into the split. The wedge will cause the handle to swell and grip the head. You can buy metal wedges. Never use nails instead of wedges. For general tightening of a hammer head, strike the butt end, not the head end, against a wood block.

Another good exercise for the ball peen hammer is to shrink one end of a copper plumbing fitting. Rest one end of the fitting on an anvil and tap firmly around and around on the end you want to shrink. Holding the anvil directly opposite the place you tap against gives the effect of hammering on the work from both sides at once. I once used this method for adapting a microscope tube to a new ocular.

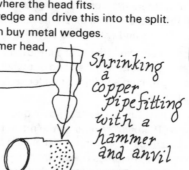

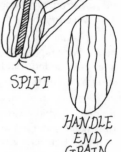

Pound down the high places

Shrinking a copper pipe fitting with a hammer and anvil

SPLIT

HANDLE END GRAIN

CHISELS

A chisel is a knife that you move by tapping on it with a mallet instead of pushing it with your hand. A chisel, like any other knife, cuts by pressing the wood fibers together, not by prying them apart, except when large portions of material are to be removed. In this case dig a deep trench around the portion to be removed and split out the unwanted material by prying the grain apart. This method works on wood, which has a grain. It will not work on plastic, which has no grain. Plastic can and sometimes must be cut with a chisel or knife, especially when the plastic is stressed, but the plastic must always be shaved away in thin ribbons. Otherwise it will shatter. Essentially there are two kinds of chisel: the straight-edge chisel and the gouge.

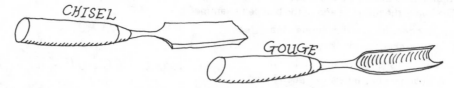

CHISEL

GOUGE

The straight chisel is used for cutting out recesses in the shape of retangular solids in wood, as for sinking a hinge into the edge of a door. The gouge cuts a trough out of a surface and can be used for the shaping of intricate curved surfaces.

The gouge is used for carving wood or for removing portions from wood surfaces. For example, if you want to remove a stained place in a wood floor and replace the stained wood, use a gouge to remove a lozenge-shaped hollow in the portion of wood around the stain. Then carve a block of wood to fit in the cavity in the floor. When the block nearly fits in the cavity, set it in the cavity and tap on it with the mallet. Then remove it. Some places will be shiny. These are the high spots. Sand them down and repeat the process until you are satisfied that the plug fits the hole well enough. Line the cavity with glue and place the replacement block in it, bracing it down by wedging a narrow board between the plug in the floor and the ceiling. Cover the ends of the board with cloth to protect the floor and the ceiling.

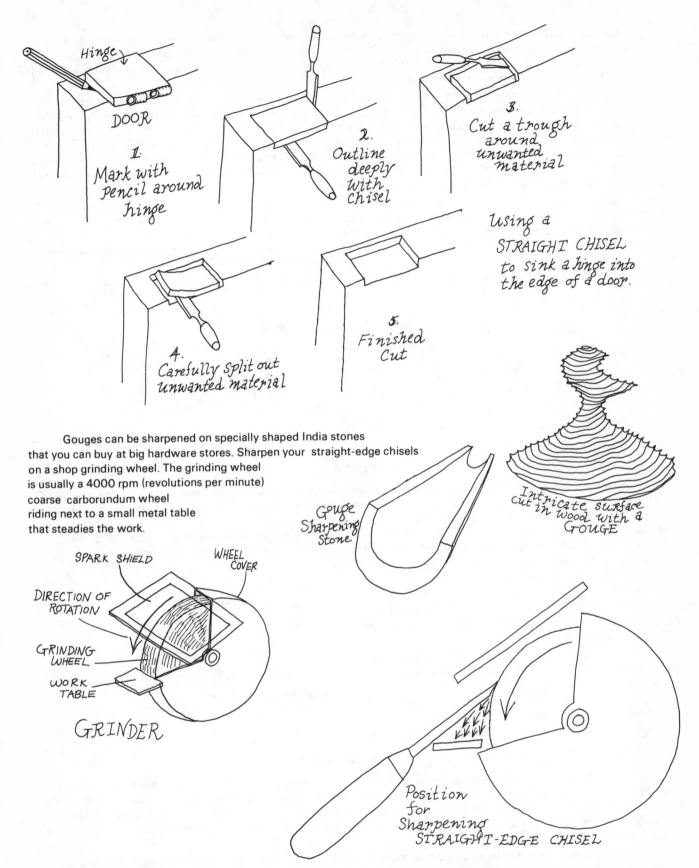

Hinge

DOOR

1.
Mark with
Pencil around
hinge

2.
Outline
deeply
With
chisel

3.
Cut a trough
around
unwanted
material

4.
Carefully split out
unwanted material

5.
Finished
Cut

Using a
STRAIGHT CHISEL
to sink a hinge into
the edge of a door.

Gouge
Sharpening
Stone

Intricate surface
cut in wood with a
GOUGE

Gouges can be sharpened on specially shaped India stones
that you can buy at big hardware stores. Sharpen your straight-edge chisels
on a shop grinding wheel. The grinding wheel
is usually a 4000 rpm (revolutions per minute)
coarse carborundum wheel
riding next to a small metal table
that steadies the work.

SPARK SHIELD

WHEEL
COVER

DIRECTION OF
ROTATION

GRINDING
WHEEL

WORK
TABLE

GRINDER

Position
for
Sharpening
STRAIGHT-EDGE CHISEL

When sharpening the chisel (or any other tool) on the wheel be careful to keep the tool moving. If the chisel stands still on the wheel the metal will heat up and lose its temper. If the metal gets a blue scorch on it you will know that it is ruined. The temper of metals is their springy quality which guarantees they will be strong without being brittle.

13

Temper (like the other formulas described here) is not fully understood but it is believed to be a function of the size, shape and orientations of the crystals in metals and alloys. Because temper is not understood, the formula for obtaining a good temper in a metal is discovered by trial and error. Such a formula, once found, is priceless, and lives have been taken in struggles to obtain formulas for well-tempered sword metal.

Simple hardness in a metal is obtained through the small size of the metal crystals. This is got by heating the metal to disturb the crystal structure and then quenching it in water. Quenching cools the metal quickly and does not allow the crystals time to grow large before they are too cold to grow at all. Metals thus tempered are hard but seldom supple. If a metal is heated red hot or nearly red hot and allowed to cool slowly, the metal crystals will have time to grow large. The large crystals are soft, and the metal is soft, and that is why a scorch on a chisel means that the chisel has been ruined by too much heat—it shows that the metal is soft. This softening of the metal by heat is called annealing. Annealing can be useful: If you want metal to be soft, anneal it. Annealing glass relaxes stresses in the glass and thus lessens the likelihood of breaking.

Incidentally if you want to see the crystals in a metal alloy, look at a well-used brass door handle, such as one on a popular public building. You will see a patchwork of rectangles up to 1/8″ in dimension crosshatching the surfaces. These are zinc and copper crystals. All metals are composed of crystals. The network surface of a cold solder joint arises when the tin and the lead crystallize out of the melt separately. This separate crystallization of materials out of a melt is put to practical use in zone refining.

Tap your chisels with a wood or leather mallet, not with a metal hammer.

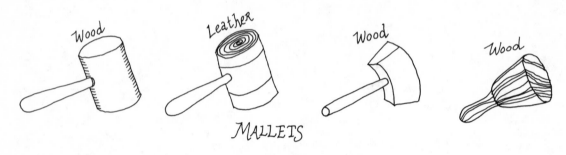

PLANE

The plane is a chisel that peeks through a slot in a flat guide. The plane usually has two uses—cutting large splinters off from the surface of wood planks and removing small amounts of wood from the edges of boards such as doors. When your door sticks in one corner, take down the high place with a plane. The flat guide of the plane ensures that the chisel will take only a controlled bite out of the surface to be cut. If the plane takes too deep a bite into the wood it will catch and rip up chunks of wood. But if the plane takes only a shallow bite out of the wood, and if it is moved smoothly and firmly across the wood, the plane will bring the wood up in uniform ribbons up to three feet long. The plane operates with the grain or across it at an angle, never against it.

The bite, or depth of cut, taken by the plane is adjusted by the knurled nut next to the handle. The tilt of the knife is adjusted by the lever in the knife holder.

Never set a plane down on its face as this will chip the blade. Set the plane down on its side. Sharpen the blade on the grinding wheel like any other chisel.

Guitar and violin makers use large precision planes for finishing the surfaces of the thin wood boards from which they construct their instruments.

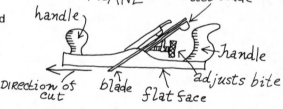

DRILLS AND BITS

A drill bit is a double rotating knife that bores into materials by chiseling shavings up from the surface of the material. The bit has a slot to carry away the shavings produced. The bit is turned by a drill—a hand powered or eggbeater drill, a handheld electric drill, or an electric drill press. The bit cuts clockwise and is held in a chuck. Most common chucks will hold any bit up to 1/2″ diameter. The chuck is built of three pins that grip the bit, and a slotted barrel that guides the pins and presses them together around the bit.

Tighten or loosen the pins by turning the barrel without turning the shaft that the chuck is mounted on. For hand drills, steady the shaft by holding the crank and the handle in one hand, and turn the barrel with the other. For power drills this whole operation is done with a toothed key. Most people chain the key to the drill press, or tape it to the cord of the electric drill, to keep from losing it. Insert the peg of the key into one of the three holes that accommodate it in the side of the chuck, and mesh the teeth of the key with the teeth of the chuck. Rotate the key, the barrel will turn, and the pegs will open or close.

For practice choose a bit, about 1/8'' to start, and open the jaws of the chuck just wide enough to accommodate the bit. Insert the bit in the chuck and close the jaws around it, hand tight. Not with all your strength, just hand tight. The bit should not be inside the chuck so far that the jaws press down on the grooves in the bit. Make sure that the bit is centered in the jaws and is not stuck between just two of them but touches all three equally. If you have an eggbeater drill, turn the crank a few times to get the feel. If you have a motor drill turn on the power and let it run until you get used to the noise. Then turn it off.

WARNING: When using any power tool, keep your long hair, necktie, shirt tail, cummerbund, suspenders, hair ribbon, French cuffs, etc. out of the way of all moving parts. People get maimed and killed routinely when they get caught in power equipment, and it is always their fault. Before you get near a power tool or machine look around to make sure you won't get caught in it. Tuck in your shirt or wear an apron. Put your necktie inside your shirt. Tie your hair back securely. Roll up your sleeves. Look both ways and make sure that no one is walking around near you. Don't be nice: Wait for them to get out of the way or ask them to wait or move. Don't talk to anyone. Then turn on the machine and devote your whole attention to it. Remember to keep your fingers out of the way of moving parts. This means anticipating where the moving parts are moving toward and having your fingers away from there. For example when using the drill press, keep your hand away from the place where the bit will emerge on the other side of the work.

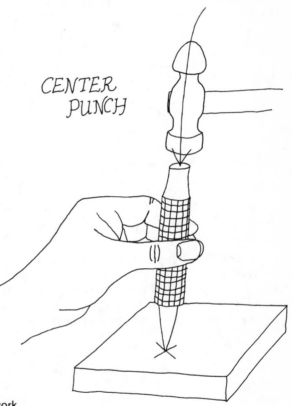

CENTER PUNCH

Now drill a hole through a piece of scrap wood or plywood.
Set the piece to be drilled down on a wood block so that
when the drill comes through the underside
it won't drill into the table.
Select the place you want to drill
and mark it with a pencil.
Then make a mark there
with the center punch.
Place the point
of the center punch
on the pencil mark
and tap the center punch with
a hammer to make the mark in the work.
Start the drill and direct the bit into the mark.
The point of the drill is not a point at all, but a square,
and the corners of the square will "walk" around over the work
when the bit turns unless the bit is started in a mark or pock
that will hold it still. The only way to drill holes exactly
where you want them is to use the center punch.

If you use a power drill, start the motor
before you lower the bit onto the work.
Press the bit gently and firmly into the work.
Debris will pile up as the grooves carry shavings
up from the place where the bit is cutting.
If the shavings stop coming, the grooves are clogged.
Remove the bit from the work and THEN turn off the motor.
If you have an eggbeater drill keep it turning until the bit is out of the work.
Keeping the bit turning will help keep it from getting stuck. If the bit gets stuck
in spite of these efforts, stop the drill and back it out by hand. This is the equivalent of unscrewing it.

Never stop a bit inside any material that might melt, such as plastic. If the bit is hot
and the plastic melts around it, the plastic will harden when the bit cools and you will never
get the bit out. Try to keep the bit turning until it is out of the work. Pick the debris out of
the grooves and start drilling again. Even if the drilling is going smoothly you will want to
remove the bit from the work often to allow both a chance to cool.

If you are drilling metal or plastic try using some cutting oil on the work.
The oil will keep the work cool, carry away plastic or metal shavings, and lubricate the bit
so that it won't catch and break.

The procedure for drilling sheet metal,
metal blocks, or plastic is the same as that for wood,
except that for these materials
the work is likely to grip the bit
and start turning with it. This is dangerous.

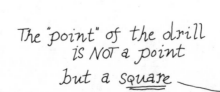

The "point" of the drill
is NOT a point
but a square

Hold the metal sheet or plastic down with a vise or C-clamp to make sure it won't get away from you. If the center punch won't put a mark in plastic where you want to drill, cut a starting mark with the point of a knife. If you use bits routinely you will dull them routinely and break them routinely, and if you have a grinder you can sharpen them routinely.

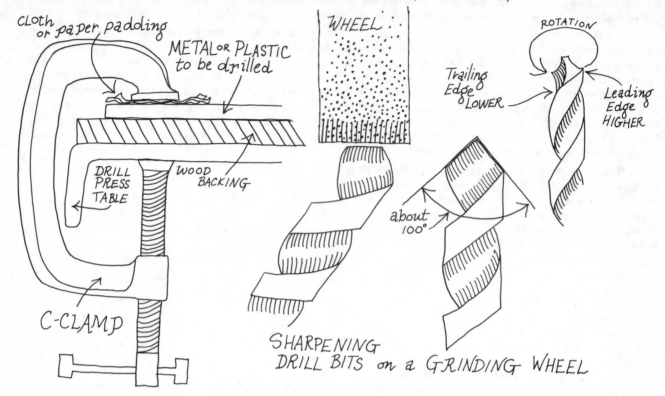

Hold the bit at about a fifty-degree angle to the front face of the turning wheel (as shown) and with the hollow of the groove facing you where it meets the wheel (as shown). Press the bit against the wheel and rock it toward you and up, all at the same time. This motion will leave the trailing edge of the cutting face lower than the leading, cutting edge. It takes a little practice to learn to sharpen dull and broken bits, but after you learn you will never hesitate to use the drill for fear of breaking a bit. Compare the shape of your own sharpening job to the shape of a new bit.

POWER DRILLS

The drill press operates by pulling a lever that lowers the bit onto the work. If you want to drill holes to some specific depth you can set a stop on the drill press to catch the drill at any depth you choose. The drill press table can be raised and lowered (release it by turning the handle on the clamp where the table grips the post) to bring smaller and larger pieces of work to the bit.

The advantages of the drill press are twofold. First, the electric motor saves you elbow grease. In addition, the centered drill with the table below gives great accuracy in placing the bit in the work at whatever angle you choose. The drill press will give you precision work down to hundredths of an inch.

The advantages of the hand-held electric drill are also twofold. The hand-held electric drill is portable as far as you can get electricity to it. Also, the electric motor saves you elbow grease. The sculptor Steve Sears says "I believe in electricity." The hand-held electric drill and the eggbeater drill share the disadvantage of being wobbly and inaccurate. In cases where you need good accuracy of drill placement but must use a hand-held drill, get two friends to stand ninety degrees apart with respect to the drill, and tell them what angle you want. They will tell you if you are off.

DRILL CUTTING EDGE *must* contact *work* in order to drill

Contact at Cutting Edge

this bit will spin forever *without* cutting

Contact at Under Surface

PROCEDURES

The drill bit has cutting edges lining the grooves. These cutting edges cut the sides of the hole that the bit bores into the work so that if the material being cut happens to shrink a little it won't grip the bit and hold it. You can't sharpen these cutting edges with the shop grinder, but you can take advantage of them as long as they are sharp. For example if the hole you drill is a little too small for your purposes, enlarge it slightly by rocking the bit around in the hole. Tapered hand-held reamers are available for doing this in sheet metal.

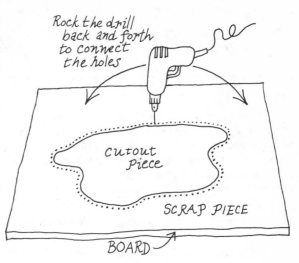

Rock the drill back and forth to connect the holes

cutout piece

SCRAP PIECE

BOARD

If you want to cut a large or irregular piece out of a sheet of material (plywood, sheet metal, plastic, or masonite) and you can't get a sabre saw (the operation of the sabre saw is explained in the sabre saw manual) mark on the sheet of material the outline of the shape you want to cut. Then drill a string of holes around this outline. Drill the holes outside the line if you want to use the cut-out piece, and vice versa. Drill the holes close together and remove the material between the holes by rocking the drill back and forth in the direction from each hole to its neighbors. When the cut out is separated, finish the edges with the rasp.

FILES AND RASPS

In the old days files and rasps were made from a plank of steel by striking it with a hammer with a blade-like edge. The edge of the hammer raises a curl of metal from the plank. Long rows of these metal curls compose the cutting surface of files. The grooves of a file are usually straight and parallel. Sometimes the grooves of a file are crosshatched.

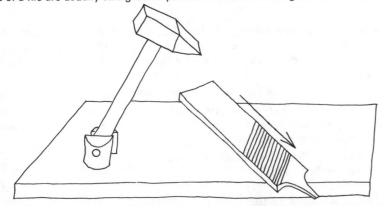

Metal plank advanced with each stroke of the hammer

Files are usually used for cutting metal. Rasps have rows of teeth instead of rows of grooves, and rasps are usually used for cutting wood. The large size of the teeth of the rasp, and the separation between the teeth, help keep wood dust from collecting in the rasp and clogging it.

The metal of files and rasps is very hard. A file will grind stainless steel to powder. The metal of files and rasps is very brittle. To see how brittle a file is, get an old and useless file and clamp it in a vise with about 3″ of the file sticking straight up above the vise. Stand at the side so that you are looking at the narrow edge of the file, and gently swing a light hammer at the file. Start about two feet back from the file and and follow through on the swing. You will effortlessly split the end off the file.

A file is a metal plane with many blades. Filing is planing. A file is not a grinder, and filing is NOT grinding. For practice filing, find a piece of thick metal sheet or plate with a rough edge. Clamp this in the vise, lining the vise with scrap plywood to protect the surfaces of the metal from the vise jaws. Choose a fairly fine metal file. Hold one end (it doesn't matter which end) of the file in your right hand, and the other in your left. The end of the file in your right hand must be nearer to you, thus:

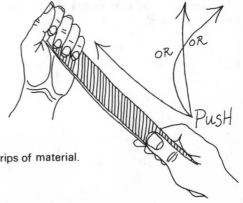

OR OR

PUSH

If you are left-handed this will be a little awkward at first, for the grooves of files are cut for right-handers. The sensuous gadgeteer must cultivate the use of both hands so this is a good place to start. Run the file over the edge of the metal sheet in the vise. Hold the file flat against the metal edge, and perpendicular to the plane of the metal sheet. Push the file straight along its own axis or straight away from you. Bear down on the file just hard enough so that it doesn't chatter over the metal, no harder. If the file is new and sharp you will feel it cut the metal. When you get the knack of filing, the metal filings you produce will be little wires of metal, not powder. Remember that filing is planing not grinding, and planing turns out long strips of material.

Filing the rough or sharp edges and flashings off sheet metal is a wise workshop routine because the fewer sharp edges lying around the fewer the chances of getting cut. File (bevel) the edges SQUARE—never round because if the edge is round you can't see the edge, and the sheet loses its shape for the eye. If you must make sure the edges are safe, chamfer them slightly.

When you use a metal file try to keep the grooves from loading up with the filings from the material you are working. Using the right pressure, as described above, is the first good way to do this. Avoid cutting lead with the file if you can. If you must file lead, just decide you are going to ruin that file and go ahead. As you work with the file, stop frequently and brush the debris out from the grooves with your hand. If you do this often you will keep the debris from packing together and accumulating. If material does get packed into the grooves, it can sometimes be brushed out with a tough wire brush called a file card (sometimes available at hardware stores). Don't let files touch each other because they will dull each other.

The rasp is used just the same way the file is used, except that it has teeth instead of grooves, so it is only for use on wood. The rasp is good for shaping convex wood surfaces where a knife would be too slow, or where a knife would leave flat spots.

Here are some common shapes of files:

All are useful depending on what shape surface you are working. The best file for a job is the one that most conveniently presents a cutting face to the surface you want to cut. Use a coarse file for cutting quickly through thick sections. Use a fine file for cutting accurately or for cutting a smooth surface. Needle files are available for the finest work. Convex rasps for wood and plaster are sometimes available at sculptor supply houses.

Files cut wood and metal faster than they cut skin, so you can use your fingers and thumb to guide the file over the work.

A flat file will put an absolutely straight edge on a sheet of metal, provided that the edge is not too much longer than the file itself (depending on the skill of the worker). For example imagine that you have cut a piece of sheet copper with a tin snips, and you find that the edge is a little wobbly. The flat file will straighten it.

Place the flat file on the table in any position you find comfortable. Hold the sheet of metal perpendicular to the table with the edge resting along the file. Push the metal sheet over the file keeping the edge of the sheet pressed against the cutting surface of the file. This will straighten the edge. If you need an absolutely straight edge for any purpose use a steel ruler as a guide for a scriber, and scribe a straight line exactly where you want your straight edge to be. Then cut just outside this line with a tin snips or a jigsaw. Then file the edge down to the scribed line. This procedure is also good for obtaining accurate right (or other) angles in sheet metal—just file the edge to the line. The method of edge filing gives astonishing accuracy. You will need this accuracy when you want to silver solder edges of sheet metal together, as for a gas tank.

Place Pressure About Here

cutting movement

Inspect the edge for flatness by placing it as shown and holding it up to the daylight. You will easily see any high places.

In the filing of curved edges of sheet metal, and in the filing of curved surfaces of domed objects, obtain smooth curves by constantly changing the angle of attack of the file. If the file is cutting while the angle of attack is not changing, you will file a flat place which is almost impossible to get out.

Desired Cut

Flat
Actual Cut

waste
Restored Cut

SCREWDRIVERS AND SCREWS

Start with the round-head regular wood screw.   Get one about 1″ long. The round head has a slot cut in it, and the slot takes a regular straight screwdriver. Use the largest size screwdriver that will sit all the way down in the slot. Choose a solid steel forged screwdriver, not one of those plated jobs with weak metal under the plating. Get a screwdriver with a large handle.   The thin plastic handles with the deep grooves are weak and dangerous. (Thanks in part to *Whole Earth Catalog*.)

Start the screw into the wood either with the center punch or with the hammer directly on the screw for rough jobs. For elegant jobs, drill a hole of whatever size is necessary (this depends on the hardness of the wood) to accommodate the screw,   giving the threads the greatest possible bite into the wood without cracking the wood. Estimating that takes a little practice. If you hear the wood starting to crack, take the screw out and drill a slightly wider (not deeper!) hole, and try again. Sometimes   you may want to drill a deep, narrow hole and a shallow, wider one on top of it for an excellent fit in very hard wood.

Before driving the screw into the wood spit on the screw and grate the threads on a bar of soap. The soap will lubricate the screw and ease its journey into the wood, and after the spit dries up the soap will hold the screw in place.

Usually screws are used for fastening gadgets, such as locks and handles, down to wood. Screws are also used for fastening pieces of material together.

Screws come in brass and steel, in sizes depending on what your local hardware store happens to have in stock. The best ones are the ones with the deep sharp threads. (The worst ones are the ones with the shallow blunt threads.) Brass is more expensive than steel and doesn't rust. Steel might be just a little stronger. Use brass screws for best durability and looks, except when you are screwing steel fixtures down. Brass will set up an electric cell with the steel and both will corrode. When screwing down fixtures, use the same metal in both.

To get the greatest efficiency out of your arm muscles, drive screws in (clockwise) holding the screwdriver in your right hand, and take screws out (counterclockwise) holding the screwdriver in your left hand. This will be awkward at first but it will cultivate the use of both hands.

In addition to the round-head wood screw there are also flat-head wood screws.

Head →   *Thread →*   *Round Head Wood Screw*   *Flat Head Wood Screw*

You must countersink the heads of flat-head wood screws into the wood (you have to drill or cut a crater-shaped seat for the tapered head to sit down in) and the head will lie flush with the surface. Use flat-head screws for joining pieces of wood when you don't want the heads of the screws sticking up above the surface, as in the making of tables or bookcases. Use flat-head screws for attaching hardware to wood when the hardware is pre-machined with seats to accommodate the flat-head screws. Some hardware stores carry a drill bit that will in one operation tap a hole to accommodate a flat-head screw and countersink the head.

End Plate of Door Handle Pre-machined to accomodate Flat head screws   *DRILL BIT*   *to countersink Flat head Wood screws*

Both flat-head and round-head screws are made in regular and Phillips styles. With Phillips heads the screwdriver is a little less likely to slip and rip the groove in the screw head than with the regular screws.

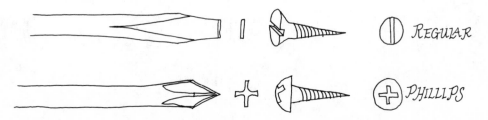

REGULAR

PHILLIPS

Self-tapping screws are for fastening together pre-drilled sheets of metal.

Screws cannot cut their own threads into (cannot tap) blocks of metal. To put screws into solid sections of metal, drill a hole in the metal where you want the screw to go, then cut threads into the hole with a tap. The tap is a hard tool-steel screw with grooves cut lengthwise in it. The edges of the grooves act as knives to cut the threads into the metal, and the grooves are receptacles that give the metal shavings a place to collect. Oil the tap before using it, and wipe it clean after using it. Turn it slowly and tenderly into the metal, never forcing it. Remove it from the work frequently to clean away metal shavings.

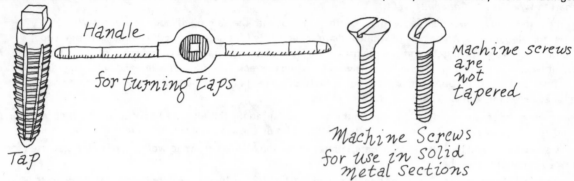

Handle for turning taps

Tap

Machine screws are not tapered

Machine Screws for use in solid metal sections

The correct tap to use for any machine screw is the one marked with the same diameter and the same number of threads per inch as the screw you intend to use. Screw sizes are listed as a pair of numbers, for example 6-32. The second number is the number of threads per inch. The first number indicates the diameter, and the diameter of a screw is 0.013 times the first number listed for the size of the screw plus 0.06. Thus the example screw 6-32 is 0.138 inches in outside diameter. Use a 6-32 tap for tapping a hole for this screw. The smallest screw, the O gauge is 0.06'' in diameter. Twelve is the highest gauge. After that, the diameters of screws are listed in inches. Screws come in all lengths.

Some books publish tables of drill sizes appropriate to use for each tap and screw. My experience has been that the drill size recommended is too big, and I suggest that you use a drill that has the same diameter as the solid part of your tap. That way the tap will cut threads of the greatest possible height and strength, but it will not have to carve its own way through solid metal.

For mass-production jobs where you must tap large numbers of holes, get a friction clutch tap holder that fits on any power drill. The tap holder has two drums. Hold the drum farthest from the drill, and press the drums together. The tap will turn clockwise and tap into the hole. Pull the drill back and the drums will separate. The tap will turn counterclockwise and unscrew itself out of the hole.

POWER DRILL with Friction Clutch Tap Attatchment

Dies are the negative of taps, and they cut threads into metal rods. Dies have their own special handles for holding and turning them. Once you learn to use taps you can easily use dies, so no special description of their use is necessary, except to remind you to oil them the same as you would a tap, before using them.

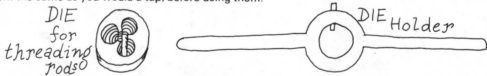

DIE for threading rods

DIE Holder

NUTS AND BOLTS

The nut-bolt pair is a fastener that will hold together pre-drilled metal plates, with a washer placed between the nut and the work so that as the nut tightens down it will not rip up the work.

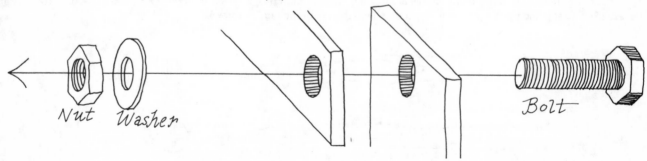

Nut   Washer

Bolt

Tighten down the nut-bolt pair using a pair of open-end wrenches or with an open-end wrench holding the bolt steady and a socket wrench to turn the nut. Don't use an adjustable wrench or pliers. Be careful to use a wrench that tightly fits the nut and bolt you are using. A wrench that is too big will round down the corners of the nut. As the corners round down they will release their restraint of the wrench and you will smash your knuckles. In addition a nut with rounded corners will be very difficult to remove because no wrench can get a grip on it. It is for this reason that you should use open-end or box wrenches instead of an adjustable wrench: The adjustable wrench might come loose and round down the corners of the nut. Use an adjustable wrench only for emergencies; for example you might want to carry one with you on your bicycle.

Pliers are not for loosening nuts and bolts because when the pliers apply as much force as is needed to tighten nuts and bolts, they apply enough force to rip up the metal of the nut and round it off, ruining it.

A lock washer is a split washer made of spring metal. A lock washer will cut a nick into the nut and the work, and hold the nut tighter than the plain, flat washer will.

Special wrenches, notably the pipe wrench, grip tighter the harder you pull on them, and they are specially designed for installing permanent water pipes.

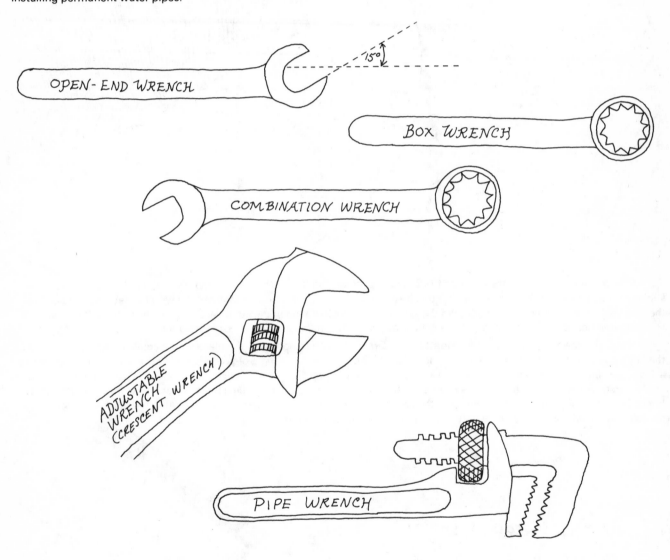

WOOD SAWS

"Hell it's only wood, it doesn't have to be all that accurate."

Wood saws are for cutting plywood, masonite, wood planks, boards, and timbers. At its best the saw cuts by carving out ribbons of material when the teeth move over the surface being cut. Each tooth acts as a tiny knife. Crosscut saws have pointed teeth, and are intended for cutting across the grain, ripsaws have flat-ended teeth and are intended for cutting with the grain (in the same direction as the grain).

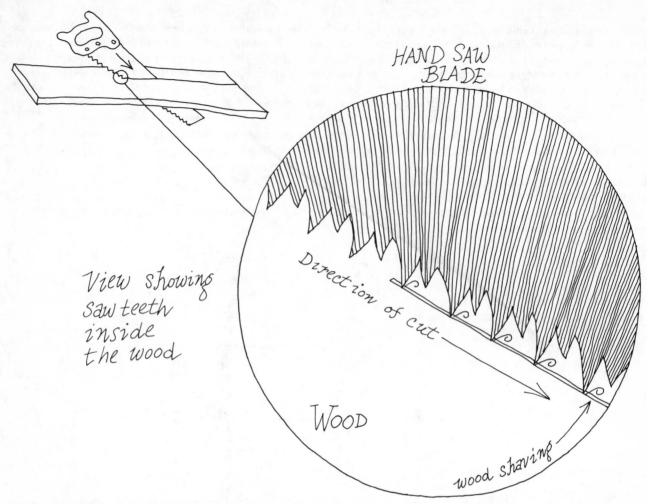

HAND SAW BLADE

View showing saw teeth inside the wood

Direction of cut

Wood

wood shaving

The big, flat wood saws are stamped from a sheet of steel, and the teeth bend alternately to the right and to the left, as shown in the picture. Most saw teeth are cut this way so that the saw will cut out a slot into the wood wider than the body of the saw itself. Because the cut is wider than the saw, the saw will not bind in the cut unless it is twisted or bent. It is this alternate bending of the teeth that gives you control over the saw and allows you to cut a straight line.

Begin by sawing a straight cut through a board. Draw a line on the board at the place where you want to make the cut. If the cut is to be at right angles to one of the sides of the board, use the right angle of your 45-45-90 triangle to line it up, or use a T-square or a carpenter's square. Make the line straight and true right out to the edge of the wood. It is essential to get the line accurate at the edge of the wood because the saw starts cutting there, and if the cut starts out wrong it will be difficult or impossible to straighten out. Remember that the saw cut has thickness, so you must decide whether the finished cut ought to fall to the right side of the line, to the left of it, or right down the middle of it.

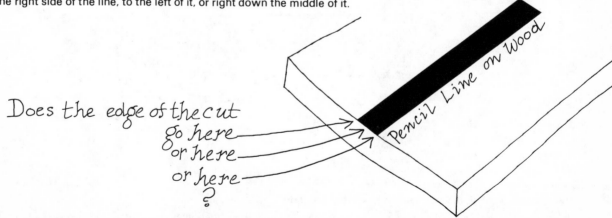

Does the edge of the cut go here or here or here ?

Pencil Line on Wood

Steady the work to be cut by placing it on a bench, table, or chair where you can lean some weight on it and at the same time get a clear shot at it with the saw. Remember that the saw will travel, so make sure it won't travel into your hand or into the side of the table.

Remember that the saw will cut a slot wider than the blade of the saw, and if the board you cut is too short by the width or even by half the width of a saw cut, your bookcase won't hold together, or your light-tight animal testing apparatus will have leaks in it, and it will just be too bad. Know where the saw ought to travel down the pencil line, and rest the teeth of the saw against the wood so that the edge of the cut will come out where you want it. Hold the edge of the wood with one hand, and set the thumb against the saw to steady it. Draw the saw toward you carefully to start a notch where the saw will travel. Start with a very small notch and see if it lies where you want it, if not, change it while you can.

When you have a good notch where you want it (made by drawing the saw toward you over the work) begin the cutting by pushing the saw away from you. Use a strong smooth movement. Go slow. Watch the cut to make sure it is following the line where you want it to.

Put the work on a chair or bench. If you are right-handed hold down the work with your left foot, and the other way around. Cultivate the use of both hands for sawing. Put plenty of weight on the wood to keep it steady. If the saw gets a little off the line, twist it to get it back on the line with the next stroke of the saw. If you get it right at the beginning of the cut you can keep it for the whole length of the cut. As the saw cuts deeper and deeper you will be able to steer it this way less and less, but if the cut is true you will need only a tiny leeway to keep the saw right on the line (or wherever you want it).

To get full power out of the saw stroke, push it not straight back and forth, but bring it back straight, and bear down on it in a curve. The curve in the power stroke will press the teeth down into the wood and cause them to take a bigger bite out of the wood than they would do without this added force behind them. Get your shoulder into it. Keep your eye on the end of the saw so it won't hit the floor and nick it up. Make sure that all the angles in your line of vision are right angles so that your eye has an easier time following the cut. When the cut is nearing completion reach around with your free hand and hold onto the block of wood that is being sawed off. Support it to keep it from falling of its own weight and taking a big sliver of your wood with it. If you are cutting a square or nearly square piece of wood with the hand saw, rotate the piece after the cut has progressed about a third of the way through, and after cutting a little rotate it again and then a fourth time so that all four sides have been cut. Then the last cutting of the wood will be on the inside, not the outside, and the danger of ripping off a corner with the last cut is eliminated.

Cutting without twisting the saw and binding it takes practice. So practice. The best practice is to get on a project that uses plenty of sawing. The best practice for sharpening drill bits is to get a cigar box full of dull drill bits and spend an afternoon sharpening them. The best way to practice hammering nails is to get in a project that uses plenty of nails. After you have hammered one or two thousand nails you will know how to do it. Practice is everything.

The hand jigsaw, or coping saw, works the same way the big ripsaw works, except that the blade is so narrow that it can perform sharp turns in wood. Mark a clear line on the wood. The coping saw gets out of control easily, so clamp the work down securely to the edge of the workbench, or hold it securely in a vise. Remember to keep the blade traveling at a right angle to the plane of the wood surface. Otherwise you will cut out a sloping slot. Follow the line on the wood by steering the saw and keeping the cut next to the line. Keep the saw on the line by keeping the path of the blade parallel to the line.

These saws are hand-held tools and they have their electric counterparts. The ripsaw's electric counterparts are the hand-held power saw, the table saw and band saw. Like the ripsaw, these saws cut in a straight line. For the hand-held power saw, just read the manual that comes with it or ask the person whose saw you use. Hold down the work with one hand, foot, or knee and turn on the power. Hold the saw in your free hand and push it against the work while pulling the trigger. The pressure from your hand will push back the blade guard and expose the blade to the work.

There is no special art to using the hand-held power circular saw. Keep your fingers out of the way, cut with a smooth steady motion, make sure you are not going to saw into any nails, and always allow for the width of the cut. The hand-held power saw is portable as far as you can get electricity to it.

The table saw is a power saw with a circular blade that peeks out from a slot in a table. The table saw is not portable but it is stable and accurate. Most table saws have a crank that will adjust the height that the saw protrudes above the table, so you can use the saw for cutting slots. Keep the blade as low in the table as you can for each cut you want to make: The saw should stick up about 1/2'' above the wood you are cutting. In some table saws you can tip the blade or the table to make edges cut at an angle. Use angle saw cuts for the corners of boxes.

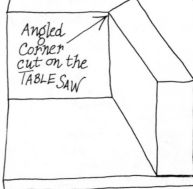

Most table saws have a groove in the table and a guide that slides in the groove. Hold the work against the guide and slide both together as you cut the work against the saw. This will give a perfectly straight cut.

To get good angle corners on small boards, as for picture frames, use a mitre box and a back saw. The saw rides in the slots and the work is clamped in the trough for cutting.

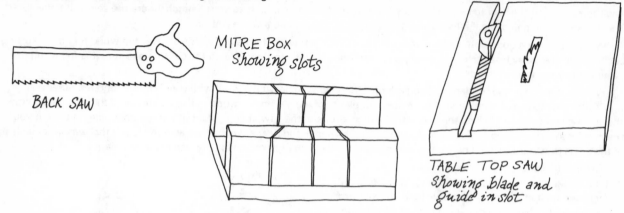

BACK SAW

MITRE BOX
Showing slots

TABLE TOP SAW
Showing blade and
guide in slot

The electric counterpart of the coping saw is the electric jigsaw. Its use is fairly obvious. The teeth cut DOWN, not up. In most jigsaws the circular motion of the motor is converted to linear motion which drives the saw up and down on a gear arrangement under the jigsaw table. The saw blade moves up and down through a slot in the table and connects to a spring above the table. The blade must cut on the down stroke or it will lift the work up off the table with each stroke. The spring above the table keeps the saw blade taut throughout its up-and-down motion. To do this the spring must be slightly tensed when the blade is at the top of its journey.

Learn how to replace the blades in your jigsaw because they will break often. Usually they are held in place at top and bottom by a set screw. Sometimes in cheaper saws they lock in with the little pegs that are at the ends of the blades. The circle in the middle of the jigsaw table comes out so that you can see what you are doing when you are changing the blade.

If you want to cut out a hole in a sheet of material and don't want to have the cut connect to the outside of the sheet, drill a hole in the material on the line you want to saw. Take the blade out of the jigsaw and thread it through the hole. Then carefully install the blade back in the saw while it is still threaded through the work. Cut your hole, and remove the blade the same way you put it in. Make sharp turns by turning the work on the table without pushing it forward at all.

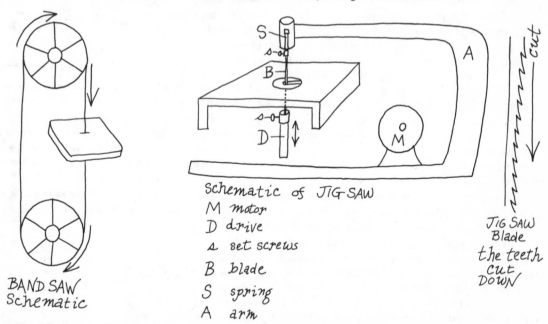

BAND SAW
Schematic

Schematic of JIG SAW
M motor
D drive
s set screws
B blade
S spring
A arm

JIG SAW
Blade
the teeth
cut
DOWN

The band saw is the virtuoso saw. The blade is a continuous loop welded in one spot, and it rides on wheels that guide it above and below a table. Because the blade moves down into the table smoothly and constantly it never lifts or otherwise disturbs the work it is cutting. The band saws with the thinnest blades do the work of a fine jigsaw. Only they do it more delicately because they don't have a reciprocating drive that bounces with every stroke and lifts the work. Band saws in big lumberyards have a blade 3/6" thick and 1 1/2" wide that will saw through whole trees. Some metal cutting houses have a band saw that runs through the ceiling and down into the floor and back up the wall. That way if you can get a piece of metal in the room you know you can cut it. They cut iron and steel sheet into intricate shapes by placing the sheet on a forest of pipes fitted on top with a ball bearing. The saw operator walks among the forest of bearing posts and pushes the sheet metal over the saw. They usually charge extra for cutting the metal "to the line" (extra accuracy) but it is usually worth it.

The kerf saw is a miniature back saw. The teeth are not bent so that it saws a very narrow slot which is useful for seating guitar frets.

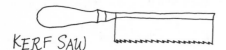

KERF SAW

SABRE SAW

The sabre saw is one of the new inventions that is a genuine addition to craftsmanship. The sabre saw is a hand-held electric jigsaw with a reciprocating blade and its own sliding table. The sabre saw will cut outlines of any size and shape out of masonite and plywood. The manufacturer makes a compass attachment that connects right to the sabre saw enabling you to cut out perfect circles.

TIN SNIPS

Tin snips are large scissors for cutting thin sheet metal. Their use is obvious; practice until you can follow a line. Tin snips leave the sheet metal with a curl at the cut edge, so don't use them if the edge must be absolutely flat, or if you do, file the curled edge down. You can cut sheet copper and aluminum and soft iron and even bronze by placing the sheet of metal on a scrap piece of plywood and cutting both together on the band saw or jigsaw. Big shops have a guillotine for cutting sheet metal.

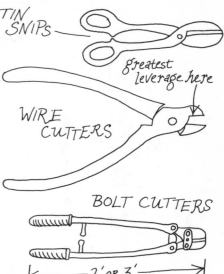

TIN SNIPS

greatest leverage here

WIRE CUTTERS

BOLT CUTTERS

2' or 3'

WIRE CUTTERS

Wire cutters are mostly for cutting copper wire, which is soft for a metal. Brass and iron wire, and even very thick copper wire will put nicks in the cutting edges of wire cutters. For cutting hard or heavy wires, use the cutters on big electrician's pliers. For the hardest wire and cable, use a bolt cutter or a hacksaw. A rough-and-dirty trick for cutting a wire is to hammer it in two against the edge of an anvil.

PLIERS AND VISE GRIPS

The word pliers means "benders-and-shapers," and pliers are are for bending and shaping metal wire and metal sheet. Use large pliers for heavy sheet metal and wire, small pliers for thin sheet metal and wire. Most pliers have serrated gripping surfaces that will not easily slip off the work. Some pliers, notably for the making of metal jewelry where a clean and scratch-free product is mandatory, have polished gripping surfaces.

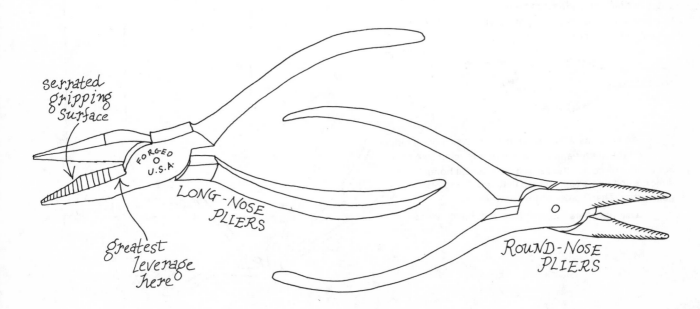

serrated gripping surface

FORGED U.S.A.

LONG-NOSE PLIERS

greatest leverage here

ROUND-NOSE PLIERS

Bend a loop into the end of a piece of iron wire. Use a piece of wire that is long enough to let you get a grip on one end with the pliers and with your hand at the other. Use two pliers at once for the most difficult work. If you get only one pair of pliers get big ones. You will be surprised what delicate or fine work you can do with large pliers. If you want to work some material like coat hanger wire you will absolutely need big electrician's pliers to cut it and manipulate it.

Bending a loop, big or small into the end of a wire—bend over the portion you want to curl (depending on the size of the loop you want) and then nibble your way back from the end. If a kink gets in the wire, start over with a new wire because kinks never come out of wires. Never ever. Gentle lumps will come out with gentle massaging with the pliers. If the loop is to be very small, the thickness of the wire will determine how tight a loop you can make.

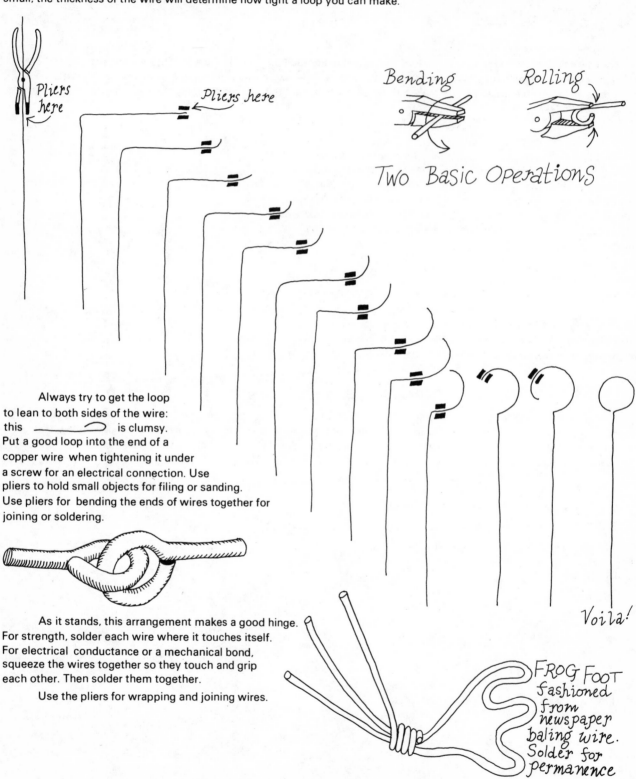

Pliers here

Pliers here

Bending   Rolling

Two Basic Operations

Always try to get the loop to lean to both sides of the wire: this ⌒ is clumsy. Put a good loop into the end of a copper wire when tightening it under a screw for an electrical connection. Use pliers to hold small objects for filing or sanding. Use pliers for bending the ends of wires together for joining or soldering.

As it stands, this arrangement makes a good hinge. For strength, solder each wire where it touches itself. For electrical conductance or a mechanical bond, squeeze the wires together so they touch and grip each other. Then solder them together.

Use the pliers for wrapping and joining wires.

Voila!

FROG FOOT fashioned from newspaper baling wire. Solder for permanence

With the pliers, bend a soft iron wire into a cube-on-a-wire, with handle.

Solder the joints, dip it in a soap solution,
and look at the bubbles that form in
the cube. Bend some wires into a
variety of different shapes
(all on a wire with handles) and dip them in soap solution.
Architects use the bubbles that form to study the nature of stress in materials

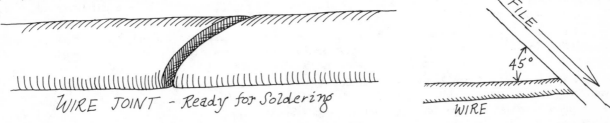

Use heavy electrician's pliers for forming coat hanger wire into any shape you can. To make a continuous loop of wire with no visible joint, file off the ends of the wire at forty-five degree angles, and twist the wire until the ends meet flush. The filing may need some adjustment. When the ends meet, solder them together with silver solder.

WIRE JOINT - Ready for Soldering

FILE

45°

WIRE

For the biggest jobs, such as working concrete reinforcing rod, do with the hammer what you have been doing with the pliers. To make sharp corners hammer the pipe or rod around the edge of the anvil, or grip it in the vise and hammer it to the angle you want. To make gentle curves, grip the pipe or rod in the vise along with a heavy iron water pipe. Tap the rod with the hammer to wrap it around the pipe. This will work for copper, brass, aluminum, and the softest iron. For harder or heavier pieces you will need to heat them up with a torch or a forge. The oxy-acetylene torch is tricky because it heats up the metal so hot that it melts or cracks. Try to work the metal cold. If you must heat it up, heat it gently.

Your local hardware store has a big assortment of pliers. Every household has an adjustable pliers for ruining the plumbing. For sculpture and laboratory apparatus, get two pairs of pliers, a big and a small. Get a long-nose pliers for light work and a medium size electrician's pliers for heavy work. The electrician's pliers has a strong hinge that will not wobble, and these pliers will be excellent for both heavy and precise work.

wire cutters

ELECTRICIANS
PLIERS

gripping surfaces

VISE GRIPS

The vise grip is one of the few new-fangled inventions that is a genuine addition to craftsmanship.

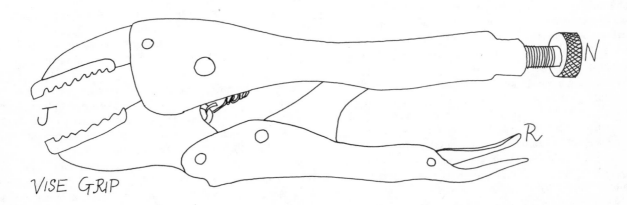

J

N

R

VISE GRIP

Turn the nut N to adjust the jaws J to desired distance apart. Then clamp the jaws on the work by squeezing the handles. If the jaws don't hold, remove the vise grip and bring them a little closer together by turning the nut a little more. Then try again. The jaws will hold absolutely. Release the jaws by pressing the release lever R. Use the vise grip to hold metal pieces down for welding. Use the vise grip to hold a piece of metal by one corner when great stress is to be placed on the rest of the piece in a way that would pull it away from a pliers. Used as a permanent grip pliers the vise grip will save fatigue of the hand muscles.

MATERIALS

The ancients possessed for the fashioning of their world the meager handful of materials which nature provides ready-made.

wood
leather
wool, cotton and a few dyes
bone, horn and shell
a few metals: gold, silver, copper, tin, lead
a few useful stones: the Sio^2 family, and marble
beeswax
clay
pitch
straw

From these they made stone, clay, wood bowls, ladles, pots, horn ladles, bone needles, and harpoon points.

The novice gadgeteer will be encouraged to know that with ingenuity and these few materials the ancients sailed south of the equator and back, the ancient Greeks built marble temples that are still standing and are still the standard of beauty for the world, practiced metal casting, and measured and weighed the earth. With these few materials Archimedes invented the art of engineering, and Praxiteles developed the art of great sculpture. The ancient Egyptians, the Easter Islanders, and the Mayans built stone mountains and monuments by the use of hand tools.

Contemporary materials engineering equips today's gadgeteer with an arsenal of materials (notably the plastics) so varied that their enumeration and description is a study in itself, and so complete that the gadgeteer can almost wish for a material with any properties he chooses, and then get on the telephone and find it.

The rich variety of materials available currently ensures that today's gadgeteer will seldom fail to complete any project for want of appropriate materials. Moreover the diversity of materials available empowers us to think of things we could never have thought of if we were not aware of the possibilities in the material.

The bewildering variety of materials available currently threatens to enslave the inalert gadgeteer by tempting him to work strictly within the limits of the materials he encounters, bringing out what is already there. Such work may be indisputably beautiful but it is not creation. The true potential of the material and the inventor will come out when the inventor decides what he wants and then works his will on the material until he gets it and creates something where before there was nothing.

Imagine that a carver has carved a smooth stone statue and then decides that he wants veins to stand out on the limbs and belly. It is too late. That is why you must know what you want before you start. You will push the material and yourself farther by knowing what you want and working your will on the material than by working within what seems to be the natural inclination of the material.

When you get a material it will be a solid of some shape, or it will be in a bottle or a can, and the temptation is to leave it alone or to follow the surface or the shape. There is a moment of bravery, fear, and danger when you cut below the surface and assume the responsibility of altering the shape of the material so that there can be no turning back to the familiar guidelines of the old surface. Now the shape is yours, to your credit or embarrassment. When you trust yourself to sieze the materials and change them you are créating with them.

ABRASIVES

All substances abrade all other substances, so that the softest alabaster eventually wears the hardest diamond to dust: The word abrasive is only a relative appraisal: A substance is called an abrasive if it wears down other materials faster than other materials wear it down. Convince yourself that steel abrades carborundum by looking at the surface of a well-used sharpening stone. It starts out flat and ends up saddle shaped. Because everything grinds to dust everything else it touches, abrasion is everywhere, and the entire oil, lubricant, and bearing industry is devoted to the postponement of the inevitable. When some material wears away other materials effectively, and when we can control the amount of wearing away that it will do, and when we can get rid of it quickly when it has worn away what we wanted it to, we put it in a can and sell it as an abrasive.

Most commercial abrasives are hard grit of different particle sizes. The grade of the grit is designated by a number indicating the number of particles which, laid end-to-end in a straight line, make one inch. Thus a line of two hundred and twenty particles of 220 grit, laid end-to-end, is one inch long. The grit size must be rigidly controlled because a single particle of coarse grit intruding into a fine grinding operation will permanently scar, for example, a telescope mirror or motor shaft. The scar will not be removed until the entire surface is ground down lower than the lowest part of the scar.

The most popular abrasive grits are quartz (the most common hard substance in the world), garnet (a little harder than quartz), carborundum (an artificial, silicon carbide rock produced by heating sawdust and sand in a furnace), corundum (natural and artificial Al^2O^3, or sapphire), and diamond (pure carbon, the hardest substance in the world, forty times harder than the runner-up, sapphire). Tungsten carbide is becoming popular in the carbide wire saw, carbide scribers, carbide mortars and pestles, carbide masonry drill bits, tungsten carbide blades for surgical scissors, and tungsten carbide gripping surfaces for surgical hemostats.

Abrasives can be bought on a variety of vehicles.

QUARTZ, GARNET, AND EMORY SANDPAPER

Quartz and garnet are the sand of ordinary sandpaper for sanding wood. They are not hard enough for sanding metal, but they are hard enough for sanding plastic. When sanding wood, sand with the grain. Start with medium paper (you seldom need coarse), then fine, then extra-fine.

Sometimes you will have a wood that becomes rough when it gets damp. The roughness is the ends of the wood fibers curling up. Paint the wood with a little water and let it dry. Then sand down the rough fibers with extra-fine sandpaper. Repeat this until you are satisfied, then sand the wood one last time and varnish it to prevent more water from getting into it.

Flint paper is quartz. (Flint is one of the quartz, or Sio family of metals). Some people say that garnet paper is slightly better than fine quartz sandpaper because garnet is slightly harder than quartz. In general a harder abrasive is more satisfactory than a softer abrasive.

The method of sanding you use depends on the kind of results you want. For wood, always sand with the grain. For plastic or metal, sand in the direction you want the scratches to go. For sanding large, flat surfaces, get a block of wood and wrap a strip of sandpaper around three sides of it. Tack the sandpaper on the two opposing sides and push the block over the surface to be sanded. This procedure will preserve the flat surface and will be economical because it will use up the whole surface of the sandpaper, except where it is tacked or held on the sides.

Sandpaper
Wood Block
Thumb tacks

For sanding small objects with curved surfaces, concave or convex, rip a 2"x2" square from one corner of a sheet of sandpaper and sand with that, backing it up with your finger tips. The work will heat up. Stop and give it time to cool. When cutting metal or plastic it is best to use emery paper or emery cloth. Emery cloth and paper come in a great variety of grit sizes, and the finest of these is crocus cloth, the finest sanding sheet made. Crocus cloth will almost, but not quite, polish metal. In general, emery cloth is not much more expensive than emery paper or sandpaper, and the hard emery grit cuts faster than quartz, while the cloth is more flexible than paper.

When sanding metal or plastic, wet the work and the sanding sheet with water or oil unless these for some reason, will ruin the work. The lubricant will carry away metal or plastic dust so that the sanding sheet will not get clogged, and dust will not fly into your lungs. The lubricant will conduct heat away from the point of abrasion and keep the work cool. You will have a more sensitive feel for the work if you lubricate it than if you don't.

Hand polish plastic by rubbing it with some toothpaste on a cloth; lubricate the work with water.

Polish metal by hand in three ways. Rub it with green chromic oxide and water, white tin oxide and water, or jewelers' rouge and water on a cloth. Burnish it by rubbing it with a piece of harder metal that has been polished to a mirror shine. Tap all over its surface with the ball of a ball peen hammer that has been polished to a mirror shine. The hammering tempers the metal surface and protects it from corrosion. Polish metal and plastic on a motor-driven cloth buffing wheel charged with jewelers' rouge. If you want a complete polishing outfit get two buffing wheels, one for coarser polish and the other for finer polish.

With a little patience you can sand a metal, wood, or plastic surface absolutely flat. The standard of flatness for this is plate glass. Every gadgeteer should have a sheet of plate glass not only as a standard for flatness, but also as a table for accurate inspection, which will be taken up later. Tape a sheet of emery cloth (grit up), cut or torn to a convenient size, to the sheet of plate glass. Tape opposite edges down securely with long strips of tape. Don't tape down just the corners.

Emery Cloth taped to Plate Glass

Lubricate the abrasive with oil or water if these won't ruin the work and place the surface to be flattened on the grit. Hold it steady in your fingers to keep it from rocking, and draw it carefully over the grit in the direction you want the scratches to go. Done carefully, this procedure will give a perfectly flat surface to plastic, metal, or wood.

QUARTZ SAND

I don't know any place where you can buy bulk quartz grit in controlled grain sizes, but you can make some pretty good grit yourself with ordinary sand. Often if you search carefully around the pile of sand at a sand lot you will find places that have been sifted by water runoffs during rains. These will concentrate grains of different sizes in puddles where you can scoop them off. Sometimes the grains will be so small they will almost hold together like mud.

The finest sand of all is clay. Use sand as an abrasive for soft stones, such as marble or alabaster, and use fine sand as a filler for making slurries with liquid plastics, which will be taken up later.

If possible, put some sand in a tumbling mill with water. If you don't have a tumbling mill, put 2" of sand in the bottom of a one-half gallon jar and fill the jar three-fourths full of water and shake it. Let it settle for one minute and then pour off the water to rinse the sand. Replace the water, shake up the jar again and let it settle thirty seconds. Pour off the water into another jar, being careful not to pour off the coarser sand at the bottom. If you are patient, and especially if you use a tumbling mill, you can get quartz sand so fine that it will never completely settle in a jar of water. If for any reason you dry out the fine sand, wear a dust mask to protect your lungs. Wear a GOOD mask when you work with any dry powder because powder in the lungs will kill you dead. The father of a friend of mine died (at age thirty-eight) from breathing rock dust, and gentle reader, you can be sure that if you breathe rock, metal, or plastic dust you will do the same.

SILICON CARBIDE

Carborundum is the backbone of the abrasive industry. Carborundum is not the hardest abrasive available, but it is the cheapest very hard material, and some grinding equipment, especially high-speed shop grinding wheels, is made from carborundum only. You can buy carborundum grit in a range of particle grades from 80 to 660 or so. Use these for grinding telescope mirrors, lenses, optical flats, lithograph stones, precious stones, valves, and every use where precision surfaces are needed.

Because several good books exist on the subject of mirror and lens grinding, not to mention an article in *Scientific American's* department "The Amateur Scientist," there is no sense for me to describe mirror and lens making here. I will give only one example of glass grinding, for historical interest.

It is reputed that the technique for grinding optical flats was invented by Sir Isaac Newton, a renowned gadgeteer. To grind an optical flat, Newton used three discs, all the same diameter and thickness, of annealed, bubble-free glass. We can use flint or crown optical glass for windows or pyrex glass for mirrors. Make a seat for the glass pieces by nailing three wood stops down to a plywood board. Seat one of the glass discs down in the stops and pour water or kerosene over the surface. Make sure the surface of the glass disc is higher than the wood blocks. Sprinkle #80 carborundum grit on the surface on the glass and grind one of the other glass discs against it, using a cyclic motion. After grinding a few strokes, move a few degrees with respect to the stationary piece of glass. Repeat this moving every few strokes so that the entire lower piece of glass receives uniform grinding from all directions.

After grinding once or twice around the bottom glass disc, set aside the top glass disc and grind the third disc in its place. Remove the bottom glass plate and place one of the other plates where it was, and continue grinding. Keep trading off the three glass plates in this way, grinding each against the other two, with each sometimes on the top and sometimes on the bottom. The grinding process will yield three optically flat glass surfaces.

It is not known precisely how the grinding and polishing action of abrasives operates. If the abrasive and water slurry is kept at just the right consistency the top glass disc will seem to roll across the bottom glass disc, and I think that the abrasive particles roll between the glass plates and cut them by pressing shell-shaped chips from the glass surfaces. I think that the abrasive particles do this because the sharp points of the particles concentrate all the pressure between the glass plates on a very small area of the glass, and that the pressure in these tiny areas is enough to cause chipping. Accordingly you will cut the glass faster by bearing down on it hard, and not by scrubbing it fast.

As the grit grinds the glass it also grinds itself, so wash away the mud with water and apply a charge of fresh abrasive. You can recover good abrasive particles from the grinding mud by scooping the mud into a jar of water and stirring it. The coarsest particles will settle to the bottom quickly. Pour off the rest, and re-use what settles first. Clean and dry the glass plates and inspect them for uniform grinding texture. If the ground surfaces seem to be of uniform texture rub one plate over another a few times as if grinding them, then separate them and examine them for any white patches. Any white patches that do not cover the entire face of the glass uniformly are high spots in the grinding. Keep grinding until you don't get any high spots, then go to the next finer grade of grit. When you change grits remember that even one single coarse grit particle left over from the preceeding grinding operation will ruin the next stage in the grinding. Wash everything thoroughly. Grind with the finer grit until the glass surfaces are of a finer uniform texture. The grinding and inspection techniques are the same through the finest abrasive powder.

After grinding the optical flats with the finest grinding grit, polish them. Melt some optical pitch and pour it over one of the optical flats or over a glass disc just like them. As the pitch cools, rest one of the optical flats against it so that the pitch surface will be flat. Make sure that the pitch is cool enough so that the glass won't stick to it. With a cold saw or knife, score channels into the pitch surface.

Channels scored in the surface of optical pitch

Sprinkle some polishing material on the pitch. Sprinkle the polish from high enough so that no cakes of it collect on the surface of the pitch. Use green chromic oxide, white tin oxide, jewelers' rouge, or Barnesite. I don't know which of these is best, but the telescope mirror people recommend Barnesite. Sprinkle a little water mist over the polish and grind the glass flats on it. Move the glass in straight lines instead of cycles.

While polishing the glass be careful not to get your fingers near the edges of the glass disc. The heat from your fingers will make the glass expand, and when it cools there will be hollows in the glass flat. Some people like to attach a wood handle to the back of the discs with optical pitch or sealing wax. Let it sit a few days to make sure it is not warm. When you get the hang of the method you can grind prism faces.

Grind telescope mirrors the same way as optical flats. Keep one glass disc always on the bottom and the other always on the top. Grind with circular motions and turn both the bottom and top pieces with respect to each other and with respect to yourself every minute or so. The top piece will come out concave (the telescope mirror) and the bottom place will come out convex.

GEMS

If you want to become a rock hound and grind gems for fun and profit, get a book on rock grinding, a diamond saw, some slow carborundum wheels, and a rubber polishing lap with tin oxide. But if you want to polish just one small stone up through the hardness of an emerald (8-1/2, about the hardness of carborundum, definitely softer than $A1^2O^3$, corundum) you can do it for a little elbow grease and about a dollar.

Stones are prized according to their color, clarity, and hardness. It is difficult to get a polish on a very hard stone, but once the stone is polished it is difficult to scratch. That is one of the things people like about diamonds. They don't scratch easily. Sapphires and rubies (corundum) are about forty times softer than diamonds, but they are still very hard and difficult to scratch.

Sapphires and rubies can be grown in a furnace. The hammer (1) strikes the hopper (2) full of $A1^2O^3$ powder (3) which falls into the furnace (5) where hydrogen and oxygen gases (4) enter and burn in a hot flame (6). The powder lands on top of a refractory rod (7) where it collects in a puddle. As the puddle grows deeper a rack and pinion (8) retract it slowly from the flame. As the rod moves below the hottest part of the flame the $A1^2O^3$ at the bottom cools and crystallizes, while fresh powder falls at the top. The process leads to the production of a sapphire boule which is a single sapphire crystal. If impurities are added to the $A1^2O^3$ powder the stone produced will have some color. Chromium yields red ruby.

It is by this process more or less that the synthetic star rubies and sapphires are produced. The stars in the natural star rubies and sapphires are not always as perfect as those in the artificial stones, but they have a certain delicacy. The artificial stars are a little loud. I have heard that it is possible to artificially produce stones delicate enough to compete in beauty with the natural ones, but that the marketing of them is illegal. In any case it is possible to mass-produce quite large boules of perfect sapphire crystal. The boules are about 3/4" wide and can be almost any length. Because of its hardness the stone makes good knife bearings for balance scales, ball bearings for gyroscopes, as well as sleeve bearings for watches. Sapphire makes good bearings because once it is polished (and therefore slippery) it STAYS polished and slippery. NASA uses tiny ruby ball bearings in a gold-plated race for some of its navigational gyroscopes.

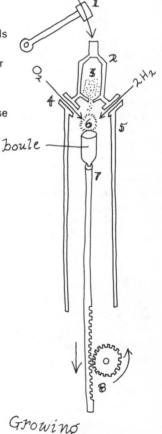

boule

Growing
SAPPHIRES and RUBIES
in a furnace

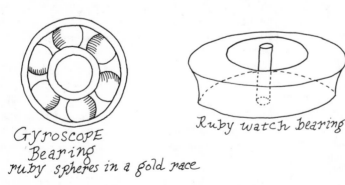

Gyroscope
Bearing
ruby spheres in a gold race

Ruby watch bearing

Chromium atoms dispersed in clear sapphire crystal will lase, and the material of some crystal lasers is the synthetic ruby, grown in an oxygen-hydrogen furnace.

You can conveniently cut by hand any stone up to 1/2" in dimension and softer than sapphire, namely (in order of descending hardness)

beryl (emerald, aquamarine)

topaz

garnet

quartz (crystal, moonstone, agate, moss agate, onyx, calcedony, opal . . .)

tourmaline

feldspar (labradorite, amazonstone)

apatite ·

jade, and many other, rarer semi-precious stones such as the diopsides.

Cut your stone into a pillow shape (cabochon) because good faceting requires accurate, if not elaborate, equipment. It is possible to do only simple, medieval faceting by hand, but it is possible to a fine cabochon by hand. Select your stone and decide what shape you want it to be. Then carefully rough chip it to approximately that shape.

Cabochons

Buy a small (3") carborundum sharpening stone. Glue the gem to a stick of dowel (called a dop stick) for convenience of handling. The dop stick is optional but helpful. Use model airplane glue or special dopping cement (available from rock hound supply houses) or some cement that will come off the gem because something like epoxy will never come off. The dop stick is helpful if you accidentally drop the stone: It can't go down the drain.

Stone on Dop Stick

Turn on the water in the sink to a slow trickle and soak the sharpening stone in the water. Grind the gem by rubbing it against the abrasive stone under the water. (If you are right-handed you will probably hold the stone steady in your left hand and move the gem over it with your right. When your right hand gets tired, hold the stone in the right hand and the gem in the left. Move the stone over the gem. This uses different muscles and will keep you grinding longer.)

Rub the gem on the abrasive stone under dripping water

The gem will grind a trough in the sharpening stone, essentially ruining it for sharpening knives. Grind the high spots in the gem first, coaxing it to the shape you want. Keep the stone turning and tilting at all times. It is impossible to over-emphasize that the gem must turn and tilt constantly as it is being ground. If the gem travels over the flat, abrasive stone without turning and tilting, a flat place will develop in the gem, and we have already discussed the difficulty of removing flat places. The hollow that the gem grinds in the surface of the abrasive stone helps guarantee that the grind stone will not have any flat places to grind into the gem, so that even though the stone is ruined for sharpening knives, it is improved for grinding the gem. It only costs 75¢ anyway, part of the cost of production.

When the gem is cut to exactly the shape you want, and when the surfaces are absolutely smooth and free of flat spots, wash off the stone and remove it from the dop stick. A soaking in water will remove the gem from the dop stick. Grind the back of the gem. Transparent and translucent stones should be polished on both sides. Opaque stones need to be polished only on the top side.

Get some 220 and some 660 carborundum grit. Tack a sheet of coarse cloth rag (linen or fine denim) to a sheet of plywood and soak this in water and dust it with the 220 grit to make a thin paste on the cloth. Grind the gem over the cloth until the surface is as fine as it will get. Then wash out the grit from the cloth, the plywood board, and the stone, and repeat the operation with the 660 grit. Then repeat everything with green chromic oxide, white tin oxide, jewelers' rouge, or Barnesite.

When done patiently this hand method will turn out a polished gem that glistens like a drop of water. It takes a long time, but if you only want to make one gem this is the least expensive way to do it, and you get the feel of the grinding. After that you can grind on a machine and have a feel for what is happening.

Now that you have some acquaintance with grinding, try to answer this question—how would you grind an optical flat? Before Newton came up with a way, it was difficult. One of the aims of this book is to make available the feel for how these processes work. How do you grind an optical flat? You do it with three pieces of glass. Just that answer alone ought to be plenty. Following is an explanation of how it works. Mull over the explanation until the answer "with three pieces of glass" makes the whole process obvious.

When two plates of glass are ground together, and one is always on the bottom, the pressure of the grinding always falls on the edges of the lower piece, grinding them down until the two pieces of glass can move freely over each other without any concentration of pressure between them at any one area. The curves formed are spheres, one concave, the other convex. This is the method used for grinding telescope mirrors.

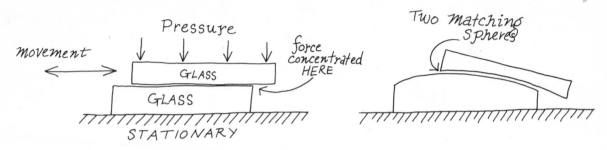

If the lower and upper plates of glass are exchanged every so often, each will have a surface the shape of which will be the sum of two spheres, one positive and one negative. The result will be a zero sphere, or flat plate, if both plates receive exactly the same amount of grinding. Since this is very hard to do, three plates are used, so that if any one of them has a curve it will be ground against a plate that has an unrelated curve, and the sums will have a better chance of being zero.

GRINDING WHEELS

Almost all grinding wheels are silicon carbide, carborundum. We have already used the grinding wheel in the section on drill bits and chisels. When you buy a new grinding wheel make sure that the rpm (revolutions per minute) of the motor in your shop grinder does not exceed the maximum safe rated rpm for the stone. The maximum safe rpm for the stone is printed on the label glued to the side of the stone.

The grinding wheel is for hard iron and steel only—*no* copper, brass, lead, plastic, wood, or aluminum. Use bronze carefully. These materials will clog the wheel with their non-abrasive residues and ruin the wheel.

Even though the grinding wheel is coarse, the movement of the wheel presents an average face to work being ground so that surfaces cut on the wheel will be quite smooth, not pitted or scratched.

Usually you will grind on the narrow face of the grinding wheel, and on the angled corner, so that the edge will become rounded and worn. Restore the sharp edges by running the wheel against a wheel dresser.

The wheel dresser has corrugated or spiked steel wheels that turn on a shaft and grind the stone to powder by vibration. WEAR A DUST MASK while restoring the grinding wheel.

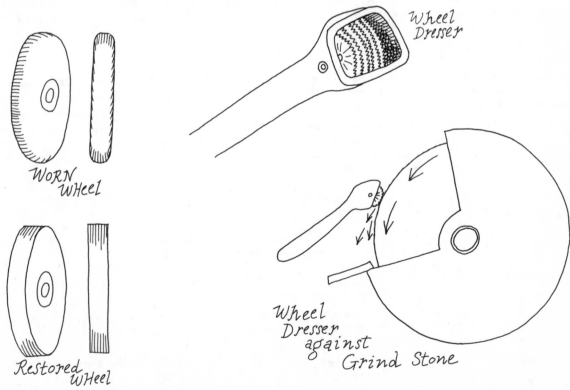

When the wheel is sharp at the edges, practice using it by grinding a Phillips tip into the end of a steel rod.

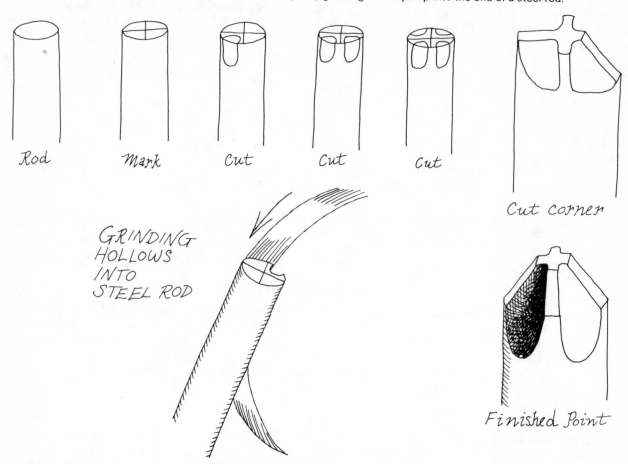

Rod   Mark   Cut   Cut   Cut   Cut corner

GRINDING HOLLOWS INTO STEEL ROD

Finished Point

Use the edges of the wheel to grind the hollows for the Phillips tip. Be careful not to scorch the metal and ruin the temper. Flatten the other end of the rod and make a handle for a homemade screwdriver. If you have an impact wrench, a screwdriver that turns (screws) when you hit it with a hammer, restore your broken Phillips tips with the grinder. On big jobs this will save considerable time and money. The restored tips last longer and grip the screw tighter than the tips that come with it when you buy it.

KNIFE

After you have learned to use the grinder you might want to make your own knife. I ground the blade for my knife on a grinder. Make your first knife blade from an old file. Decide what size and shape knife you want, we discussed that already, and pick out a file small enough so that you don't have to grind it forever to get it down to the blade size you want.

Use an old, worn-out file so that you don't have to waste a new one. Decide how long you want the blade and handle of your knife to be, and mark these lengths on the file, beginning from the end of the tang.

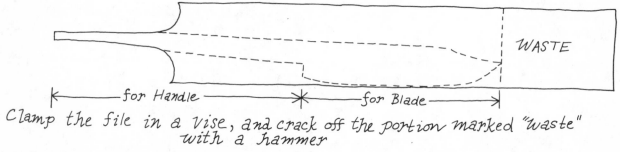

WASTE

|← for Handle →|← for Blade →|

Clamp the file in a vise, and crack off the portion marked "waste" with a hammer

Remove the file from the vise and take the brittle temper out of it by heating until red hot or nearly red hot over a Meaker burner or blowtorch. The file metal does not need to be re-tempered later. The knife blank is now ready for grinding on the grinding wheel.

Grind the sides of the file blank to remove the grooves. Grind until all traces of the groove hatching are removed, then glue to the side of the blank a paper tracing of the profile of the knife you want to make; the tracing should include the tang.

Paste your design (you do not have to cut it out) onto the side of the file with Elmer's Glue-All, and grind around it right down to the line. Remember to keep the knife moving at all times during grinding so that the metal doesn't scorch. Hold the file flat against the grinder table and grind around and around the outline until the blank is finished. The scratches on the edges will all slope off to the bottom of the blank.

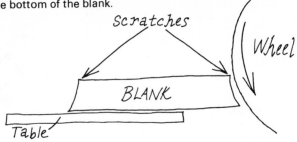

Turn the blank over and gently trim the other side on the wheel so that the scratches meet in the middle of the edges.

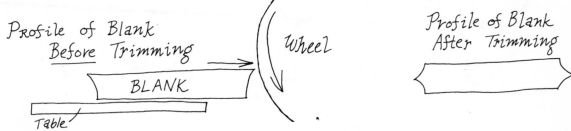

Round out the back of the knife so that it will not raise blisters when the hand is pressed against it.

Carefully grind the sides of the knife so that they taper to a point at the front. Chamfer the edges of the tang slightly.

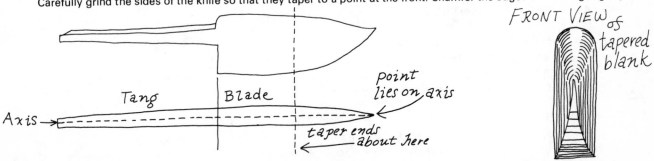

Center the knife point directly on the axis of the blank. This is not easy to do, and will take a patient eye. During the grinding take the knife off the stone repeatedly and examine it point-on and tang-on, and note if it is fatter on one side and hollower on the other. Remember where the high places are and grind them down.

When the blank has a satisfactory taper begin grinding the cutting edge. Remember that the thickest part of the blade is up next to the back and is NOT in the center of the blade.

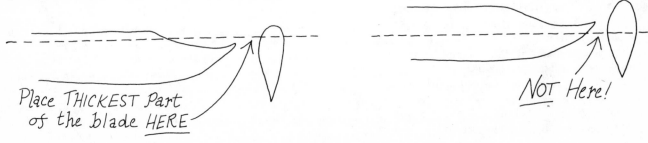

Leave a block at the rear of the blade to sit up against the handle or finger guard of the finished knife.

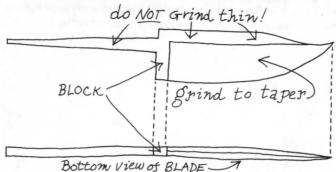

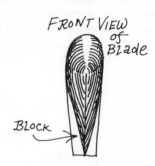

Because the annealed file metal is fairly soft you can cut the cutting edge into the knife blank by hand with a file. Filing the cutting edge by hand instead of grinding it in the grinder affords a chance to work slowly, and avoid ruining your first knife. File from the rear to the point of the knife.

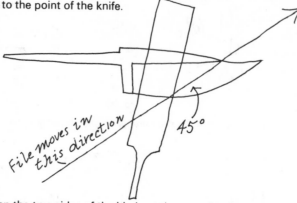

Always keep the two sides of the blade at the same level of completion so that the sides of the blade come out symmetrical and the cutting edge comes out straight. The motion of the file helps greatly in this, as if the forward movement generated a straight cutting edge naturally through averaging.

When the blade is shaped, make sure that the taper to the cutting edge is thin because the sharp edge must touch the work at a steep angle.

Smooth the blade with fine emery cloth lubricated with oil, then polish it with crocus cloth lubricated with oil. Then burnish the blade by rubbing it on any piece of shiny, smooth, stainless steel. The head of a stainless steel bolt will do.

For this work and all other hard grinding, filing, polishing, sanding and sawing, the same result is effected by moving the work over the tool as is effected by moving the tool over the work. Fasten down the one that is most convenient to fasten down, and move the one that is most convenient to move. For example it is often most convenient to hold a saw in a vise in one's lap and move the work over the saw than it is to hold the work in the vise and move the saw over it.

The knife blade is ready for a handle and a finger guard. The finger guard is optional. If you choose to make a finger guard, make it first. I put a finger guard on my knife (the only concession I made to the weapon) to remind me when my finger was getting near the blade. The finger guard gives a little extra leverage and control in pushing and twisting the knife.

Make the finger guard from a sheet of steel or silver. Nickels are good for this use, but it is illegal to cut up coins. A knife with a blade made from a file is not worth a silver finger guard. The finished finger guard should have this shape:

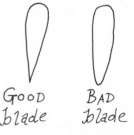

but cut out the hole FIRST—then cut out the shape around it.

Cut out the rectangular hole by drilling two holes in the place where the rectangular hole will be. Center punch the holes separately and drill them separately, then connect them by pushing the piece against the rotating drill bit. Use drill bits of diameter smaller than that of the finished rectangular hole. When the holes are connected slide a needle file in and cut the hole to the shape of a rectangle. Enlarge the rectangular hole by degrees until the finger guard will barely slide over the tang and up to the base of the blade. Then the hole is completed.

Flatten the face of the finger guard that will touch the knife handle by laying the guard on a file and moving it back and forth over the ridges, holding it against the file with two or three fingers. Use the file to dome off the side of the guard that will face the blade. Now begin the handle.

Make the handle out of wood—mahogany, teak, walnut, manzanita. Antler, bone, rosewood, and ebony make good handles, but it seems a shame to put an antler handle on a knife made from a file. Cut the handle from a piece of wood in the shape of a rectangular solid.

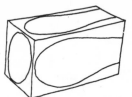

Outlines of KNIFE HANDLE traced on surface of wood block

Draw on the sides, ends, top, and bottom of the wood block the outlines of the handle that you want. Now drill out the hole that will accommodate the knife tang. Orient the hole at the angle at which you want the blade to exit from the handle. Because the tang on the blade is probably tapered you will also want the hole in the handle to be tapered.

Select the place at the butt end of the handle where you want the hole to exit the handle, and mark the spot. Turn the wood over and mark on the front face of the handle the place where you want the tang to enter the handle. Mark this place with a rectangle the size of the hole in the finger guard. Inside the rectangle mark two places with the center punch so that two holes can be drilled side by side without the bit falling into the first hole while it is drilling the second. When two holes are drilled through the rectangle so that both exit the wood at the single place marked at the butt of the handle, they will make the outline of a tapered hole that will accommodate the tapered knife tang.

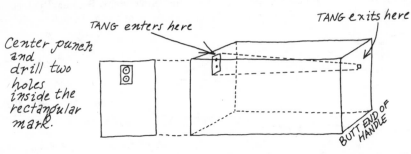

Center punch and drill two holes inside the rectangular mark.

TANG enters here

TANG exits here

Use the vise and the drill press to direct the bit into the wood at the desired angles.

BUTT END OF HANDLE

In order to accommodate the knife tang the double-round hole in the handle will have to be squared off to rectangular cross section. Begin by joining the two slant holes with a drill. Cut into the wood between the holes and twist the bit so that it chews away the wood. Be careful not to drill into the sides of the hole and ruin its future rectangular shape. There are several ways to square off the corners of the hole.

1) Cut them square with a coping saw. This is tricky. Take the blade off the saw and thread it through the hole in the handle, then spring the blade back into the saw. Press on the back of the blade with your thumb so that the toothed side of the blade is convex, and cut into the corners. The blade must slide along the walls of the hole as it cuts or it will saw a deep notch into one of the walls. The notch will be impossible to get out.

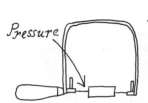

Pressure

Apply pressure to the BLADE with one hand so that it will bow out in a convex shape. Move the handle over the saw blade with the other hand, scraping the walls of the hole against the teeth to flatten them.

2) Cut them square with a scraping tool made from a windshield wiper spring.

90°

Scrape the sharpened cutting edge in the corners of the hole until they are worn square.

3) File them square with a needle file. This is the easiest, quickest, most accurate way if you can get a needle file thin enough to fit down the narrow drill holes. Remove the file from the wood constantly and clean the sawdust out of it. Use a square or triangular needle file.

As you cut the hole for the tang, put the tang into the hole every so often and peek inside as far as you can to determine the places where the metal contacts the wood. Cut at these places only. It is safe enough to force the tang into the handle blank provided you force it only by hand power, without hitting it. Eventually the tang will fit all the way down into the handle blank.

Remove the blade from the handle, slide the finger guard on the tang, and replace the tang into the handle blank. Trace onto the wood around the finger guard, and remove the finger guard and blade. Draw a line across the middle of the traced finger guard.

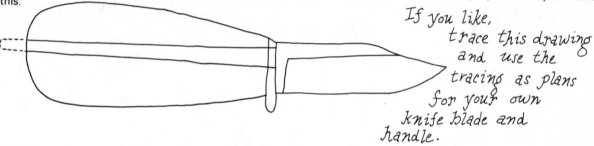

trace

Set the finger guard
in place on the front
of the handle blank
and trace around it

line

Remove the finger guard and
draw a line across the middle
of the tracing of it.

Area A in the illustration
is the front end of
the knife handle

The area enclosed above the line is the front of the knife handle.

Now, ignoring the old lines for the knife handle, draw new handle outlines on the handle blank. Replace the blade and finger guard in the handle and imagine how the finished knife will look. Take the time to arrive at a shape you like. My own knife looks like this.

If you like,
trace this drawing
and use the
tracing as plans
for your own
knife blade and
handle.

After you arrive at a plan for the handle, draw it boldly on the handle blank.

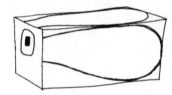

Cut away what you can with the jigsaw, then cut away the rest with a wood rasp, coarse file, and sandpaper. Finish the handle with crocus cloth and human face oil, linseed oil, Butcher's wax, or lemon polish. Don't use varnish or paint because these will give the handle an absolutely smooth surface that will raise blisters.

Cut off the end of the tang just beyond the end of the handle.

When the handle is nearly finished put the blade and finger guard in it and see how the end of the handle and the finger guard match. Bring them together with crocus cloth. The crocus cloth will bring the edges together with thousandths-of-an-inch accuracy. Make sure the back of the finger guard is flat, and that the front and bottom (which protrudes below the handle and blade) are rounded at the edges.

After the handle and finger guard (if any) fit satisfactorily in your completed handle, glue the blade in the handle with epoxy. Follow the instructions on the package. Usually the instructions direct that you mix equal volumes of resin and hardener to a uniform paste and apply them to roughened, absolutely clean, dry surfaces.

Line the hole in the handle with resin and slide the tang in. Try to fill the space between the tang and the walls of the hole with epoxy. The twenty-four-hour epoxy stays runny for four to six hours, so you will need to keep checking the knife and rotating it to make sure the epoxy doesn't run out. If the epoxy plastic hardens in drips on the blade or handle it is nearly impossible to remove, and the knife is essentially ruined. The fifteen-minute epoxy sets up in about three or four minutes, so you don't have to tend it as long, but you will have to work correspondingly faster with it once you have it mixed up.

Epoxy is water soluble while it is still runny, so you can wipe it up with a damp, NOT wet, rag. Use the rag sparingly to reduce the danger of letting water drip into the handle and ruin the epoxy there.

While the glue is drying, clamp the blade securely into the handle in exactly the position you want it, thus:

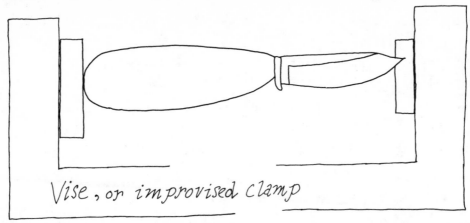

Vise, or improvised clamp

Don't let the clumsiness of the knife's position in the clamp prevent you from inspecting the underside of the knife for glue drips. After twenty-four hours your knife is ready. If necessary, grind or file the end of the tang to meet the end of the handle exactly. Oil the handle every few days until it doesn't need oiling any more.

If you want to make a case for the knife I suggest you sew a case out of leather.

The case described below fits the knife plan described above.

Get a piece of heavy belt leather from a leather store. Such stores often sell remnants at reduced prices; get a piece that will yield the pieces described here.

Cut out a piece for the blade guard.

Do not sew the blade cover yet.

Cut out another piece for the handle strap.

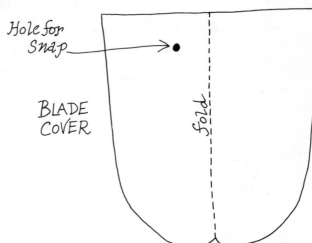

Hole for Snap

BLADE COVER

fold

HANDLE STRAP

Hole for Snap

Fold the blade cover over with the smooth side of the leather out, and place the blade in the pouch thus produced.

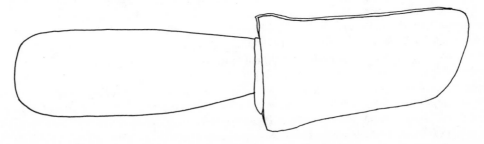

Fold the cover over the handle so that it falls down on both sides of the blade cover.

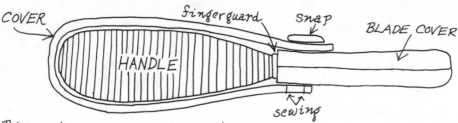

COVER — fingerguard — snap — BLADE COVER

HANDLE

sewing

BACK VIEW of KNIFE in its COVER
Buy a snap from the shop where you bought the leather and have them install it in the leather pieces at the holes marked on the patterns.

Adjust the cover, the blade guard, and the knife so that they are comfortable with each other. This requires some kneading of the leather. Avoid saddle soaping the knife cover more than once because the finished cover ought to be fairly stiff. When the case is adjusted decide where to put the holes for the snap. The places marked in the patterns above are appropriate. Go back to the leather shop and have them install a large brass snap in the unsewn case. Use brass because it won't rust. Then sew the other end (away from the snap) of the handle cover to the back of the blade cover (the side away from the snap).

For sewing the knife case, get two sewing needles and some carpet-and-button thread. Use the thinnest needles that you can thread with this thick thread. Cut a four-foot length of thread, and thread one needle at each end. Put the cover against the blade guard as shown in the illustration and punch the needle through both sheets of leather at the place where the arrow marked "stitching" indicates. Pull the thread one-half way through.

From this point on, stitch the leather by pushing the needle through both pieces, pull the thread through tight, then push the other needle through the same hole from the other side. Probably the leather will be so tough that you will need to drive the needles with pliers while backing up the leather with a sheet of plywood.

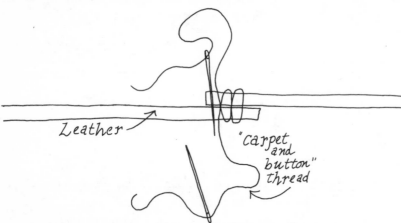

Leather

"carpet and button" thread

Keep the stitching even and straight by marking the places with a pencil where the holes are to go. By these means you can achieve stitching of great strength and evenness.

When the handle cover is sewn in place, fold the blade guard and sew it with the same piece of thread. Knot the end of the thread between the halves of the blade cover.

Now that you have the necessary practice, make another knife blade, same size and shape as the first, out of better steel such as a car leaf spring or a planer blade from a big sawmill. This steel is springy and harder than a file, so rough out the knife blank using a tungsten carbide wire saw and plenty of cutting oil (and elbow grease). The carbide saw will cut a straight line.

outside half of snap (button showing)

KNIFE CASE outside view

Smooth side of leather showing for both pieces

inside half of snap (high part showing)

Stitching

The better steel is too hard to file so you must cut out the outline of the blade on the grinder.

Paste a paper outline on the roughed-out metal and grind it to the outline, using the wheel. Follow the procedures for the last knife. Round out the knife back.

NEVER SCORCH THE METAL. If it scorches even once it is ruined. Keep it moving when it is touching the wheel, and remove it every few seconds to dip it in cold water.

Because good metal is hard, you will have to cut the taper into the knife on the wheel, instead of with the file. Set the blade on its back on the grinder table so that the future cutting edge stands up to meet the turning wheel. Grind the sides of the blade down to the curve of the wheel.

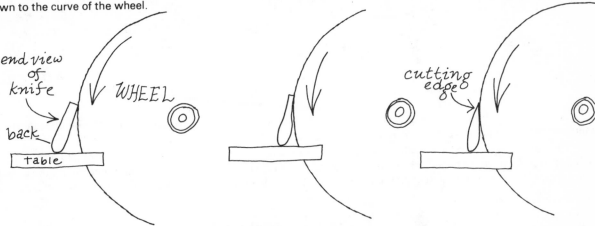

Observe the work from the point of view illustrated, by looking at the point of the knife and along the axis. Keeping the blade moving will help guarantee a straight cutting edge (one that lies all in a single plane). When the cutting is finished both sides ought to lie flat against the turning wheel. In practice they won't quite do this, so you never get a hollow ground blade.

When the blade is ground to shape, polish it with fine emery cloth, crocus cloth, then chromic oxide, or burnish it with a piece of polished stainless steel.

Now you are pretty proficient with the shop grinding wheel.

CUT-OFF WHEEL

For grinding thick, hard metals such as massive stainless steel plate use the pipe cut-off wheel. The cut-off wheel is a fiber disc about 9" in diameter with a steel reinforced hole in the center for mounting it on a turning shaft. The fiber material is impregnated with carborundum or sapphire chips. Mount the cut-off wheel on a slow table lap, or Skil saw, or on a hand-held grinder.

Use the biggest grinder you can find (they can often be rented) and wear ear plugs, goggles, a dust mask, a leather apron with sleeves, steel-toe shoes, gloves, and a hat to protect you from the noise and dust. I know a fellow who used the grinder and cut-off wheel while he was wearing only a T-shirt and pants, and the hot carborundum grains embedded themselves in his belly. Use the grinder for fairing out welds in plates, and for straightening wavy edges in even the heaviest steel plate. The strategy is identical to that used in straightening wavy edges in sheet metal with a file.

When the cut-off wheel is worn down to about 4" in diameter throw it away and get a new one.

Some cut-off wheels are more flexible than others, and the more flexible ones are easier to use. The hard ones seem to take too big a bite out of the metal with too little effort from the operator, although with practice one can do the most delicate work with the hard wheel.

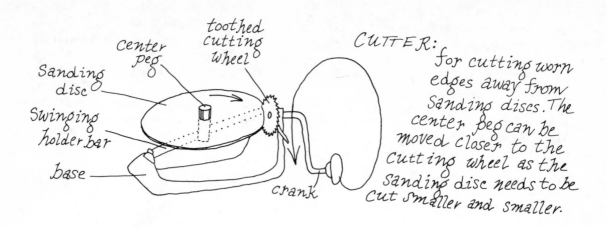

center peg

Sanding disc

Swinging holder bar

base

toothed cutting wheel

crank

CUTTER: for cutting worn edges away from sanding discs. The center peg can be moved closer to the cutting wheel as the sanding disc needs to be cut smaller and smaller.

Use the grinder for turning sanding discs. These are cloth discs coated on one side with Al_2O^3 grains that will grind and texture the surface of metal, stone, or concrete.

The sanding disc must have a rubber wheel backing it up. Buy a set of rubber backing wheels of different sizes, and use the largest first. Grind at the edge of the wheel, and when the abrasive is worn away at the perimeter, cut off the outside edge of the sanding disc and back it up with the next smaller rubber backing wheel. In this way you can use the entire surface of the sanding disc.

TUNGSTEN CARBIDE

Tungsten carbide is the hardest cheap abrasive, and we have seen it in the carbide wire saw. It is used for the cutting blades in masonry drill bits and rock drill bits available in hardware stores. Carbide tip scribers are also easy to get and fairly cheap—about $1.75 or so for a pencil-shaped scriber that will mark metals and even glass. The scriber is not a glass cutter, but some glass cutters are made with a carbide wheel. My experience with these has been that the carbide wheel cuts glass well enough, but the holder hurts the hands more than do the more common steel wheel glass cutters.

I have used a tungsten carbide scriber for cutting my signature into drinking glasses cut from wine bottles. The scriber is not a glass cutter; the glass cutter employs a wheel which does not scratch the glass but applies to a very small area of glass all the pressure that your arm brings to the cutter. Thus the cutter starts a small crack in the glass which you deepen by tapping.

Big scientific supply houses carry tungsten carbide mortars and pestles.

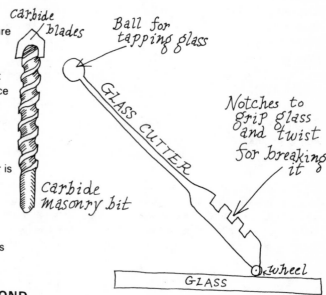

carbide blades

carbide masonry bit

Ball for tapping glass

GLASS CUTTER

Notches to grip glass and twist for breaking it

wheel

GLASS

DIAMOND

Diamond is the hardest of all materials, and the harder a material the better an abrasive it is. Buy a diamond scriber (a small one costs about $2.00) and compare it to the tungsten carbide scriber. Sign your name twice on the same bottle, once with the carbide scriber and once with the diamond scriber. The diamond is like milk and honey by comparison. There is no comparison. That is why hardness is an elegant and excellent quality in a stone.

Serious jewelry supply houses carry diamond dust (called bortz or diamond bort) in different grain sizes. It cost about $5 a carat when last I looked, but that was a long time ago. Whatever it costs, it is worth the price. Diamond dust is unsurpassable as an abrasive for fine drilling into stone for jewelry, and for fine grinding of stone surfaces.

It is likely that the world diamond concerns have enough diamonds to flood the market and bring the price down considerably. The high price of diamonds holds up science and medicine to a certain degree by impeding the access to diamond windows in high pressure apparatus for study of the solid state:

indestructible microscope lenses

super sharp knives for eye and heart surgery

super sharp microtome knives for electron microscopy

durable abrasives for science and industry

The diamond crystal is octahedral Diamonds are pure carbon, and can be burned in oxygen to obtain CO_2

Gem quality diamond are the clearest and are said to be of the first water. Some gem quality diamonds have color, such as cinnamon. The Hope diamond is blue. Industrial diamonds, used for cutting and grinding in industry are opaque and black. A history of diamonds would fill a bookshelf of adventure books.

WOOD SCRAPER

Some people prefer to smooth the surfaces of wood with a steel scraper instead of sandpaper. The scraper is a rectangular steel plate with the edges ground so square that they are sharp.

To grind the steel plate into a scraper, or to restore a sharp edge to a dull scraper, grind the plate on a flat sharpening stone. Grip the plate in a pipe clamp protecting it from the jaws with wood, cloth, or paper. Rest the steel against a flat, oiled sharpening stone and rest the other end of the pipe clamp on a vise or any other elevated object. Adjust the heights of the pieces so that the steel meets the stone at a right angle. If you use a vise, place pegs in the vise on either side of the pipe clamp arm so that when the clamp moves during the sharpening operation the arm will not fall off the vise.

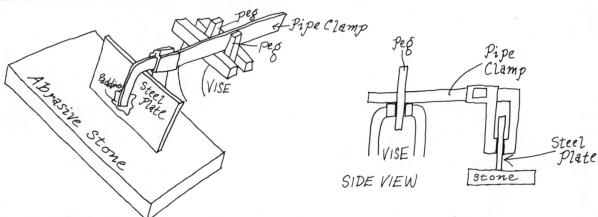

Grip the plate with both hands and flex or bend it gently to ensure that it will meet the stone at right angles. Move the plate over the stone in a figure eight motion, pressing lightly enough that the metal plate never wobbles in the pipe clamp, as wobbling will round the edges. The sharpened steel plate will smooth and polish hard wood. Use a plate about 1/16'' thick. For curved surfaces use a piece of broken glass.

METALS

Copper, brass, bronze
Lead, lead-calcium alloy
Aluminum
Iron, steel, stainless stell
Silver, mercury

Solders: lead-tin, silver

The gadgeteering metals share a few properties in common.
1)   They are *malleable*. If you beat on them they will dent and if you press on them hard enough they will flow. In addition they are *ductile:* if you pull on them they will stretch into a wire. They can be rolled into plate, sheet, and foil; they can be cut with a hacksaw or a file. They are not brittle, unless specially treated to be brittle. They will not stay rigid under pressure and

then snap abruptly as will glass. Instead they bend before they break. When they break they tear; they do not chip into shell-shaped (conchoidal) pieces as does glass, or split along fracture places as do minerals. If metal sheet or wire is bent the crystal structure deteriorates in that it is pulled apart in a way not thoroughly understood. This pulling apart of metals when they are bent is called metal fatigue.

Cut a length of coat hanger wire and bend it back and forth in your hands. Notice that after the place of bending is established it stays put, so that the wire bends back and forth around the same point. That point is a weak place in the wire. Touch the weak place and it will burn you because internal friction in the metal generates heat as the metal rubs over itself. Eventually this metal fatigue will break the wire. It was metal fatigue that caused the Electra airplanes to crash during the early '60's. The planes rocked back and forth and the wing braces slowly fatigued, just like your coat hanger wire, until the wings fell off in flight.

The most dramatic evidence of the malleability of metals is that they can be pulled into wire. Gold, the most malleable of metals, can be pulled into wire so fine that a mile of it weighs only one gram. Gold can be beaten into foil so thin (leaf) that light will pass through it.

2) The gadgeteering metals conduct electricity.

3) The gadgeteering metals conduct heat and expand when heated.

If heat is applied to any part of a metal object, the whole object will heat up. The reverse goes for a cold object applied to a piece of metal. That is to say that a high or low spot in the temperature level of a piece of metal will spread out. Thin sections of metal and thick sections of metal behave differently in this respect, because the thick section of metal provides the heat more pathways to follow.

Temperature gradient continually encounters new paths of thermal conduction so that heat is rapidly conducted away from the hot object.

HOT OBJECT

THICK METAL SECTION

HOT OBJECT

THIN METAL SECTION

Temperature gradient quickly encounters insulator (air), so that relatively few pathways of thermal conduction are available to conduct heat away from the hot object, which will remain hot for a relatively long time.

The thermal behavior of metal is one of the properties that the gadgeteer must deal with when working with metals, and one that he can put to use. For example, if you want to change the temperature of a thing, touch it with a thick piece of metal at the temperature required. A doctor who wants to use dry ice pencils for the freezing of warts can use this method for sharpening his dry ice pencil.

1) Pulverize a piece of dry ice by wrapping it in a sheet of cloth and pounding it with a mallet.

2) Form the pulverized material into a pencil shape by scooping it into a tube mold and tamping it from above, then use the tamper to push the dry ice rod out of the tube mold.

3) "Sharpen" the pencil to a point by rotating it against a steel flat-iron face at room temperature. The sheet metal light shield on a desk lamp will not sharpen the dry ice pencil even though the temperature of the metal is near the boiling point of water. This is because the metal is thin and provides few paths for thermal conduction.

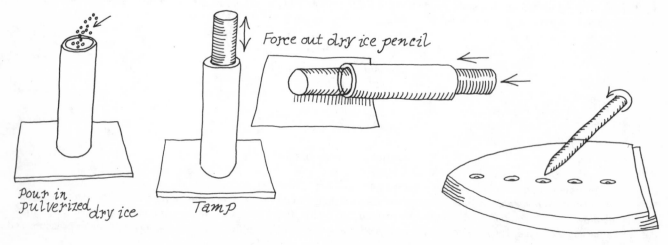

Pour in pulverized dry ice

Tamp

Force out dry ice pencil

Motor and engine manufacturers take advantage of the heat conducting characteristics of metals when they put vanes on connectors or cylinders. The heat-conducting metal carries excess heat from the cylinder to the vanes, and the vanes conduct the heat to the air. This use of broad areas (the vanes) for conducting heat into or away from water or air is used in all radiators.

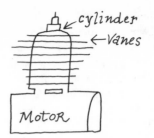

The heat conducting characteristics of metals will be of the greatest importance in the next section on soldering.

The true character of metals will be appreciated only from experience with large, thick pieces. A large block of a metal will reveal to you the specific gravity $\frac{weight}{unit\ volume}$, hardness, color, heat conducting, and acoustic properties of metals. Find an opportunity to examine a large block of each of the gadgeteering metals, and learn to recognize all of them by their color. Look up the entry for each of them in a good encyclopedia. If possible, obtain a block of each of these metals for your own use.

A piece of sheet or foil, or even a disk the size of a large coin is not enough. Get something at least an inch on every side. Heft the metal pieces to get an idea of their weight. Scrape them with your fingernail, a knife point, a piece of broken glass, and some coarse emery cloth to get the feel of their hardness. Scrape especially at the edges and corners. Hit the metal with the round of the ball peen hammer to feel its malleability (don't hit iron or steel with the hammer, as this will dent and ruin the hammer).

Cut the metals with the hacksaw and file. Look at the color of freshly exposed surfaces and compare it to the color of older oxidized surfaces. Burnish a freshly sanded surface with a piece of shiny, round stainless steel, such as the head of a stainless steel screw. Drill and tap your pieces of metal and drive identical steel screws into the holes, turning them until the threads rip out. You should have a feel for the way the metals behave, and you will be able to select the right metal for any job you are doing.

ALUMINUM—Has a silver color with a faint pinkish or bluish cast. Aluminum is fairly light but still strong enough to use as a structural material. When you pay a high price for a lightweight ten-speed racing bicycle, you are paying for aluminum. Aluminum is also popular in lightweight ladders and engine blocks. Magnesium is even lighter than aluminum but it is much more expensive.

Aluminum is soft, even tender, and must be treated carefully. It can almost be carved with a knife. A hacksaw cuts it like butter and aluminum powder will pack into a lump, ruining your grinding wheel and clogging your file unless you are careful.

Aluminum can be soldered with special aluminum solder which is made from pure tin. I have never used this and can't offer any advice on its use, so check the instructions on a box of aluminum solder at a hardware store. You can get aluminum foil, sheet, plate, block, and round or square rod for different uses.

LEAD—Lead is heavy and lead is beautiful and lead melts at a low temperature and it is useful for these three properties. Freshly exposed lead surfaces are a bright silver color that soon tarnishes to purple and then grey. Lead is also very soft and not useful as a structural metal. Sometimes lead is alloyed with metallic calcium to increase its strength, so if you have two pieces of lead, one softer, and one harder, one is probably a calcium alloy. Unless you need a lot of lead in a hurry you can usually get all you need by collecting the wheel weights that garages put on car wheels to balance them. They fall off the wheels and can be found on any road. Keep them in a box and when you need some lead, you have it. Also the telephone man will sometimes leave a piece of soft lead pipe lying around. Take this home and put it in your lead collection. Dig bullets out of firing ranges. If you need to, you can buy lead at large hardware stores.

While you have your eye peeled for lead you will notice other useful items such as copper wire, plate glass, or a bronze door latch. Take these home with you, too. Good gadgeteering is a full-time occupation, and the sensuous gadgeteer sees the possibility for a work of art or a piece of apparatus in almost every cast-off scrap of material that society bequeaths him in the garbage.

Lead (chemical symbol Pb) is the Latin metal *plumbum*. Because lead is soft and melts at a low temperature it is easily formed into pipes and sheets for the transporting of water. The Roman aqueducts which carried water from the mountains into Rome were troughs lined with *plumbum*, and the man who works the water pipes today is a *plumber*. One theory of the demise of the Romans is that lead oxide got into the drinking water as the water made its long journey down those lead troughs, and the Romans drank the lead and were poisoned.

The roof of the Nôtre Dame de Chartres cathedral is protected from the rain by many tons of sheet lead, bought at great expense. The lead was formed into sheets, and the sheets rolled up and carried to the roof where they were unrolled and carefully welded together at the edges. The roof is magnificent to see, and it is absolutely watertight. The weight on the end of the mason's plumb line is a plumb (lead) bob.

You will probably use lead for weights, sculptures, or bullets and the methods of working lead are the same for all. There are so many people ready to tell you how to make lead bullets and equip you to do the same that there's no sense in me telling about it here. Sometimes for weighting things with lead (such as holoow plastic chessmen) it is useful to simply mix lead shot or B-B's with plaster or epoxy and to pour the mixture into a cavity. Other times it is practical to have the lead weight concentrated in a specific place or shape.

Work lead with the hammer, hacksaw, sandpaper (or file if you are prepared to ruin the file; set aside one file exclusively for cutting lead), knife, chisel, tin snips, wire cutters, and pliers. You can both push and cut lead. You can easily melt lead with a blowtorch, and daub it while it is melted. Using a blowtorch and a lead rod, you can daub new material onto a lead surface. Shape the new surface with cold tools as needed.

Buy lead wire as thick solder wire in a hardware store, or cast lead rods by pouring molten lead into molds. Melt the lead over a gas stove, in a metal or porcelain saucepan that must NEVER AGAIN BE USED FOR COOKING. The lead will melt quickly, but it should be poured soon because when it is melted the surface oxidizes quickly and the oxide dissolves into the melt, making it refractory, so that the molten lead will curdle. (See Cellini, *The Casting of the Perseus.*) Scrape off the slag and pour the metal. Make a mold by shaping a double thickness of heavy aluminum foil around a pencil or dowel rod,

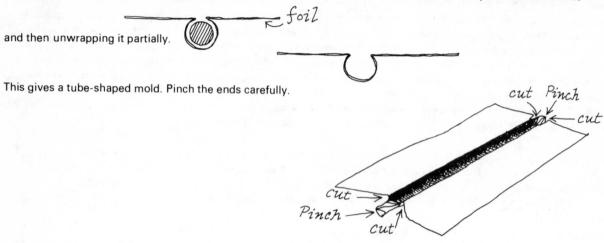

and then unwrapping it partially.

This gives a tube-shaped mold. Pinch the ends carefully.

Metal foils require special care to manipulte. You will probably get foil in a roll. Unroll it carefully, making sure to keep the stresses in the foil distributed over as large an area as possible to keep from creasing it. Sometimes if foil gets creased the creases can be removed by placing the foil on a sheet of plate glass and massaging the crease with a thumb nail.

If this doesn't work, the metal has been stretched in some places but not in others, and the crease will never come out. Bend foil to roll it or crease it by pulling gently on the foil at the opposite ends of the place where the bend is to be.

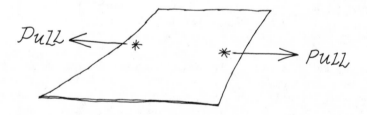

Let the foil hang over the stressed part like a sheet on a clothesline, then sweep it onto a table top. Then press the bend into either a roll or a crease. Use metal foil for a light shield. It is thin, it is not heavy, and it is absolutely light tight.

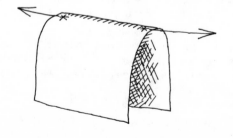

Place the mold on a large sheet of plywood or in a box of sand (to catch spills) and gently pour the lead into the trough. Let it cool. If molten lead touches your skin it will burn you, as it has burned me, and the burn will remain miserable for weeks. Use aluminum foil for casting tubes and rectangular solids (and other solid shapes) from lead. Cast lead into cut wood. If you cast lead into plaster of Paris, bake the plaster until you are sure that all the water has been driven out of it. If lead (or any other hot metal) is cast into plaster that holds any water at all, the water will boil, sending bubbles of steam into the molten metal and ruining the casting. Plaster of Paris is difficult to remove from a casting after the mold is cooled. For almost all metal casting use special investment plaster available from art supply houses, or ask you dentist. World War II escapers melted lead plumbing and cast counterfeit uniform buttons in molds carved in pieces of wood and potatoes. You can cast lead in silicone rubber molds made from the new RTV rubbers. (Room Temperature Vulcanizing) or the air-curing silicone rubber sealers.

Practice working lead by placing two large sheets together edge to edge, and weld a seam between them using a blow-torch and some solid wire solder. Build up a mound of solder using the torch and solid wire solder, or the soldering iron and solid wire solder. See the sections on soldering and casting for greater detail.

The seams of stained glass windows are lead beams of H-shaped cross section. Use lead bottles and dishes for storing and using HF solution (hydrofluoric acid) which dissolves glass and is used for etching glass. Wipe a thin layer of wax onto the glass and then cut away the wax where you want to etch the glass. Pour HF solution on the glass and wait. Then rinse off the acid with PLENTY of water, and remove the wax with acetone. WARNING: Hydrofluoric acid is dangerous. Do not allow acid or fumes to contact body or clothes.

Manufacture of Lead Beams for Stained Glass Window Seams

Troughs receive edges of glass panes

Lead Bar Passes through Rollers

Because lead is soft and heavy it makes a good anvil for working other soft metals, such as brass, without denting them. Make an aluminum foil mold and cast a lead anvil in the shape of a rectangular solid at least one inch thick. When the anvil becomes deformed through use, melt it down and cast it again. Aluminum molds are commercially available for casting of lead hammer heads, which are used mostly for working sheet metal. The lead hammer or anvil may stain brass, so if you are installing brass fittings on a leather belt and want to avoid staining the fittings, put a cloth or a piece of paper between the lead and the brass.

After handling lead or any other metal, WASH YOUR HANDS. The smudges which get on your hands when you handle metal are poison, but if you don't handle your food with dirty hands you are very safe. I know a sculptor who worked lead and ate his sandwiches without washing his hands. He got lead poisoning. On the other hand, I know a boy who used a swallow fishing sinkers and never got sick. I myself once licked some mercury to see if it tasted like metal (it did, it tasted like a penny) and I never got sick. I know many people who handle metals including lead every day. They wash their hands before eating, and they never get metal poisoning.

COPPER—One of the precious metals. The word *copper* is the name of the Mediterranean island of Cyprus, where the ancestors of European civilization mined copper. Probably man's first metal was gold and his second copper. Probably the first uses of copper and gold were jewelry. Copper is the basis for two very different alloys, brass and bronze. Pennies are copper. Copper is too soft and too expensive to be used as a structural material. It is an outstanding conductor of electricity and heat and is sometimes used as a structural metal when it must conduct one of these. Electric conducting wire is usually copper.

A large of block of copper, like a large block of gold, is an awesome sight, but you will never need such a thing except for esoteric physics experiments. The biggest pieces of copper you will encounter are scrap trolley car cable, about 1/2" in diameter. When the Transit Authority puts in copper cables, they are pretty careful to save the scraps, and when they phase out the trolleys they just pour asphalt over the steel rails in the street, but they keep the copper wire and sell the metal by the pound. If you are lucky you will find a piece of this. Use it to make a set of wax-working irons which will be indispensable for the making of wax models and wax molds.

Cut off 2" of 3/8" or larger copper wire and tap it into a shallow spoon shape using a polished ball peen hammer and a polished anvil or an anvil covered with paper to protect the copper from nicks.

Polish the entire surface of the copper spoon by tapping it everywhere with the ball of the hammer. The tiny dents produced in this way are tempered places. The tempering of the copper surface will protect it from corrosion, and it will look good, too. Now gently clamp the spoon in a vise lined with plywood and cloth to protect the copper from scratches, and adjust it so that the round side points up absolutely vertically. Center punch the center of the copper rod and use the drill press to drill a narrow hole down almost the length of the rod, but *not* coming out the other end.

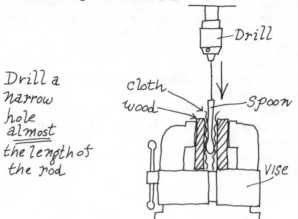

Drill a narrow hole almost the length of the rod

Buy a small pencil-type soldering iron with a replaceable copper tip, and unscrew the tip. File the end of the tip flat.

Copper tip   file tip flat

Select a new drill bit that will drill a hole just large enough to accommodate the soldering iron tip, and enlarge the hole in the copper spoon so that it can be fitted on the soldering iron tip.

Now drill two small holes through the copper spoon and the soldering iron tip. Make the holes at right angles to each other, and place brass or copper-wire rivets in the holes.

tip   Spoon   holes

Screw the spoon onto the soldering iron, plug in the iron and, as the copper spoon heats up, melt a layer of wax over the spoon. The wax working spoon is now ready for storage or use. When we get to the section on wax and molds you will probably want two waxing irons: the big one you have just made, and a smaller one made directly from the soldering iron tip. Use copper for waxing irons and for other uses where you must conduct heat or electricity.

COPPER SHEET—Sheet metal is a species unto itself. It doesn't look like the solid stuff, because solid metal sections nick under impact, while sheet metal dents and creases under impact. If dents or creases get into it, they never come out, ever. Sheet metal is thin, and therefore easy to bend, and since the home gadgeteer rarely has a foundry, forge, big milling machines, or even lathes available to him, he thinks and works in terms of what he can manipulate: sheet metal. The same thinness that makes sheet metal easy to work makes it easy to destroy, and the corrugations in garbage cans and in sheet iron roofing, like the corrugations in cardboard, are a measure to strengthen the thin, weak metal (which is also cheap and easy to work).

Corrugated cardboard   corrugated garbage can   corrugated iron

To persuade yourself that corrugations are strong, get a crisp new dollar bill and inspect if for strength. If you push on it it is weak, because when you push on it, it flops into a different plane:

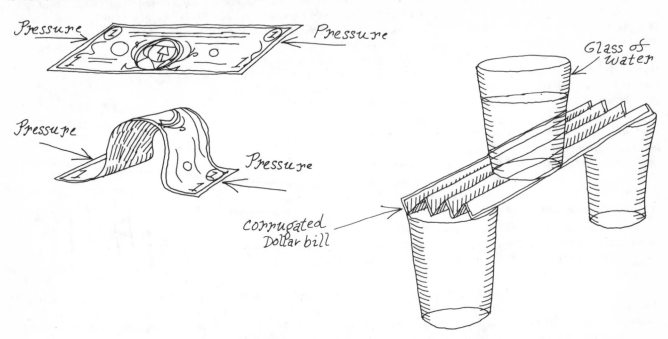

Corrugate the dollar bill by folding uniform pleats into it lengthwise, and demonstrate its strength by placing it across two glasses and supporting a glass of water on it, like a scaffold.

The creases hold the material of each pleat in a single plane, so that to bend a pleat one must move the paper fibers past each other in a single place (rip the paper) or else flatten out all the creases at once. The second possibility is easier, and it happens first, but flattening all the creases is always harder than bending the uncreased bill.

A single corrugation is a dome.

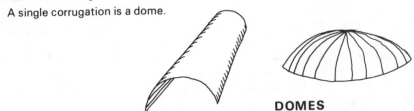

DOMES

Domes are strong because when pressure is applied to the top of a dome the stress is distributed throughout the whole dome, so that the entire mass of the dome must be compressed before the dome will be crushed.

Convince yourself that domes are strong by holding the domed ends of an egg between the thumb and forefinger of your stronger hand.

You may squeeze as hard as you can, but the egg won't break.

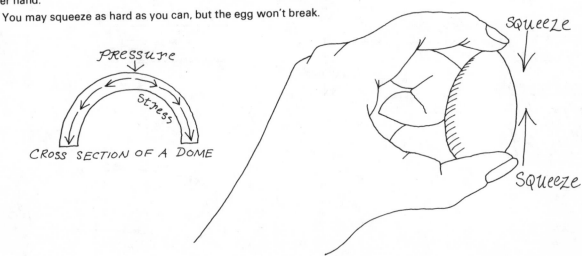

One of the great problems of antiquity, comparable to the more recent problem of the flying machine, was the problem of the constructing of a great stone dome showing no visible means of support. The early Romans could make a small dome, as large as could be carved out of a single piece of stone, but that was the limit. The problem went unsolved for years until at last an architect went to the Emperor and announced that he could build a dome of any size. The Emperor was delighted and said, "Excellent. Tell us how you plan to do it." But the man answered, "No. If I tell you how to do it, you will simply do it and not pay me. Give me a contract to build a dome, and after I build the first one, everyone will know how to build domes." The architect and the Emperor made the contract, and this is how the architect made the dome.

He built a circular building with a round, open hole at the roof and the stones lining the edges of the opening tilted inward slightly. Then he put up a wooden scaffolding just inside the lip of the opening and set in a circle of stones with a trough in them.

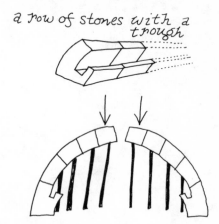

a row of stones with a trough

Then he put up a new layer of scaffolding and rested a layer of stones on the ones with the troughs, and so on, until the dome was in place. Then the architect placed a massive iron chain in the trough in the first layer of stones, pulled the chain tight, and closed it with a last link, removed the scaffolding, and the dome stood.

Use copper sheet for small jobs where it is more important to have an easily workable material than it is to have a stress-bearing finished product. Because copper takes solder easily, use copper in jobs where the use of soldering is important.

Because copper is one of the precious metals it is often used for jewelry. Copper against your skin will dissolve in your sweat and stain your skin green, but many fanciers of copper jewelry don't seem to mind. If you mind you can lacquer the copper.

Buy copper for jewelry from a big hardware store or jewelry supply house. Work the metal with pliers, saw, file, emery cloth, knife, cold chisel, and hammer. When you must hold the metal in the vise, line the jaws with wood and cloth to avoid nicking the metal. When soldering copper jewelry use silver solder (read the section on soldering before beginning) because silver solder is non-toxic and is absolutely permanent. Use as little solder as possible because solder is a different color from copper, and the silver color will accent the seams against the copper piece. This looks good only up to a point.

Begin a copper finger ring by making a paper ring from a 3 x 5 card. Fit the ring carefully to the finger that it is intended to be worn on, and glue it with Elmer's glue. Then wear it for a few minutes. When you are satisifed it fits, carefully remove it and cut it with scissors at the place where you want the seam to be in the finished ring. Choose thick, substantial copper sheet for your ring. Glue the paper ring down flat to the metal, and file or saw around the edges of the paper, bringing the edges of the metal and the paper into exact correspondence.

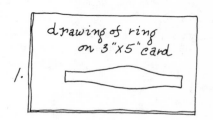

drawing of ring on 3"x5" card

1.

Soak the paper away with water. Carefully file a small bevel into the edges of the copper ring, and polish the filed places with crocus cloth. If the ring is to have decorations in the metal, cut them now. Drill three holes in a plywood board and put wood pegs in them so that the flat ring can sit up against the pegs.

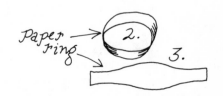

Paper ring   2.   3.

Carve the metal with a knife. If you want to stamp the metal with steel dies, place it on a steel anvil and stamp it, tapping the die gently with a light hammer. Copper is soft, and a hard hit with the hammer will send the die too deep into the metal, creating a dent and bending the ring.

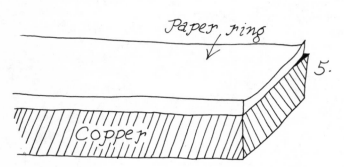

Paper ring   5.   Copper

4.   Paper   Copper

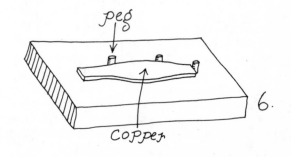

peg   6.   Copper

When the ring is decorated, polish it by burnishing or by tapping it with the polished ball of the hammer, or by holding it against the cloth polishing wheel. Then bend it around a dowel rod. Begin by bending the ring around a dowel larger than the size of the finished ring. The center of the ring will bend easily but the ends will bend only with difficulty. Wrap the ends of the ring around the dowel rod either with the hammer or by gripping the end of the ring against the dowel with the vise and bending the metal back against the dowel. When the ring is bent as tightly as it is going to bend on the dowel you have been using, get a smaller dowel and continue working until the ends of the ring meet. It is possible to use a polished steel rod instead of a dowel. When the ends of the ring meet, solder them. If you care to take the effort to make the ends come out accurate, you can have the ends meet at an angle, giving greater area, and therefore greater strength of joint. An angled seam will diminish the circumference of the ring by a small amount, so take this into account when making the original ring blank from copper sheet.

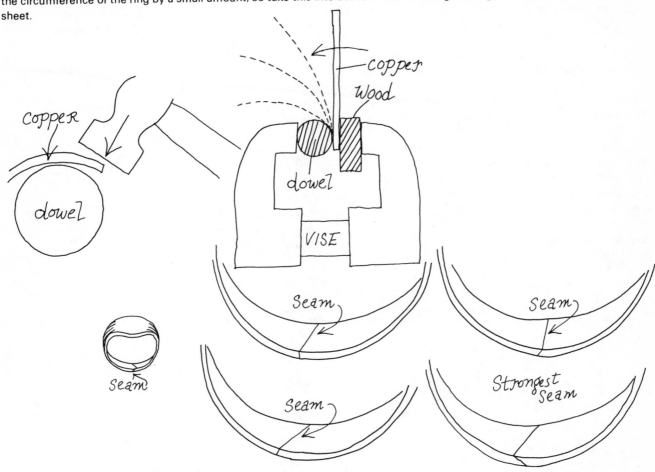

Solder the joint as follows. Make sure that the edges of the joint meet *flush* and *flat*. Adjust the ring so that the joint sits closed when the metal is at rest. Using the hammer pound a bit of silver solder into flat foil. Using the scissors cut out a little rectangle of the solder foil. The rectangle must be small enough so that the entire solder rectangle can be hidden inside the seam in the ring. GENTLY open the seam by pressing the ring between the fingers of one hand, and with tweezers or pliers slip the solder foil into the seam and release the ring so that the springiness of the metal holds the solder in place. Adjust the solder so that it is hidden inside the seam and using a toothpick apply one drop or less of zinc-chloride/hydrochloric acid flux to the seam, just enough to fill the seam with flux by capillarity.

Place the ring on a block of brick or asbestos and gently heat the metal with the blowtorch, concentrating the heat on the seam. You will notice that one part of the flame turns the copper black and one part of the flame makes the copper shiny. Use the part of the flame that makes the copper shiny. First the flux will boil, then there will be a long moment of waiting, then the solder will melt all of a sudden. The seam in the ring will close as the solder turns to liquid, and if you have estimated the amount of solder accurately, the hairline seam will be visible as a shimmering red river.

Remove the blowtorch immediately and wait for the solder to solidify (freeze). You will see it solidify if you look closely. As soon as the solder solidifies (but not before) pick up the ring on a stick or a wire (because it is still too hot to touch) and drop it into a can of water. The ring will sizzle for a moment as it boils a thin layer of water around itself, and then it will be quiet. As soon as the ring is quiet it is cool enough to touch. Take it out and look at it. If it was not sprung open during the insertion of the solder foil it will show a silver seam as thin as a hair against the background of yellow copper metal. Polish the ring with rouge on the turning cloth wheel.

If you want to set the ring with the cabochon stone you made earlier, place the stone on a flat surface and draw a band of paper snugly around it. Make the band of paper about as high as the stone itself. Glue the paper with Elmer's glue, cut it as you did the pattern for the ring, and glue this pattern down to another slab of copper sheet, thinner than the metal used for the ring.

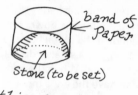

band of Paper

Stone (to be set)

Cut the copper sheet to a size a very little bit bigger than the paper and soak off the paper. Now bend the copper sheet around the stone using any dowel rods or steel rods necessary to get a snug fit. Try not to put too much pressure on the stone. If the copper piece is a bit too long, file off one end until the band fits snugly around the stone and also closes perfectly. Place the seam at a straight part on the stone or at a place where the radius of curvature in the stone is greatest.

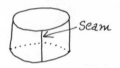

thin copper

Paper band

This copper band is the stone setting. Solder the seam in the setting. Wrap a sheet of emery cloth, abrasive side out, around a stick of dowel so that the outside diameter of this combination is just the same as the outside diameter of your ring. Sand the setting to the curvature of the ring, being careful not to bend the setting (you might fill it with hot paraffin and sand it after the wax hardens) being careful to keep the indentations at the same depth on both sides. Be careful to orient the hollows in the setting so that the stone will sit on the ring facing in the direction you want.

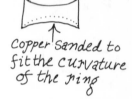

Seam

Place the setting on the ring. It should sit down snugly. Place the stone in the setting. The setting should reach high enough on the stone so that if the setting is folded inward all around it will grip the stone, but it should reach no higher than necessary. If the setting is too high, grind off the flat top with a piece of emery cloth taped to your slab of plate glass.

Copper sanded to fit the curvature of the ring

Remove the stone from the setting and place the ring with the setting on a block of brick. Hold the ring still with a rectangular block through the middle. Adjust the setting to the exact place you want it to sit. You might want to clamp the setting in place by resting a steel rod against it.

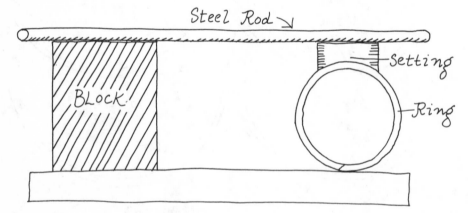

Steel Rod

BLOCK

Setting

Ring

Cut tiny slivers of solder from your sheet of silver solder foil and drop them around the seam where the setting meets the ring. Settle them in along the seam. If you want to do a safe job, get two different solders for the seam at the side of the setting and the seam between the setting and the ring. A jewelers' supply house will sell you these solders for about $9 an ounce. The solders are made to melt at three different temperatures. Use the higher melting solder for the seam in the setting. Then when you solder the setting to the ring, the setting will not come unstuck. If you are careful you can do the whole job with a single silver solder, letting the seam in the setting melt without damage to the work.

Make sure the slivers of silver solder rest snugly at the seam between the setting and the ring. Use just enough solder so that when capillarity draws the melted solder between the setting and the ring, there will be just enough solder to fill the seam comfortably. Not a bit more, not a bit less. Estimating that by eye is an art.

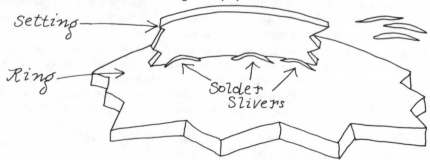

Setting

Ring

Solder Slivers

Using a toothpick, place a drop of flux between the setting and the ring. If the drop does not fill the joint by capillarity, add another drop. If the flux knocks the solder chips out of place, use the toothpick or a thin wire to push them back where they belong. When all the parts are in place, heat the top of the ring with the blowtorch until the flux boils. Don't be alarmed by the capillary bedlam cut loose by the boiling of the flux. This usually does negligible damage, and anyway cannot be helped. The solder will appear to you in a beautiful and almost magical way as a quick, silver river that wraps itself around the seam. As soon as you are satisfied that the solder has flowed, remove the flame and watch for the solder to harden. As soon as the solder is hard pick up the ring on a stick and drop it in a can of water. When the water is quiet take out the ring and polish it on the cloth wheel with rouge.

These processes might not come up to your hopes the first time, but you can quickly learn to turn them out routinely.

Rub the ring clean with silver polish on a toothpick, getting all the crevices absolutely clean. Absolute means absolved of all reservations or doubts. Place the stone in its setting.

Grip the setting around the stone by shrinking the metal lip down around the stone. Most people advise that this be done with polished pliers pushing inward on the metal. I recommend that you use the polished surface of your flatiron. Press the setting against the iron and rotate the setting, keeping up a gentle pressure. The metal lip will begin to shrink. Keep working around and around the stone until it is held firmly. The ring is now ready to wear, unless you choose to lacquer it first.

The soldering techniques described here are the ones I recommend for all mechanical soldering. Occasionally it is not possible to use these methods (as in the making of closed gasoline tanks) and we will come to that later.

The instructions for making a copper ring apply equally to silver and gold. Talk to the salesman at the jewelers' supply house about buying fine silver and gold solders that melt at slightly different temperatures for consecutive soldering of joints on the same piece of work. Don't try silver and gold until you are pretty sure of your skill, or unless you are prepared to pay the cost of a failure.

SEAMLESS COPPER, SILVER, OR GOLD RING

It is possible, by the use of a rather long and wasteful process, to make a seamless precious metal ring. Begin with a coin or a coin-shaped piece of metal, place it standing edgewise on a polished anvil, and hammer on the upper side with a polished hammer. Rotate the coin as you tap around and around its edge.

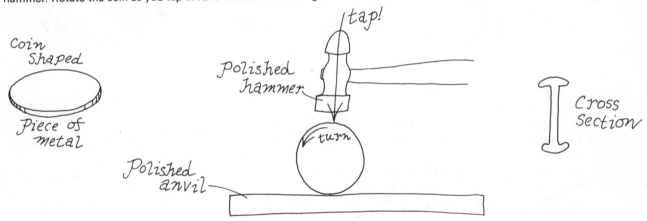

The edge will bulge and mushroom out in a way that leaves any inscriptions on the original disc preserved inside the seamless ring. Cut out the inside when the ring gets down to the size you want.

ENAMEL on COPPER, SILVER, or GOLD

Because they melt at a temperature higher than the melting point of glass, the precious metals copper, silver, and gold make excellent backing for enameled jewelry. Enamel is glass melted onto the surface of a metal. Usually it is convenient to buy the metal backs ready-made from suppliers. Manufacturers stamp out copper circles and shapes and give the metal sheet a camber, or domed shape which, as was presented in the section on domes, is stronger that a flat disc. In addition, the convex side of the dome is pleasing to the eye and most attractive for enameling.

In addition to the copper backs, the supplier will sell you a mild flux and steel wool for preparing the surfaces to be enameled. The enamel itself is powdered glass that you scoop, sprinkle, or otherwise distribute on the surface of the metal. You can also place glass cones, hairs, and curly queues in the enamel. These come out as colored squiggles in the finished jewelry.

Carefully file or sand any rough or sharp edges smooth, but not rounded. Gently rub the copper surface clean with fine steel wool, and paint on a little enameling flux. Then place the enamel powder on the copper surface. Try different ways of applying the enamel. Remember that the enameling process involves melting the glass, so the enamel will spread out on the metal surface. Don't get the enamel layer too thick unless you know you want it thick. Once you have the basic operation under control you can invent with it.

Begin by dusting some enamel on the prepared copper surface, sprinkling it from a height. As the powder falls it will distribute itself evenly. Try masking one side of the piece with a sheet of paper so that only one side gets dusted, then mask the dusted side and dust the first side with a different color.

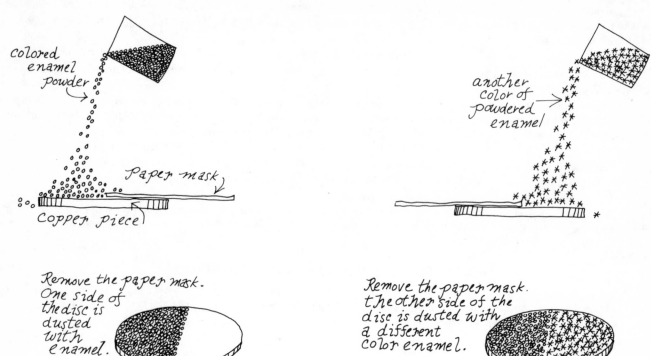

Now place the piece in an enameling oven and heat it until the enamel flows. The enamel will not flow suddenly, but will first get sticky and then it will turn the consistency of honey and flow to an even surface. Let the hot piece cool slowly. The more slowly it cools, the fewer strains will be present between the glass and the metal, and the enamel will be less likely to crack. It is not possible to exaggerate slowness of cooling. Let the piece cool until it reaches touching temperature, and then it is safe to handle.

If you don't have access to an enameling oven, melt the enamel with a propane blowtorch. Hold the piece to be heated on a metal mesh screen of the kind used for heating things in chemistry labs. Light the blowtorch by first striking a match, and then opening the valve of the torch. If you light the match before releasing any gas from the torch you eliminate the danger of explosion by guaranteeing that a cloud of unburned gas will not collect near the torch before the match can be brought near it. Hold the match next to the side of the torch nozzle so that the escaping gas can't blow out the flame. Turn the knob to adjust the size of the flame to something that is as big as the torch can handle without sputtering. If the flame sputters it is too large.

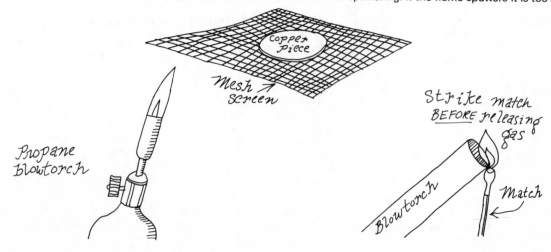

If you use a Bunsen burner the method of lighting is basically the same, except that you have to adjust the air supply to the flame. Screw the burner tube down on the base until the ventilation ports (1) at the bottom of the tube are closed.

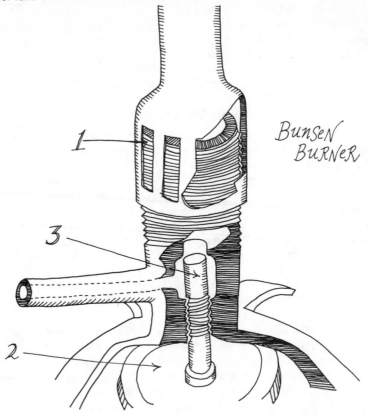

BUNSEN BURNER

Screw in the wheel (2) at the bottom of the burner until the needle valve (3) is closed, then turn on the gas at the stopcock on the wall.

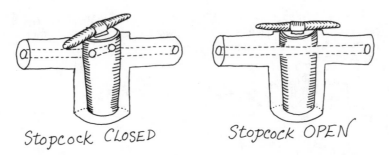

Stopcock CLOSED   Stopcock OPEN

Light a match, hold it *beside* the top of the burner and back the needle-valve wheel down a half a turn.

After a few seconds, the burner ought to light to a lazy, yellow flame. Use the needle-valve wheel to adjust the flame to about 3" high, then unscrew the barrel of the burner to open the ventilation ports (1) a little. (If your Bunsen burner has no needle valve, you will have to adjust the gas flow by some pretty delicate manipulation of the gas cock on the wall.) As the ventilation ports open, air will flow into them and the flame will burn bluer and hotter. (The yellow of the lazy flame is unoxidized carbon atoms glowing in the heat. In the blue flame, almost all the carbon atoms are combining with oxygen to form CO_2.)

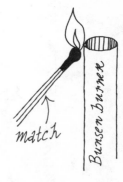

match   Bunsen burner

Adjust the flame until it is taking all the air possible without rattling up and down or lifting itself off the top of the burner. If the flame on the burner goes out or gets out-of-hand, close all the valves and ports and start over.

As the barrel heats up it can be handled at the bottom only. When the burner is first lit the metal is cold, making the barrel safe to touch and adjust, but making the air draft through the ventilation ports weak. As the burner heats up the flame gets stronger.

Place the wire screen on a holder or stand and place the copper and enamel piece on the screen, enamel side up. Heat the copper gently from below by moving the propane blowtorch or Bunsen burner around underneath it. As the piece grows hotter, hold the flame more steadily beneath it until the enamel flows. Then play the flame around under the piece as it cools, so that is will cool very slowly. If you bake the piece in an enameling oven, just turn off the oven and it will cool very slowly. Don't remove the pieces until the oven reaches touching temperature.

After you get the knack of enameling you can invent you own processes. You might want to work the metal yourself and then enamel it, or make 3-D pieces and enamel them. When you trust yourself not to ruin a piece of metal you might try enameling silver or gold, but I suggest you treat them with reverence.

COPPER ALLOYS—BRASS, BRONZE

Elegant Utility Metals

Brass and bronze are alloys of copper and other metals. Brass is usually an alloy of copper and zinc. Bronze is a whole family of metals based on copper. For example, bronze metal for sculpture casting is often 85% copper and 5% each of tin, zinc, and lead. Brass is soft, and is the finest metal for machining. Bronze is hard and tough. It is difficult to machine bronze, but bronze castings, both industrial and artistic, last forever. Marine fittings are bronze. The discovery of bronze during prehistory elevated metals from the ornamental to the utilitarian level, and in so doing, elevated man out of the Stone Age.

The best ancient bronze was an alloy of copper and arsenic, but the arsenic fumes given off during the forging of arsenic bronze poisoned and killed the smiths who worked it, and the ancients gave up arsenic bronze for tin and antimony bronze. The best ancient swords were bronze, and even after the discovery of iron the best swords were still bronze until the relatively recent cultivation of the art of steel tempering. The iron sword (and the Iron Age) supplanted the bronze sword (and the Bronze Age) because iron equipment could be produced in large quantities. Over a period of years, a bronze implement will outlast and outperform an iron one, but iron implements can be produced more cheaply and more quickly. So, it was easier to outfit an army with iron swords and replace the swords every two to four years, than it would have been to outfit the army with bronze swords in the first place.

The ancients used bronze, and we still use bronze where toughness, beauty, and durability are worth the price, especially in metal sculpture. (Techniques of casting metal will come up after the section on soldering.) Bronze won't strike sparks against steel or stone, so bronze tools are used for work in explosive atmospheres, such as petroleum processing plants, where steel tools might strike sparks and detonate explosive gas mixtures. Sleeve bearings, which run at low revolutions per minute and are a little fragile, can carry very heavy loads. They are bronze.

The gadgeteer will seldom use bronze. Casting satisfactory bronze pieces requires the constructing of dangerous and expensive ovens, and most sculptors do their bronze casting work in wax and then pay a foundry to cast it. I have never known of any person who owned his own foundry for the purpose of casting his own bronze work, but the melting oven is worth describing.

The bronze melting oven is a metal cylinder cut from an old boiler and lined with refractory fire brick. The hole in the center of the oven is about three feet deep and two feet across. The oven has a hole at the bottom, and compressed air is forced into this hole to supply the flame with oxygen, just as in the Bunsen burner.

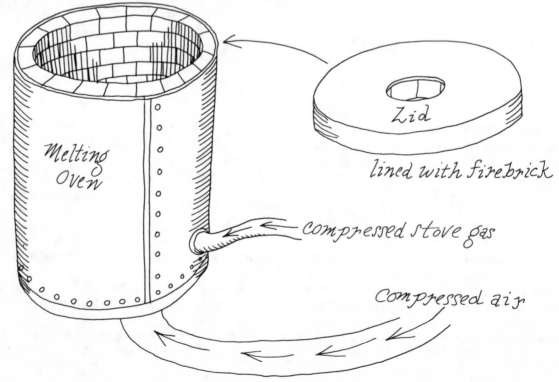

Melting Oven

Lid

lined with firebrick

compressed stove gas

compressed air

The lid can be lifted on and off in any way convenient. The outfit should be operated outside or be fitted with a pipe over the lid to remove the exhaust gas, as this might contain some carbon monoxide.

The metal to be melted—bronze, brass, aluminum—must be placed in a ceramic crucible, and the crucible placed in the cold oven. For small amounts of metal use a small oven and set the crucible on three bricks so that the air and gas can freely enter the oven and the exhaust can freely escape. For larger amounts of metal, pack the oven with a lining of coke to receive the crucible. Lift the hot crucible out with tongs.

For some kinds of casting the mold must be heated before the hot metal can be poured in (see the section on casting), and the molds are often heated in an electric oven lined with fire brick. Fire brick is ruinously expensive, but glass factories sometimes overhaul their furnaces, and they might give you some. Do not try to build any of this equipment on your own. Get someone who has actually done it before to do it with you. If you are doing enough casting work to justify your owning your own casting outfit, you will know how to go about it anyway. I include this description for curiosity only.

Bronze takes solder only with difficulty. To solder bronze, first polish it clean with steel wool and then "pickle" it in a bath of zinc chloride/hydrochloric acid flux. When the metal is good and clean, hold it horizontal and place a small chip of solder on it, and heat it from below or from the side with the propane blowtorch. The flux will boil and the solder will flow. Wipe the molten solder with a rag slightly damp with flux. The solder should spread over the bronze and plate it. The metal is now "tinned" and can be soldered easily. Drop it in a can of water to cool it. This method of tinning bronze works for both lead and silver solders.

Bronze is hard, tough stuff and very difficult to work in a home shop. Usually when you want a non-rusting metal you will choose brass because it can be worked easily. I have used bronze only once, when I had to make sheet metal guides that would be very thin but very strong. Only bronze would do. One-and-a-half square feet of 1/32" bronze sheet cost $11 in 1968. The metal was so tough that I had to take it to the physics machine shop at the local college to have it cut. The machinist there cut out intricate shapes on a huge band saw, and chopped out oblong pieces on a metal guillotine.

BRASS

The yellow alloy of copper and zinc, brass is a work-horse metal stronger than copper which will allow itself to be worked or machined to precise tolerances. Use a heavy, steady drill press to drive a new bit into a block of brass. Center punch the metal, use the lowest drill speed, and use a little oil on the bit. Drive the bit into the metal slowly, withdrawing it often, and keeping it oiled. Brush and blow the shavings away. The bit will enter the metal almost as if it were entering clay, and you will have the sensation that the bit is leaving its print in the metal. Repeat this procedure with aluminum and you will feel the bit ripping out chips of metal creating the impression that the bit is chewing its way along. Compare the holes you have drilled and you will find your impressions more or less confirmed: the hole in the aluminum will be rough and the hole in the brass will be smooth. That is why people use brass: you can drill it, tap it, lathe it, bend it, file it, stamp it—and the accuracy of the work is limited only by your own skill. Brass takes solder easily and it won't rust. Brass is a little expensive but worth it if you want to build fine parts that last. The only thing you can't make out of brass is cutting edges because it is too soft for that.

Get brass sheet, tubes, and wire at the local hobby shop or hardware store. Metal supply houses will have brass rods, tubes, plates, sheet metal, and ingots. Look up BRASS in the yellow pages of the telephone book.

IRON AND STEEL

Except for iron baling wire, coat hanger wire, and a few sheets of steel for a radio chassis or a knife blade the home gadgeteer will have little use for iron and steel, and he will not have the means to work large pieces.

PLASTICS

Plastic means "capable of being shaped and molded." The plastics are the product of twentieth century materials engineering, and the twentieth century has put plastics to its every use. Lumberjacks' wedges, lenses, car bodies (and soon motors), fishing poles, furniture, laboratory "glassware," ropes, nylon stockings, and food wrapping are now made from plastics. This may or may not be good, because the molecules of plastic are organic molecules so unlike anything found in nature that very few bacteria can metabolize them, with the result that, once created, most plastics cannot be disposed of, thus locking up the materials put into them forever. Even though I can't encourage the use of, for example, disposable plastic cups, the infinite variety possible in organic molecules gives the gadgeteer a truly wonderful range of physical properties to make use of in plastics.

Some chemists believe that it is possible in theory to construct organic molecules (plastic) which will offer zero resistance to an electric current. Wires of such plastic would give us frictionless roads, cheap round-the-world telephone calls, and efficient electricity delivery everywhere. This chapter describes techniques for working plastic without the use of complex molds, and so it will say nothing about the casting plastics—epoxy, polyster, and polyvinyl chloride, which will be taken up in the chapter on molds and casting.

The first plastics were the celluloids. The molecule of celluloid is the molecule of cellulose, the structural molecule of plants, and I have heard that celluloid was discovered (and the DuPont chemical company founded) when an early DuPont opened a barrel of cotton that had been stored for a long time under hot, wet conditions. Instead of finding cotton inside, he found a clear syrupy liquid which hardened to a smooth durable material on exposure to air. Celluloid found its first use in paints, playing cards, the ruled surfaces of slide rules—and in bombs.

The plastic which the gadgeteer will find the most workable without the use of complex molds is plexiglas. Plexiglas comes in sheets which can be sawed, carved, filed, drilled and tapped, or heated and shaped. The material is tough, not brittle, and has a shiny and therefore attractive surface which is easy to clean. It scratches easily. Plexiglas can be bought in a number of colors (including clear, opaque white, blue, black) and in a number of thicknesses up to at least 1/2". Its great strength makes it useful for monkey-restraining chairs for psychological testing, aquariums, special microscope slides, weatherproof domes, and display cases for sculptures. I have used it for the removable back of a working model of the human vocal tract, and for a mask in the shape of a cat's head.

The usefulness of plexiglas for sculpture and laboratory apparatus is partly limited by the fact that it can be bought only in sheet form and the sheets cannot be cast conveniently into complex shapes. Still, great use can be made of the sheets.

Plexiglas is very expensive, so most people draw up detailed plans of what they intend to make with it before they even buy any, and they save all scraps. New sheets of plexiglas come with a protective sheet of paper stuck to them. Draw your plans directly on the paper and saw up the plastic with the paper still attached, thus avoiding scratches in the plastic. Then remove the paper only when you are about to us the plexiglas.

If the paper gets old it may stick to the plexiglas and you will have trouble removing it. Soak it in water or alcohol overnight, and peel away as much paper as you can with your fingers or the back of a knife. Scrub away the glue with acetone and gauze. Acetone is an anesthetic, an explosive and a poison, so use it with plenty of ventilation, and keep open flames away from it. No matter what anyone tells you, acetone will not attack or dissolve plexiglas.

Learn to work plexiglas by playing with some scraps. These are almost always beautiful, so sculptures will suggest themselves. It is possible to saw plexiglas with a power saw (jigsaw or band saw) if the saw blade does not heat up. When the blade heats up it will melt the plastic, which will collect in globs in the groove left by the blade, and seal the groove closed. Thin sheets of plexiglas are less likely to seal up in this way than are thick sheets. The band saw is better for cutting plexiglas than is the jigsaw because the continuously moving band saw must move many feet of blade past the plastic before the same spot on the saw comes back to cut again. In the meantime, the heated portion of the blade has some time to cool. Because the reciprocating jigsaw brings the same section of blade past the plastic on both the cutting and return strokes, the blade is almost certain to heat up. Keep the plastic moving against the saw blade so that the blade is always cutting into new, cool portions of the plastic. Sometimes it is helpful to put a sheet of plexiglas in the refrigerator for a few hours before sawing it with the jigsaw. If the plastic insists on melting, you will have to cut it with a hacksaw or a coping saw. These are slow and for that reason can be kept cool. Touch the blade after every few strokes to feel if it is too hot. If it is, give it a moment to cool down before sawing again. Use a file to finish saw cuts in plexiglas. For the most delicate saw cuts in plexiglas, hold the hacksaw between your legs with the front of the saw back against your chest, and move the plastic over the blade with your fingers.

For the most delicate cuts in plexiglas:

saw

plastic

For drilling holes in plexiglas, start the hole with the center punch or knife point, then drill it out directly with the bit that will give you the hole of the size you want. It is not true that by using first smaller bits and then progressively larger ones you will reduce the chances of shattering the plastic. Very much the opposite. As the bit moves into the plastic it will heat up and perhaps melt a bit of plastic along the sides of the bit. To avoid this, lubricate the bit with oil and remove it from the hole repeatedly to let it cool. This process yields a smooth, clear bore but is very tedious to perform, so you must decide whether you need such clean holes. If you only want to use the holes for inserting bolts through a sheet of black plastic, then maybe all that work is not worth the effort. If you intend to fill the holes with water and examine their contents with a microscope, then the holes need to be cleanly drilled.

As the drill bit is about to exit from the sheet of plexiglas it may catch on the thin layer of material there and crack out a chip. Avoid this by moving the bit extra slowly, and by pushing on it extra gently, when it comes near to exiting from the bottom side of the plastic sheet. Always drill on a piece of scrap wood.

If you want to screw down a sheet of plexiglas but want the screw heads to be countersunk, drill the seat for the head first. This way you avoid placing the larger bit into the smaller hole and shattering the plastic.

desired countersink   *drill first*   *drill second*

Plexiglas can be tapped to accept machine screws. Treat it like aluminum. Use plenty of oil.

Like other plastics, plexiglas is a good insulator. Thus if you place a hot object against even the largest piece of plastic, the heat will not be conducted away, but will be concentrated in the material actually touching the hot object, and this small region of plastic will melt. Make use of this quality of plastics in several ways. First, use it to tap holes for screws when you have no tap set available. Use wood screws, and drill a hole in the plastic large enough to accommodate the threaded portion of the screw, but narrower than the threads.

Drill holes where you want the screws to be, and tap the holes by heating the screws gently over an alcohol lamp and turning them into the holes while still hot. Hold the screw in an old forceps and warm it over the lamp. Quickly place the screw point in the drilled hole and turn it a bit. Then quickly follow this up with the screwdriver. Be careful to turn the screw only far enough to cut threads for it, not far enough to rip the threads out. Wait a moment until you feel the plastic beginning to harden, then crack the screw away from the plastic by unscrewing it a fraction of a turn. If you do not crack the screw away from the plastic it will become permanently stuck in it.

Use the melting properties of plastics to make a "seat" for a part that needs to be positioned accurately, but needs to be removed from its mounting often, or needs to be held down securely without much pressure being applied to it. Drill a hole in a plexiglas sheet to accommodate a bolt, and drill a hole in the base of your mechanism to accommodate the same bolt. Heat the base, and quickly put the bolt through it and bolt it down to the plastic. The heated base will melt a region of plastic conforming exactly to its own shape. After that, if you must remove the base, it will be easy to return it to exactly the same position.

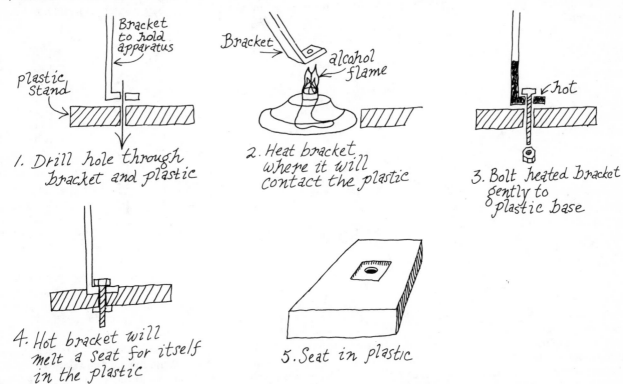

Plexiglas can be glued to plexiglas or to styrene by the use of solvents. I have tried the popular commercial ones, and the only one I found to do a satisfactory job is Micro Weld, manufactured by Martin Krasel Studios, 5914 Blackwelder Street, Culver City, California 90230. It costs about 75¢ for a bottle that will last for a year or more. If you can find out what chemical is the solvent in this "glue," you can buy it for less. Solvent "glues" such as Micro Weld do not truly glue pieces of material together, but instead weld them by dissolving a thin layer of material at both of the surfaces to be joined. The dissolving material from both sides of the joint diffuses together and grows solid again after the solvent evaporates.

A glue differs from a welding medium in that it contains a small amount of adhesive material dissolved in the solvent, so that when the solvent evaporates it leaves behind the adhesive material which will fill up cracks between the pieces to be joined. Because a welding medium contains no dissolved material, it can be used only on materials that can themselves be dissolved. Because it can dissolve only minute amounts of material at the surface of a piece, the joint between the two pieces to be welded must be nearly perfect.

Where a glue such as celluloid dissolved in acetone (e.g. airplane glue) is being used to join insoluble materials such as wood, a rough surface of the wood at the joint will give the adhesive a large area to adhere to, giving a stronger joint. In contrast, where two pieces of material must be joined by dissolving their contacting surfaces together, the closer the surface, the better the joint. In practice this means that the strongest bonds will be obtained between two pieces that have been polished to exactly the same shape.

Prepare plastic surfaces for joining by filing them until they fit perfectly. Obtain flat surfaces by using a file, or a sheet of emery paper taped to a sheet of plate glass. The smoother the surfaces, the stronger the welded joint between them. Hold the joint in place and put a strong light behind it or hold it up to the sky. If a crack of daylight shows through, the joint is not accurate enough. File or sand down the high places.

THE DAYLIGHT TEST

The daylight test is an example of extreme accuracy of inspection obtained through relatively simple means.

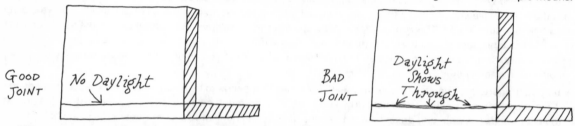

When you are satisfied that the plexiglas joint is close enough for your purposes, weld the pieces together by applying a few drops of welding liquid between them. Pick up the welding liquid with a draftsman's pen, or suck a little into a glass capillary tube. Then apply the point of the pen or the end of the capillary to the crack in the joint, and let the liquid flow into the crack by capillarity.

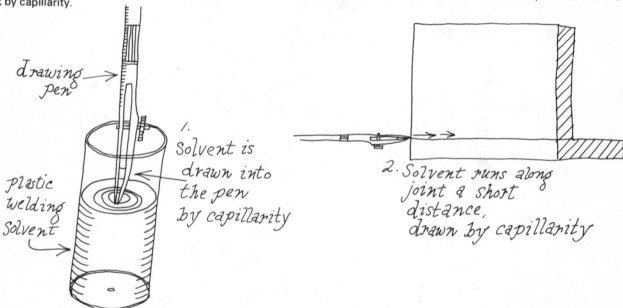

If you use the glass capillary instead of the drawing pen you can connect a tygon tube (clear flexible plastic available as gas line in hobby shops) to one end and draw a little solvent into the tube with your mouth. The solvent, like acetone, is anesthetic and poisonous, so never let any of it get into your mouth. Set the tip of the capillary tube next to the plastic joint and slowly let or blow out the welding solvent. As you do this, capillarity will draw the solvent along for a short distance, but not for the entire length of the joint, so you will need to go around the joint with the welding solvent, tacking it together.

In practice, consecutively welded places will connect to each other most smoothly if the halves of the plastic joint are held together gently at first, the welding solvent applied as quickly as possible, and the joint clamped tight immediately. In this way capillarity will have the greatest opportunity to spread the solvent before the joint is clamped tight. This procedure requires some practice to perfect.

Plexiglas can not only be sawed, filed and drilled, it can be cut with a knife. The knife must be sharp, but definitely not razor sharp, because a razor-sharp knife will cut too deeply into the plexiglas and will stick. The knife is especially useful in finishing, enlarging, or shaping irregularly-shaped holes in flexed plexiglas sheets. Carving plexiglas is no different than carving wood, except that the plexiglas has no grain. Shave thin sheets off the surface of the plexiglas, one at a time. Too much pressure will shatter the plastic, so shave off thin sheets and be patient.

The above methods for working plexiglas at room temperature work equally well for styrene, with a few modifications. The gadgeteer will most often encounter styrene as the plastic in plastic model cars, boats, and airplanes, as well as in the plastic boxes that hold such things as sewing needles. Styrene is more brittle than plexiglas, so it must be drilled very carefully. It can hardly be carved at all, although one can, with care, carve single slivers from the edges of styrene sheets. Because styrene is very soluble in acetone and in methyl-ethyl-ketone, genuine sytrene glue is fairly easy to make. Most popular plastic glue is intended as styrene glue.

While styrene can be worked only at room temperature, plexiglas can be heated and shaped. When it cools it will hold its new shape, and can be drilled, filed, and carved in this condition. Because bent plexiglas is more brittle than flat plexiglas extra care is needed in working it.

Heat plexiglas for molding and shaping by placing it in a hot oven, or under an infra-red heat lamp, or hold it over a gas burner (e.g. of a stove) or over an alcohol lamp. If you heat plexiglas over an open flame keep it moving constantly, turn it over constantly, and try to heat it fairly slowly without holding it over the flame too long. If the surface becomes too hot it will boil, then spit, then catch fire. You can blow out the fire easily, but the plastic surface will be scarred at the places where it has boiled. The hot plastic has a high specific heat and will burn your fingers even through a thin pot holder, so use several thick layers of insulating cloth to handle it, or clamp cold parts of the plastic between sheets of wood for handling.

The hot plastic will be of the consistency of limp gelatine sheet, or non-springy rubber, and in this condition it can be bent and twisted, or even indented or stretched within limits. After it cools it will retain its new shape, but if it is heated again it will return to a flat sheet.

Because polished sheets or rods of clear plexiglas will conduct light inside themselves, physicists have used twisted strips of plexiglas to conduct light from a phosphorescent particle detector to a light sensitive cell.

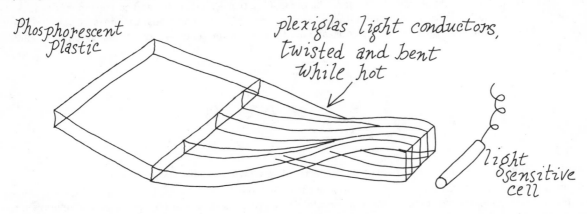

The light conducting strips were heated and twisted, then allowed to cool in their twisted condition.

The standard procedure for blowing plexiglas domes with compressed air is this: Cut out a hole in a sheet of plywood to the size and shape that you want the base of the dome to be. This shape is most often a circle, but there is no need for it to be a circle.

Cut out a sheet of plexiglas as big as the plywood board, and cut out a second plywood board as big as the first. Make a small hole in the middle of the second plywood board for injecting the compressed air.

Many arrangements are possible for injecting the compressed air through the bottom board. If you intend to make many plexiglass domes you may want to make a permanent arrangement using, for example, a copper pipe soldered to a hole in a copper plate which rests on the plywood sheet where the copper pipe goes through a hole drilled in the wood.

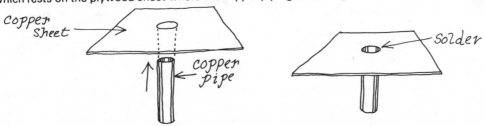

If you don't need such a permanent arrangement it is often sufficient to hammer the plastic barrel of an empty ball point pen through a hole drilled in the wood, and then saw and file off the end of the plastic barrel flush with the surface of the plywood board.

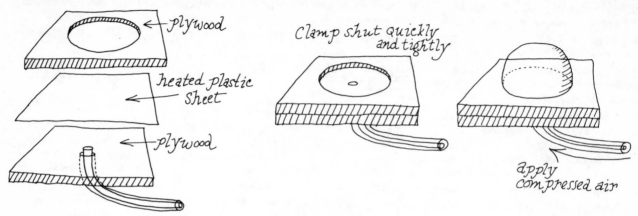

Fasten one end of a flexible plastic tube to the copper or plastic pipe in the plywood board, and connect the other end of the tube to a source of compressed air. Heat up the plastic sheet until it is limp and clamp it between the plywood boards. Attach flexible tygon tube to source of compressed air—but do not apply pressure. Apply compressed air cautiously but firmly—hot plastic will blow up in the shape of a globe. Maintain the pressure until the globe cools and can no longer collapse. Apply the compressed air cautiously but firmly and inflate the globe to the desired size. Then adjust the pressure valve so that the size of the plastic bubble is maintained until the plastic cools and hardens. Separate the plywood sheets and remove the finished globe.

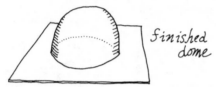

It can be cut free of the square base or used as it is, depending on what you plan to do with it.

When preparing the plastic for blowing, it is important to heat it evenly because cool spots will be stiff and will leave flat places in the finished globe. For the same reason it is important to keep drafts away from the globe as it is inflating. If too much pressure is applied to the globe as it is inflating, it will pop like any other bubble.

While there is no reason that the base of the plexiglas bubble needs to be circular, there is no reason why the surface of the bubble needs to be spherical. A wire bolted or otherwise held where the bubble is expanding will leave a curved indentation in the bubble. More useful still, the bubble can be blown into a mold cut to any shape you choose, within the limits of the plastic to stretch without breaking. While it is helpful to apply the air pressure to the bubble when the plastic is as hot as possible, success with this method of plastic blowing is mostly a matter of practice. The hot plastic will pick up dents and unwanted marks very easily, so it is essential that the mold be very smooth. Because the mold must stand the heat of the hot plastic, make it from wood or plaster. Cut a few vents in the mold to allow air to escape behind the expanding bubble.

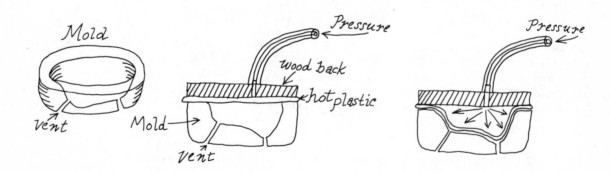

The pressure method of plexiglas blowing works best with thin sheets of plastic and shallow molds. Slightly more steeply-cut molds can be cast in plexiglas by the use of a sculptured back that presses the hot plastic into the mold. Mold and back must be cut so that at every place a channel lies between them of a thickness slightly greater than that of the plastic.

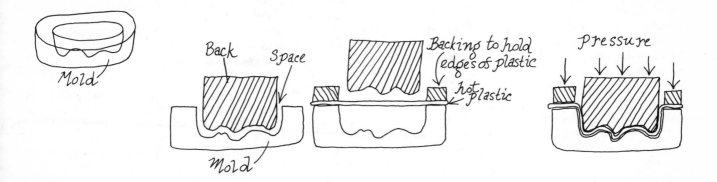

This method of plastic molding requires that great pressure be applied to both backs of the mold, and the danger of breaking the sheet of hot plastic is great. For forming shapes more steeply cut or undercut then these, see the chapter on casting.

After you have finished working a plastic surface by use of knife, file, and sandpaper, you can polish it in two stages. Begin by sanding it with finer and finer emery cloth lubricated with water, finishing with crocus cloth. Add the final polish on the buffing wheel charged with jewelers' rouge. If you do not have access to a buffing wheel, do the buffing with a little toothpaste and water on a cloth rag. Because it requires huge amounts of muscular effort, the hand-buffing method is practical for polishing only surfaces of small area. As with other materials, plastic will take a satisfactory polish only when the scratches left by each coarser abrasive have been completely removed by the next finer abrasive. If you try to polish off the scratches with the buffing compound, you will be left with a surface covered by scratches that have polished sides.

VINYL

The vinyls are a family of plastics that include rigid casting plastics, semi-flexible and flexible plastics, and highly plasticized floppy plastics. In this chapter we will consider only the two intermediate consistencies of vinyl. These are most commonly available as stiff vinyl book covers and flexible vinyl sheet in inflatable swimming pools. When I want to use vinyl sheet I buy vinyl notebook covers and swimming pool patching kits with large sheets of soft material. I have used these in constructing a miniature bellows which was a component in a working model of the human vocal tract.

The most effective glue for vinyl sheet is the liquid that comes in a can and is much thinner than honey. It contains very little vinyl and a great deal of solvent. Apply a rounded bead of glue over one of the two surfaces to be joined. If one of the two surfaces is smaller then the other, apply the glue to the smaller surface so that the finished joint will be clean.

Work quickly to avoid having the glue dry in the air where its solvent will be of no use. The rounded bead of glue will guarantee that both surfaces to be joined will have plenty of glue contacting them.

In addition to plexiglas, styrene and vinyl, which can be worked by hand, you will encounter polyethylene, polypropylene, Teflon and mylar. Polypropylene is a fairly rigid plastic used commercially for chemical apparatus because it is essentially inert chemically. You can use polypropylene ware as it is, or saw it, drill it, and tap it if the need arises. Mylar is a very expensive, tough plastic which is available in thin sheets, and is so beautiful when coated with a thin layer of copper or aluminum that you will want to own a little even though it cannot really be worked at home. Use it for sun shades, decorations, or windows in architectural models.

Polyethylene is a fairly soft, flexible and stretchable plastic that is slightly slippery to the touch. It is chemically inert for most purposes. Polyethylene is commonly seen as vegetable bags at supermarkets, and as cleaner bags. It is waterproof and flexible, and can be used to line troughs or as a temporary gasket for jars or bottles of liquid. Thick blocks of polyethylene are used as radioactivity shields in atomic submarines, and if you can find one of these you may want to carve small objects from it. I once used blocks of polyethylene for making a working model of the system of bonelets that control the pitch and camber of a bumblebee's wing in flight.

Teflon is like polyethylene (the molecules differ only in that Teflon has four fluorine atoms where polyethylene has four hydrogen atoms) but it is stronger, more slippery and more inert chemically. It is very expensive, and finds its main commercial use in laboratory equipment that must operate in extreme chemical environments. Still, it is the most slippery material in the world, and Teflon washers make the best oil-free bearings imaginable. Teflon is an excellent electrical insulator, and high-voltage components in delicate electronic equipment are sometimes mounted on Teflon posts to isolate them. The gadgeteer can cut Teflon with a knife or hacksaw, turn it on a lathe, and drill it.

ADHESIVES

Adhesives are materials which are used for making other materials adhere (stick) to each other. The adhesives we will use are welding agents (already described in the chapter on plastics), glues, and solders. Because adhesives are designed to stick to specific kinds of materials, or to specific kinds of surfaces, it is essential that these surfaces be exceedingly clean, and that they be prepared properly. In the case of welding agents for plastics, as already mentioned, this means that the surfaces to be joined should be polished to fit exactly. In the case of glue, this means that the surfaces should fit closely, but that they should be roughened instead of polished. Use sandpaper or a file.

Glues are adhesives that stick to the materials they join, but are different from them. The glue works by diffusing a short distance into the openings at the surface of materials. In some cases this diffusion occurs at the molecular level, and in others it occurs at a grosser level. In wood and paper the diffusion occurs at the level of the fibers which compose the material. Wood and paper glues derive their strength from the presence of a layer of glue surrounding the wood fibers, (i.e. the glue by itself is not as strong as the glue mixed with the fibers) so that the best glued bonds are obtained when the glue has thoroughly diffused into both pieces of material to be joined, and the layer of glue between them is continuous (no bubbles) but thin. This is why the glue manufacturers recommend that in joining pieces of wood with glue, you first apply a thin layer of glue to both surfaces to be bonded. To this I will add that you should press the glue into the wood by running your finger along the surface. Apply a coat to each of the surfaces to be joined because a bead of glue will quickly skin over as solvent evaporates at its surface. If this skin is then applied to a fresh wood surface it will prevent the liquid phase of the glue from squeezing among the wood fibers and will yield a weak joint. After both of the surfaces to be joined are impregnated, each with its own fresh coat of glue, apply a new, thinner coat of glue to one of them and immediately press them together. If the glue takes a long time to dry you may want to clamp the pieces together with C-clamps rather than holding them by hand. This is a matter of taste. As the pieces are pressed together, excess glue will squeeze out from between them. After the glue has started squeezing out do not lessen the pressure on the pieces until after the glue has dried, because a lessening of pressure will only bring air bubbles between the two wood pieces.

These instructions apply to the glueing of all porporous materials: china, leather, paper, cardboard, and wood. Although it is not absolutely essential in all cases, the instructions can be used to advantage with any glue that adheres to these materials:

> celluloid in solvent (Testor's, Lepage's, Ambroid, etc.)
> bakelite (Weldwood)
> protein (hide glue, Elmer's, [casein], Casco, Iron glue)
> epoxy

1) Press the glue into the surface of both pieces to be joined. If the glue is very runny it can be applied with a brush.

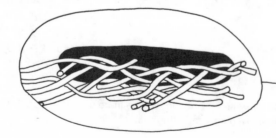

Glue flows among fibers (or particles) of porous material, gripping it.

bead of glue

Surface to be joined

2) Apply a fresh coat of glue to one of the surfaces to be joined (this guarantees that no bubbles will remain between the joined pieces to create weak places).

3) Join pieces, squeeze out excess glue, and hold or clamp the pieces until the glue is dry. Remove excess glue from edges of joint before glue becomes hard.

Press pieces tightly together

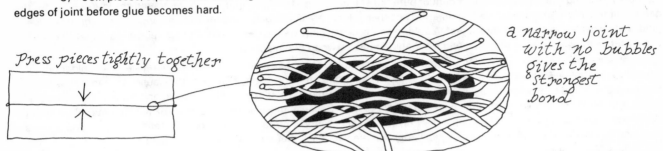

a narrow joint with no bubbles gives the strongest bond

The water soluble glue on paper tape and on the backs of envelopes is a vegetable gum that sticks in the same way that other glues do. It does not need to be applied to both paper surfaces to be joined because so much water is applied to it that a thick film of very wet glue is present at the surface. When the wet glue is applied to dry paper, much of it enters the paper by capillarity, making a glue bond between the paper sheets. The glue dries quickly because the paper soaks up the water.

EPOXY GLUE

While epoxy finds its most spectacular use as a casting plastic it is one of the best glues because it will stick to almost anything (including itself) except polyethylene and Teflon. Epoxy glue is an organic resin that will harden by polymerization when a suitable catalyst is added to it. Accordingly, epoxy is always sold with its catalyst (often called "part A" and "part B"). For practical purposes it does not matter which part is which. Mix the two parts (the resin and the catalyst) according to the instructions on the package. Because the resin and catalyst must be completely combined in order to be effective, mix the two together until the mixture is uniform. Use a popsicle stick to mix them, and mix them in a paper cup or on a sheet of cardboard because they will stick to and ruin whatever objects are used for handling them. Apply the catalyzed epoxy with the tool used for mixing it. Apply the epoxy to the cleaned, roughened surfaces to be joined, and press the surfaces together. The epoxy will need some time to harden. This time is printed on the box you buy the epoxy in, and can vary from ten seconds to twenty-four hours.

Decide how much time you need or want, and buy epoxy that hardens leaving you enough time. In practice the ten-second epoxy may leave you twenty seconds to play with, while the twenty-four-hour kind will leave you about six hours to play with. Heat from a low-temperature oven (150°F) or an infra-red lamp will speed the curing of the epoxy somewhat.

Before it cures, epoxy is soluble in water, so that drips, spills, or excess epoxy around the edges of joints can be cleaned up. When cleaning excess glue away from the edges of a glued joint, use a cloth that is only barely damp, in order to avoid ruining the joint by spilling water on it.

Epoxy will bond to wood, leather, porcelain, metal, rock, styrene, and plexiglas, NOT to vinyl, polyethylene, Teflon, rubber, or silicone rubber. Epoxies are sold for many purposes, so make certain that what you buy will accomplish what you want. If you want to use it as glue, then the tubes or cans available in hardware stores are fine. Some epoxies cure to a rock-hard plastic, while others cure to a slightly flexible plastic, so decide what you need before you buy. Some epoxies are clear, others opaque and colored. Again, decide what you need before you buy.

For glueing newspaper clippings, photographs, and any small pieces of paper into albums or onto any surface without injuring the paper, apply a thin coat of rubber cement to the back of the paper and stick it in place before the glue dries. Rubber cement comes in little brown jars with an applicator brush on the inside of the lid.

For glueing felt to the bottom of chessmen, or a layer of polyurethane foam to the bottom of a microphone stand, use contact cement. Apply a layer of cement to both of the surfaces to be joined, then position them carefully before pressing them together. Once the surfaces are pressed together they will essentially never separate. The virtuoso contact cement is Eastman 910 adhesive, which is expensive, and a drop of which, placed between two washers, can lift a car.

For glueing rubber to rubber, use the glue sold in bicycle shops for sticking patches to tires. Roughen the surfaces to be joined (use sandpaper or a scraper) apply glue to both surfaces, apply a little extra glue to one of the surfaces, and press them together tightly for several hours. A stronger bond is obtained by the use of silicone seal, a silicon rubber that comes as a paste in a tube. It can be bought in most hardware stores (in colors—clear, white, black, metal). The newly-squeezed rubber is a thick paste that can be spread with a small instrument or a finger. It reeks of acetic acid (vinegar) and cures in the air after about twenty-four hours. I have used it to stick rubber cleats, cut from an old tire, onto the bottoms of rubber boots (for running in the snow). The cleats stayed on the boots for the equivalent of about 50 miles before some of them began to peel off.

Silicone seal will stick to metal, porcelain and glass, and make a watertight seal. It will not stick to wax, and can be used for homemade rubber objects built up on a wax surface and then peeled off.

SOLDER (Electrical Soldering)

The last family of adhesives we will use are the solders. With the exception of aluminum solder which is pure tin (remember this if you ever need a small amount of pure tin) solders are metal alloys that melt at temperatures low enough for the gadgeteer to use without expensive equipment. The other solders are commonly used for joining copper, brass, bronze, silver, gold, and occasionally iron and steel sheet. A solder joint is usually intended to achieve one of two purposes: good electrical conductance between pieces of metal, or a mechanical joint between two pieces of metal.

Buy a small roll of rosin-core TV-and-radio solder (about 40¢), and a small roll of low-temperature silver solder (about $1.00). Obtain a feel for the physical properties of these by cutting off a short length of each and pounding them flat with the hammer. Cut new bits of solder and flatten them with the pliers. Hold the solder wire in your hand and bend it. The silver solder is soft and the TV-radio solder (an alloy of lead and tin) is softer. Because these solders are essentially soft materials, a strong solder joint is not obtained by building up a thick layer of solder around a metal-to-metal joint. Instead a strong solder joint is obtained by causing the solder to move by capillarity between surfaces that are polished to an exact fit.

In a sense solder is a glue that adheres to metal surfaces by diffusing among the atoms of the metal. The strongest bond has the thinnest layer of weak solder between the surfaces of the parts joined. This rule works in practice as well as in theory.

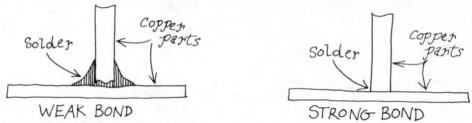

As a rule, then, the solder that you see at a joint contributes nothing to the strength of the bond; it is only the solder you don't see that builds strength.

Begin learning the use of solder by practicing electrical soldering. Buy a forty-watt (approximately) soldering iron, and practice joining wires using it and the thin TV-radio solder. This wire solder is especially practical for wiring electrical circuits because thin wire requires the least heat energy to melt it, and the less heat applied to delicate transistors and diodes, the less chance of melting the silicon chip inside and ruining it. A good way to lessen the chance of melting a transistor or diode is to clamp the wire being soldered with a "heat sink" between the soldering iron and the electrical component. The heat sink (a surgical hemostatic forceps, a heat sink bought specially for the purpose, or just the point of a needle-nose pliers) will conduct heat away from the wire and protect the electronic device.

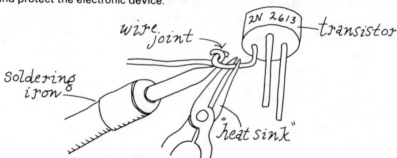

For all electrical soldering, use rosin-core solder rather than solid or acid-core. Acid-core solder is thick, so that it will require too much heat and may create the danger of melting electrical components during soldering. In addition, the acid in the solder will eventually corrode and ruin the wires in your electronic device. The guarantee that comes with electronic kits is void if the kit is constructed with acid-core solder or with a soldering iron cleaned on a sal ammoniac block.

After buying a new soldering iron, the first thing to do is to prepare the tip by tinning it. Tinning is coating the tip with a thin layer of solder which will transfer heat quickly and cleanly to the wires being joined. Plug in the soldering iron. As the heating element heats up it will heat the tip.

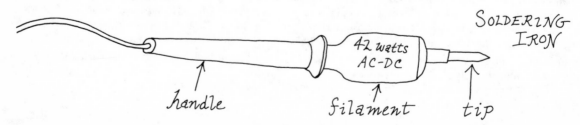

When the iron is hot, the only part of the iron that is safe to touch is the handle. If you work with the iron for several hours at a time you may want to make a wire stand to set it in when it is not in use, or you may want to buy a cage for holding the hot iron. The cage has the advantage of preventing you from accidently touching the hot part of the soldering iron.

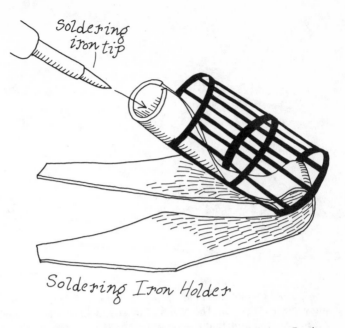

Soldering Iron Holder

As the tip is heating, clean it by whatever means are necessary. If the tip is crusted with dirt and oxide, you may need to clean it with sandpaper and a file. Cut down until bright metal is exposed. If the tip is fairly clean, then just wiping with a damp rag or sponge may be sufficient. When the tip begins to be very hot, touch the end of the rosin-core solder to the tip. Even though the solder will not melt at first, a small amount of the rosin core will melt and flow over the iron tip. This coating of rosin will keep oxygen in the air from oxidizing the metal of the soldering iron tip. (Even though the soldering instrument is called an iron, tips are made almost exclusively from copper.) Later, when you are soldering wire junctions, the rosin will flow over the solder joint and will keep the solder from oxidizing.

As mentioned in the section on lead, the oxide would dissolve into the solder and cause it to become refractory. By the same token a layer of oxide on the surface of a metal such as copper will cause it to become impervious to solder and thus un-solderable. For this reason metals that must be soldered should never be heated too hot or too often.

After a while the solder will melt on the tip of the iron. "Paint" the solder onto the tip until it covers the entire front portion. Wipe the excess solder away with the damp cloth or sponge.

Make a good mechanical joint   or   1.   2.   3.

Although this is difficult in practice, try not to let the solder spread all the way up the tip into the place where the tip screws into the heating element, as this makes the tip difficult to change later, if you decide you want to change it.

If the solder doesn't "take" on the tip of the iron even though the tip is hot enough to melt it, unplug the iron, cool the tip down, clean the tip, and try again. When the tip is properly tinned it can sit in its stand hot essentially all day and will remain useable if you use it only occasionally and wipe it with a damp cloth or sponge after and before each use. For this purpose a little plastic tray with a sponge in it is advisable. Pour a little water on the sponge, and set it on your desk for use when needed. The sponge will not only remove oxide from the soldering iron tip, it will also remove excess solder.

Make a good solder joint by beginning with a good mechanical joint. With the pliers, wrap together the wires to be joined.

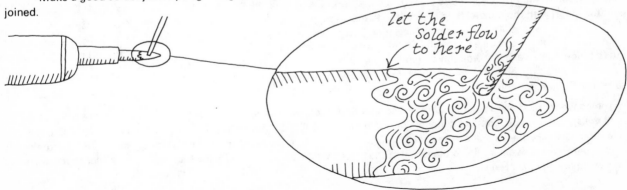

Let the solder flow to here

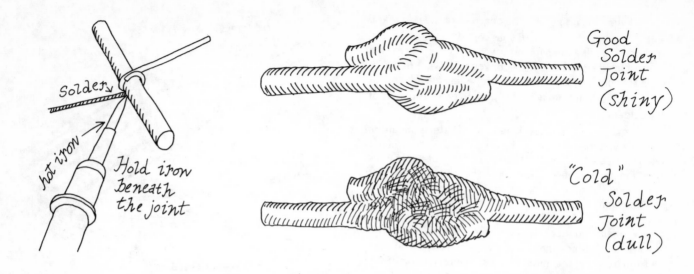

Solder

hot iron

Hold iron
beneath
the joint

Good
Solder
Joint
(shiny)

"Cold"
Solder
Joint
(dull)

Hold the hot iron *beneath* the mechanically joined wires, pressing it firmly against the joint, and press the solder between the wires and the iron. The object of these procedures is to heat the wires as quickly as possible. The advantage of this is that the shorter the time that the wires are hot, the less time the heat will have to be conducted along them and ruin electrical components, and the less time the metal will have to oxidize. As the solder begins to melt it will conduct heat to the wires and further increase the speed of their heating. The solder will flow by capillarity into the narrow crack between the joined pieces of wire. *After* the solder has flowed you may want to touch the solder to the top of the wire joint to add a bit of solder there. Usually this is not necessary.

When the solder has flowed satisfactorily, remove the solder wire and the soldering iron from the wire joint, and let it cool until the solder hardens. Then you can touch it or bend the wires if you need to. Moving the wires before the solder freezes will result in a "cold joint" which has a curdled or dull appearance, is mechanically weak and conducts electricity only poorly. A good solder joint is smooth and shiny.

TV-Radio
Solder

rosin

The fanciest TV-radio solder is 60% tin, 40% lead (written 60/40 tin-lead), is very thin, and has up to five or seven tiny rosin cores inside it.

STRUCTURAL SOLDERING

With a few exceptions, lead solder is used as an electrical conductor rather than as a structural material. One of the exceptions is the case when two large surfaces meet, and they must be joined without the use of high heat or where high heat is not available. The latter can sometimes arise in large sections of metal: even if you heat them with a blowtorch, they may conduct the heat away and dissipate it to the air so fast that the material never gets hot enough to melt high temperature solder. Fox example, to solder a brass pipe to a brass plate, use a blowtorch to avoid scarring the metal with solder stains at the place where a soldering iron would have to touch it. The procedure is essentially the same as that used for the ring we made earlier: set the flat end of the pipe down on the metal plate and let two or three drops of acid flux flow between them. Place a few bits of lead solder around the base of the junction and heat the metal with the blowtorch, directing the flame sometimes at the base of the tube and sometimes at the plate. As soon as the solder flows, remove the flame and let the solder cool. When it has cooled enough to harden, drip water on it until it is cool enough to touch, then wash it thoroughly to remove the excess flux. The large area of the junction between the pipe and the plate will give a strong joint even with lead solder. The same is not true for a thin copper pipe.

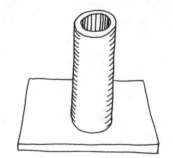

The above method will work for restoring the spout on a copper tea kettle that has been left on the stove without water in it until the spout melts off. First cut away the old solder because it is oxidized and refractory. Cut down to bare copper if possible. Anchor the kettle and clamp the spout in place against it. Use the same procedure as for soldering the pipe to the plate: using a torch will avoid straining the metal at the places where an iron would have touched it. Work fast because you are working on an already oxidized surface.

As described before, a good way to get solder slivers is to pound the end of a solder wire flat, and cut the slivers from the flat part with scissors.

The last use of lead solder that we will take up concerns the making of contoured metal shells. These are steel, copper, or brass sheets soldered together to make a hollow form (such as a head, or a sculpture of a person) or other object in which a good appearance is important but great structural strength is not. In this precedure the lead solder not only holds the metal sheets together, it is the substance of rounded and contoured corners. The making of these requires that the solder be syrupy (not runny) even when melted. Only a thin wire of low-tin, rosin-core solder will do, because thick or solid solder wires will require so much heat that as new material is being added, old joints will melt open. High tin solder or silver solder melts to the consistency of water, much too runny for this purpose. I have found Kester rosin-5 TV-radio solder satisfacory.

Begin with steel root beer cans, or the like. Burn off the paint with the blowtorch and clean the surfaces with fine sandpaper. Cut off the joint and the ends of the can to obtain a metal sheet, and flatten this out. You will need two pairs of pliers, plenty of solder, plenty of zinc chloride flux (available at hardware stores), scissors and files. First tin the parts that are to be joined, just as you tinned the soldering iron, by sanding an edge clean, wiping flux on it, and holding it up in the flame of the blowtorch. The purpose of pre-tinning the seams is to guarantee that a good solder joint can be made along each edge. If for any reason the solder won't take at any place along an edge, it is best to know before a piece is partly installed in the work. In addition, pre-tinned pieces can be soldered more easily than pieces that are not pre-tinned, because the sometimes difficult job of getting the solder to take is already done.

Hold the flame just below the top of the edge to be tinned and hold the solder against the metal. When the solder melts it will run down. Let it run, moving the work up so that the flame stays just ahead of the falling drop of solder. When the drop becomes too small to continue running down, replenish it by touching the solder wire to the metal again. With a little practice it is possible to turn out a thin layer of solder tinning on the edge to be soldered.

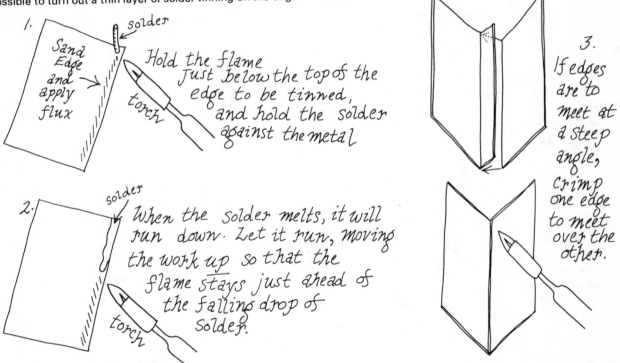

1. Sand Edge and apply flux — solder — Hold the flame just below the top of the edge to be tinned, and hold the solder against the metal — torch

2. solder — When the solder melts, it will run down. Let it run, moving the work up so that the flame stays just ahead of the falling drop of solder. — torch

3. If edges are to meet at a steep angle, crimp one edge to meet over the other.

In joining edges it is best to get them as close together as possible, as with the joining of plastic edges. Here we will not try to obtain a perfect fit, but will smooth over an approximate fit by adding more solder. If edges are to meet at a steep angle one of the edges should be crimped over to meet the other.

Hold the two pieces together as accurately as possible and apply the flame to one corner to tack it in place by forming a solder joint. It is good to do this where there is a drop of solder sticking to the metal. After the corner is soldered down the two pieces will stay together pretty well; solder them down starting from the other end. Always keep listening for the unwelcome creak of already soldered joints coming open in the heat, and learn to remove the heat quickly. Work around joints, pressing pieces together with the hammer where necessary.

apply hammer to round corner down

When the joint is complete there will still be some spots that show daylight, and these can be patched in two ways. The first is to melt the solder enough to get it to stick but not enough to let it run. This is tricky and requires nimble use of the torch. The other way is to hold the work so that the hole to be patched is the lowest part of the seam. When you heat a small area around the hole and feed some solder in, the liquid solder will flow down and fill the hole. Hold the work in position until the solder cools to avoid letting it flow out of the hole. After the seams are completed, finish them with file and sandpaper so that there are no sharp edges.

The exposed can metal rusts quickly, so protect the work by lacquering it or painting it immediately after it is complete.

Both the rosin core of the lead-tin solder, and the zinc chloride-and-hydrocloric acid cleaning liquid are popularly called flux even though the functions they perform are completely different. The rosin flows over the surface of melted lead, preventing it from oxidizing in the air and causing the molten solder to curdle. Rosin flux is good only at the relatively low temperatures at which lead-tin solder can be used. The zinc chloride solution dissolves grease off from the surfaces of metals, rendering them chemically clean so that the solder can diffuse easily into the metal. When using zinc chloride or acid flux, heat the metal to the melting point of the solder as rapidly as possible so that oxidation will have as little chance as possible to proceed.

SILVER SOLDER

Where lead-tin solder will last for years, silver solder is absolutely permanent. Because silver solder is harder and stronger than lead-tin solder, it is used as a structural bond in pieces that need to take great mechanical stresses, such as jewelry, a lightning rod cable, holding a retaining ball in place at the end of a winch cable, or closing gas tank seams. We have already gone through most of the important information related to silver solder, but it might be useful to organize it here.

1) Silver solder will bond most easily to copper. It will bond very nicely to brass and iron or steel; it will bond to bronze with difficulty.

2) Because silver solder melts at temperatures too high for use with a covering flux, it should be heated and cooled quickly to minimize oxidation in the solder and the substrate.

3) Because silver solder melts at higher temperatures than lead-base solders, it must be applied with a torch rather than with an iron.

4) Melted silver solder is as thin and runny as water. Therefore seams to be sealed by silver solder must meet perfectly, i.e., they must pass the daylight test.

We have already seen some sophisticated silver soldering in the making of a silver or copper ring. A simpler but instructive exercise is to silver solder a machine screw to a metal plate. You might need to do this if you wanted to bolt things down to the plate but do not want to drill holes in the plate to accommodate screws. With the file, remove any bumps from the flat face of the screw head, so that the head will pass the daylight test when it sits on the sheet metal.

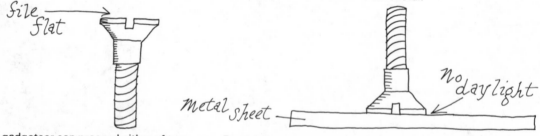

The gadgeteer can proceed either of two ways. For the first method, apply a drop of zinc chloride or acid flux between the screw head and the metal plate, allowing the liquid to spread by capillarity. Pound the end of a silver solder wire flat and snip off a sliver of the flattened solder. Straighten out the sliver (which will curl as it is being cut) and slip it into the slot where the screw ordinarily receives the screwdriver.

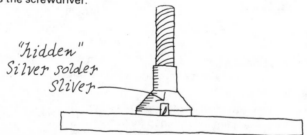

Do not attempt to heat the solder by sending the blowtorch flame down the slot. Instead, warm the screw and the metal plate with the flame until the flux boils away. Then apply the flame directly under the plate so the heat from the plate will melt the solder. In this way you guarantee that when the solder melts, the metal is hot enough to receive it. When the solder melts capillarity will carry it to the edge of the screw where it will appear as a red ring. Immediately remove the torch from the metal plate and watch the ring of solder. As soon as it freezes (an event which is easy to recognize because it occurs suddenly) you may sprinkle water on the metal to cool it, or pick it up with pliers or other heat-protective devices and drop it in water.

Hiding the solder in the slot intended for the screwdriver gives four advantages. First, it eliminates the need to touch the screw with a solder wire after the screw has been set in place. Thus the danger is eliminated of knocking the screw out of position when touching it with the solder wire. Second, it allows you to control exactly how much solder will be applied to the solder joint. (If you care to, you can weigh the solder sliver before inserting it). Third, it minimizes the danger of oxidation by guaranteeing that the solder will melt as soon as the metal is hot enough. In contrast, you would have to constantly test the temperature of the metal with a solder wire, and the metal might reach the required heat between tests. Fourth, it guarantees that the solder will go exactly where you want it to go, and nowhere else. In order to apply solder directly from the wire, you would have to touch the plate with the tip of the wire. In doing this you would inevitably leave a solder stain on the place where the wire touched the plate, and there would be no guarantee that the solder would flow under the screw.

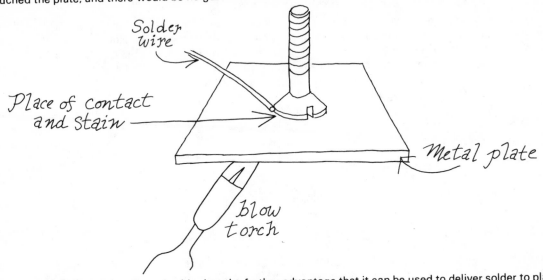

The technique of hiding the sliver of solder has the further advantage that it can be used to deliver solder to places which might be entirely inaccessible to other methods of solder application. Imagine for example that you wanted to solder the screw to a surface at the bottom of a well.

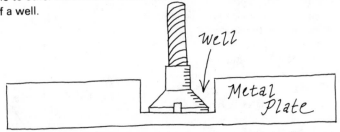

The difficulty of inserting a solder wire down the well would be prohibitive. If the solder was hidden in the slot in the screw, the problem would be eliminated. If you need to solder down some metal piece which does not have a slot conveniently cut in it, you can drill a hole or saw a slot to accept the hidden solder slug.

If the hidden solder technique is used for soldering together two pieces of large area, and the solder is not really hidden but only stuck in, an interesting effect results—for example in soldering a pipe or solid bar to a plate, as in the first example in this chapter, the solder might simply be stuck under the pipe or bar, and would prop it over slightly.

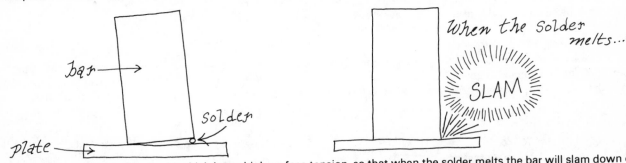

The silver solder melts to a thin liquid which has a high surface tension, so that when the solder melts the bar will slam down on the plate with a clatter, and will be held in place so strongly that even while the solder is still molten you will have a hard time sliding the bar across the surface of the plate or pulling it off. The hidden solder technique is essentially the one used for making the ring described earlier.

The second method for soldering down the screw is that of tinning the flat face of the screw, tinning the surface of the metal plate, cleaning both tinned surfaces, and then sealing them together with heat. The method has the slight disadvantage that it sometimes brings an excess of solder to the joint, so that the pieces do not meet flush. This method invariably stains a wide area of the plate around the place where the screw is placed. The method also reduces the accuracy with which the screw or other object can be located on the surface of the plate.

The method of tinning is best used when a metal does not take solder easily (bronze) or when very small pieces are to be soldered where there is no place to hide any solder. The method of tinning bronze with silver solder is the same as that for tinning bronze with lead solder: cover (dip or paint) the area to be tinned in acid flux, then hold it horizontal and place a sliver of silver solder on it; heat if from below. The solder will spread by itself. Wipe it with a damp cloth to help it spread. If you want to solder both sides of the plate, repeat the procedure for the other side.

For tinning the ends of wires I use this method. Cut a bit of silver solder about this big ▢ (about 1/16" on each side) and place it on a block of porcelain (the back of a tile will do) and melt it in the direct heat of the blowtorch. Dip the wire to be tinned in flux, then touch it to the bead of molten solder. Withdraw the wire, cool it in water, then dip it in the flux to clean it, and wash the flux away with more water. Sometimes I cool the hot wire directly in the flux, but this spits hot flux and acid fumes.

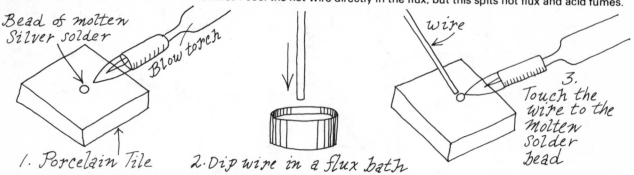

Bead of molten Silver solder — Blow torch

1. Porcelain Tile

2. Dip wire in a flux bath

wire

3. Touch the wire to the molten solder bead

As you solder larger and thicker metal objects the heat-dissipating character of the metal becomes important and should be turned to your advantage. When you heat with the blowtorch any sheet metal object that is larger than about 3" in any dimension it is essentially impossible to maintain the temperature of the entire object at a level that will melt silver solder. Thus if you are sealing a seam between sheet metal edges you can heat one part of the seam while the rest of the seam remains relatively cool. Prepare the joint carefully so that it passes the daylight test. The two sides of the seam must touch when the metal is at rest, because there is no opportunity to manipulate them when they are hot. Clamp the sheets in place if necessary. Apply plenty of liquid flux to the seam. Heat the seam, starting at the upper edge, until it barely reaches the melting point of silver solder (determine this by constantly touching the metal with the end of the solder wire *without* placing the solder wire directly in the flame).

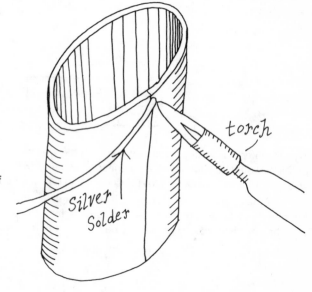

torch

Silver Solder

Take the flame away from the work momentarily if necessary. When the silver solder melts it will flow like water and, if the seam you are soldering has passed the daylight test, the solder will flow down it delightfully quickly. As the solder runs down the seam, bring the blowtorch with it. You can control the rate of flow by controlling the speed at which you move the torch. Seal the seam as quickly as possible to avoid oxidation. Long seams of this kind are most easily made with copper (slightly less easily with brass) sheet.

I used the above method to solder seams in the mold I used for casting the tube in my working model of the human vocal tract. The tube had to be of lens-shaped cross section ◇ (not oval ○) so that the mold needed to have sharp, soldered seams along the edges. The procedure will work for silver soldering seams in any sheet metal mold, tank, or other contrivance.

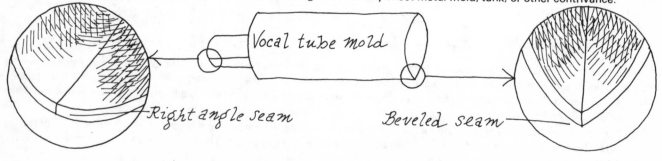

Vocal tube mold

Right angle seam

Beveled seam

Occasionally, when working with a very large or thick plate of metal, you will find that your torch will not bring the metal to the melting point of silver solder. Try to get a bigger torch. If this fails, you will need to find a different way to fasten down your joint or seam.

For fancy jewelry work, silver solders are available that melt at different, known temperatures. These are used in order, starting with the highest temperature solder, when a series of solder joints are to be made in a single small piece. After the first joint is made with the highest melting solder, the next joint is made with the next highest melting solder. Heat is applied only until the second-highest solder flows, and so on. In this way the jeweler can make several solder joints in sequence without melting previously finished joints as he makes new ones. This special silver solder is sold by the ounce and is needed only for jewelry. For utility purposes the silver solder available in hardware stores will do well enough. Buy jewelers' solder at supply houses.

MOLDS AND CASTING

Casting is the ancient art of manipulating a material when it is a liquid and using it when it is a solid. The power of this technique is so great that it has stood the test of time, and ranks with such inventions as the axle, the knot, and the ship's hull in its contribution to human cultural history—art, science, and industry. In addition, the materials can be poured into re-usable molds that are themselves made from a single original, giving us the power to manufacture identical parts in essentially any quantity desired. For example, the sockets of socket wrenches are cast by the millions—and they are all alike, so they all fit standard bolts. Engine blocks, fountain-pen bodies, plumbing elbows, bathtubs, lenses for car headlights, and motor casings are all cast. The uniformity of the castings guarantees that when you order a six-foot bathtub, that is what you will get, and you will not have to rebuild the bathroom plumbing to accommodate it.

By the use of casting a sculptor can convert a clay or wax original into a plaster or bronze finished piece, and then he can duplicate the piece into an edition of as many copies as he chooses. By casting, the artist or scientist can make sturdy plaster or plastic objects of any shape or size he chooses, and the only materials he needs to manipulate are plaster or wax. The architect can design a large wall constructed of a repeating module, and can manufacture the individual pieces to such precise tolerances that when the modules are assembled to make the wall, they will meet perfectly.

Repeating modules

We have already done a little casting when we cast lead rods in an aluminum foil mold formed around a pencil. In this operation the lead eventually "replaced" the pencil in the mold: we took away the pencil and poured lead in its place. The principle can be extended to other molds, the first of which we will consider is the sand mold.

Casting in a sand mold is called sand casting. Although much industrial casting is done in sand molds (e.g., large gears and wrenches) the home gadgeteer will seldom use the technique because it requires too much expensive and dangerous equipment. In addition, the equipment used for sand casting is dirty and is essentially useless for anything other than sand casting. Still, the technique is instructive, and is undeniably useful for making plaques and brass cannons, and perhaps you will find a use for it.

The basis of sand casting is a sand that will pack and hold its shape even when it is dry. A commercial foundry will tell you where to obtain some. Perhaps they will give you some. I have heard that the best natural sand for this use comes from the bottom of the River Seine in France, and that some modern foundries use zircon sand instead.

Begin by making a plaque (or solid cannon, without the bore) out of any suitable material such as wood, plastic, or wax. Because the plaque must be lifted free of the sand while leaving an impression of itself in the sand, the original must have no undercuts.

1. Cross section of plaque —
No undercuts.
This will lift easily out of
the sand, leaving an
impression of itself.
It *can* be Sandcast.

2. Cross section of plaque —
With undercuts (at arrows).
This will lift out of sand only
by taking with it the sand held
beneath the undercuts.
It *cannot* be Sandcast

Make or buy a sturdy (preferably steel) dividable box with polarizing pins to guarantee that it can be taken apart and put back together in exactly the same position.

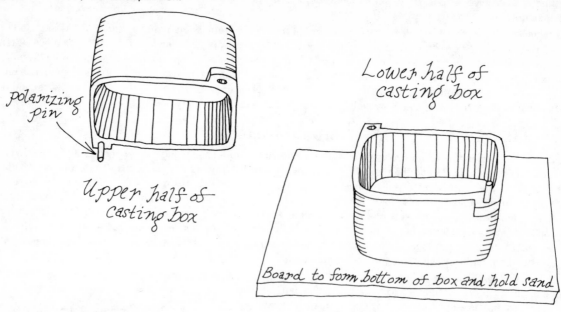

polarizing pin

Upper half of casting box

Lower half of casting box

Board to form bottom of box and hold sand

The basic idea of the sand casting procedure is to make in the sand an impression of the original, and to pour the hot metal into the impression. When the metal cools it will form an exact copy of the original piece. By this technique you cut a wax or wooden article, and exchange it for a metal one.

Begin by placing one of the box halves on the board, with the polarizing pin and hole facing up. Fill the box with casting sand, and knock it until the sand is firmly packed. Run a straight-edged board across the top of the box to make the sand surface absolutely flat and flush with the top of the casting box. Add more sand, tap the box, and use the board again repeating these operations until the sand is packed and flat.

Shake the sand in carefully to avoid lumps
or sift it in through a strainer
1.

2.
Smooth the sand surface with a straight-edged board

3.
finished sand surface

Dust the flat sand surface with releasing powder, an agent which ensures that when you add a new layer of sand on top of the first, the two layers will not stick together. Talcum powder will do.

Place the plaque, flat side down, on the flat surface of the sand, and dust it with releasing powder.

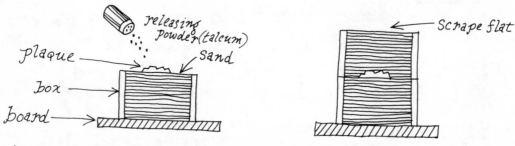

releasing powder (talcum)
plaque
sand
box
board

Scrape flat

Now set the upper part of the casting box in place and fill it with sand.

Notice that as the sand falls on the sculptured surface of the plaque (or other object) it will fill all the hollows and contours exactly, and in a way that would not be possible if the object were pressed into a soft sand surface. It is for this reason that shaking or sifting the casting sand over the contours of the surface to be copied is the essential procedure in sand casting. For the same reason, if you want to cast a medal or brass cannon, or other object that has a shaped surface on both sides, the first step is to cut the piece in half down the center, so that the back of each side is flat. This procedure allows you to shake new sand onto each side separately, as you will see.

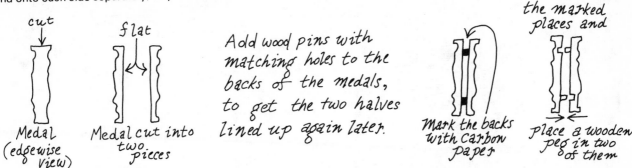

Place the medal, flat side down, on the bottom board, and fill the box with sand, covering the medal. Then turn the box over, leaving the medal back showing on the exposed surface.

In order to produce a sand impression of the second half of the medal it is necessary to pour loose sand over it. Place the second half of the medal on the first half, fitting the pins into their slots, if you have installed pins as guides.

Sprinkle releasing powder over the second half of the medal. Set the top half of the box in place, and fill the box with sand.

Using a hollow pipe a little less than 1'' diameter, dig two holes down through the top of the box of sand to the level where the two layers meet. If you gently poke the tube into the sand a short distance and remove it, it will bring some sand packed inside. Repeat the operation until the holes reach the required depth.

Measure the depth of the hole by comparing the depth to which the pipe penetrates, against the outside of the box. Put the pipe down in the hole as far as it will go and hold it with your thumb barely touching the surface of the sand. Withdraw the pipe and hold it alongside the box, with your thumb just touching the edge of the box. The distance that the tube extends down the side of the box indicates the distance that the hole extends inside the sand. The sand will hold its shape because it packs and sticks to itself.

Once again separate the two halves of the mold by lifting off the top part of the box. Remove the pieces which are the originals for the medal. With a sheet metal scoop, carefully scoop a trough connecting the edge of the impression left by the pieces to the holes that extend to the top of the mold. Make the holes as deep as possible without scarring the faces of the finished medal. One way to do this is to cut half of the trough into the top box of sand, and half of the trough into the bottom box of sand. Now put the two halves of the mold back together again.

Before going on with the casting, consider what an elegant device we have obtained through simple procedures. By the use of casting sand which first flows and then packs tight, we have created a hollow which is in the exact shape of a model or original which we have previously made out of wood or wax, or other easy-to-work material. It is then possible to fill the cavity with molten metal (which will cool to give an exact metal duplicate of the original) by pouring the metal down the channels cut for that purpose.

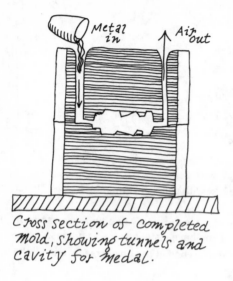

Cross section of completed mold, showing tunnels and cavity for medal.

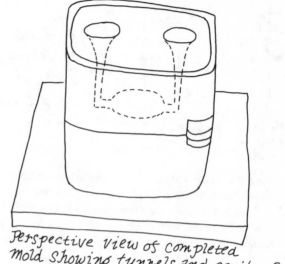

Perspective view of completed mold showing tunnels and cavity for medal inside the sand.

Melt the metal (lead, copper, brass, bronze) and pour it gently but quickly down one of the holes in the sand. If the metal is poured slowly, some of the material at the advancing edge may solidify and plug the mold, preventing any further metal from entering it, and ruining the mold. The molten metal will flow down the tube it is poured into, and will fill the cavity where the medal is to be. As the metal enters the tunnels and cavity, it will drive the air out the other tunnel.

Let the mold cool for at least an hour before removing the metal casting.

After removing the casting from the mold, saw off from the piece the metal that fills the tunnel through which it was poured.

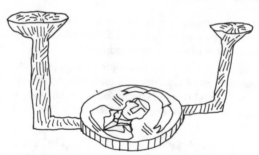

In practice sand casting leaves a rough-textured surface which is not a startlingly accurate copy of the surface of the original piece. Sand casting works best for small objects (up to about 10″ x 10″ x 5″) which will be machined after they are cast. Thus it is good for casting brass cannons, and plaques with lettering that will be ground off flat after the piece is removed from the mold. Because bubbles may become trapped in the mold in spite of the porous nature of the sand, there is danger that castings may come out perfect on the bottom, but with voids (bubbles) on the top. For this reason sand casting works most effectively in casting plaques that have flat backs.

back →
face →

Cast with back side up. Metal will flow down into features of the face, filling them.

For a variety of reasons already mentioned, sand casting is not practical for the home gadgeteer, although the technique is used every day in heavy and light industry. Sand casting is illustrative of the strategy common to most casting.

To obtain objects made of a durable, and therefore difficult-to-work material, begin with some more easily worked material. Work the material into the precise shape desired and replace it with a more durable material. Then surround the object with some medium that will hold its shape, and remove the original piece, leaving in the surrounding medium a cavity of precisely the same shape as the object desired. Pour the durable material into the cavity as a liquid, and let it harden into its durable form. Remove it from the mold.

In practice removing the finished piece from the mold sometimes requires destroying the mold.

No praise can do justice to the ingenious invention of casting, which enables us to work the toughest materials into any intricate shape we choose, with almost no waste.

There can be no hard rules governing the use of materials for molds or casts: I have already described a mold made from copper sheet. Still, the gadgeteer can learn the techniques of casting by practicing with a few of the commonest and most useful materials.

WAX

The best wax for use in mold making is one that is pliable (not brittle), and that is solid at room temperature, soft at hand temperature, but does not melt until it approaches the boiling temperature of water. Good wax has little memory, so that if you bend a piece of it, it stays bent and does not creep back to its old position. In addition, it must not transmit pressure through itself, so that if you scoop out a portion of a ball, the far side of the ball must not expand under the pressure. Such expansion is behavior of the wax beyond your control, and the basic factor in gadgeteering is control.

The wax must not be brittle, so that it can be twisted or cut with a knife without cracking. It must stick to itself, so that it can be built up in layers. (A sculptor may want to build up the features of a face by adding material, or a scientist may want to weld corners by pressing them together.) Last, a good wax must be a dark color, and opaque; otherwise you will not be able to see the shape of its surface. The opaque, dark color is not a picky detail but is a basic essential, as you will find when you begin to work wax.

Because it is brittle and does not stick to itself, paraffin, the wax sold in grocery stores for making candles and for canning jellies, is definitely useless for the mold making we will be doing.

The best wax I have used was a brown microcrystalline wax produced by Mobil Oil company. The last I heard they had stopped marketing the stuff, and you may have to buy it from a local hi-tech wax company. Ask a foundry where to get microcrystalline wax, or look up wax in the yellow pages. Before buying it, try out the wax to see if it has the correct properties. If the wax is light yellow, you can get pigments to dye it dark brown. Ask the company that produces it, or try the wax dye from a candle supply store.

In order to be usable the wax must be in the shape of thin sheets of not more than 1/2″ thick. The sheets can be cut into any shape for making the walls of molds, or the sheets can be cut up into little pieces (2″ x 3″ or so) which are dropped in a bucket of hot water to soften. As they soften they can be kneaded together into any shape you choose.

Form the wax you have bought into sheets by first melting it in a double boiler. It can be melted over a direct flame, but that requires constant attention to make sure the wax does not overheat, boil, or catch fire. When the wax is melted, pour it in thin layers of 1/4″ to 1/2″ thick on the surface of *hot* water placed in cookie sheets or other pans. Using hot water ensures that the wax will not harden as soon as it touches the water and leave lumps and membranes of wax mixed with water. When the water and the wax cool, the wax sheets are ready. Cut them away from the edges of the cookie sheet and store them for future use. The wax will stick to the edges of the cookie sheets tenaciously, so it is a good idea to get one or two cookie sheets (and one double boiler) and use them for wax only. The wax in the boiler pot is not usable because when it is melted it is too hot to touch, and when it hardens it is too hard to work. Pour the sheets. The sheets of wax, if poured carefully, will be remarkably smooth, and the top and bottom surfaces will be absolutely parallel.

Microcrystalline wax is related to paraffin but has a longer carbon chain in its molecule. Some microcrystalline wax is very hard and brittle, so be certain to try it out before you buy it. The wax should not cost more than 25¢ a pound.

In an emergency, beeswax can be used instead of microcrystalline, but is is more difficult to work and can raise blisters on your hands. It is too hard to work when treated as we treated microcrystalline; also, if you buy the wax from the beekeeper it will contain dirt and dead bees.

Melt the beeswax, stir it up, and pour it hot into a cone-shaped vessel (or at least a vessel with a narrow bottom) lined with aluminum foil. When the wax is cool, remove the aluminum foil and cut away the dirty wax at the bottom. Or clean the wax by melting it in a tin can and letting it cool. Remove the wax by heating the whole outside of the can, melting a thin layer of wax next to the metal. Turn the can upside down and knock out the lump of wax. The clean wax at the top is usable. Melt it again and pour it on warm water, but before it has a chance to congeal completely, knead it in your hands into little tiles about 2″ x 3″ x 1/4″. Knead the wax thoroughly. As you press it, it will chip into little plates which are so hard when cool that they cannot be worked by hand. Break each of these plates to bits. The wax tiles will be a light yellow color, but essentially opaque, and suitable for use in sculpting. Wax that has not been properly kneaded will appear translucent. If possible, avoid beeswax and use microcrystalline. Beeswax costs a dollar a pound and up.

Learn to work the wax by hand by making a life-size wax head or other object such as a bird—your choice. A head is a good thing because it is easy to cast (although not easy to make), and perhaps you can ask a friend to pose for you. Begin by getting a bucket of very hot water and dropping in several of the wax pieces. When the wax softens, make some quick sketches in wax of the head you intend to make. Because the hot wax will stick to lumps of cooler wax, you can press new wax onto the head as it progresses, building up features here and there. When you are satisfied with the wax sketches, make a life-size head of wax.

Make a wooden base out of a large square of plywood (1' x 1') with a 2" x 2" x 8" wood block standing up in the center. Use the base not so much as the pedestal to make the head on, but as a peg to hang it on when your arm gets tired. Hold the wax in one hand and work around and around the head with the other, adding new wax from the bucket of hot water when it is needed. As in carving, work around and around the piece, keeping all parts at the same level of completion, never allowing any part to get ahead of the others. To make the head easy to hold and light in weight make it hollow on the inside. Set the finished head on the base.

If, during the making of the wax piece, you need to weld together the edges of wax sheets, or smooth a surface, do this with the waxing iron you made earlier. Hold the edges to be joined together, and run the hot iron between them, making the melted wax flow into the crack. If necessary, add extra wax from a wax "worm" rolled between the hands. Seal the weld from both sides, making sure the pieces are "melted together" thoroughly. The uses of the waxing iron are limited only by the user's imagination.

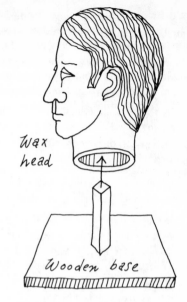

Wax head

Wooden base

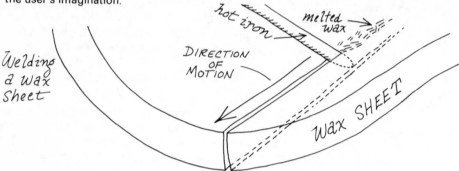

Welding a wax sheet

hot iron   melted wax

DIRECTION OF MOTION

WAX SHEET

I will describe the making of a clay head, and then explain how to cast the wax or clay heads, which are fragile, in plaster, which is much more durable.

CLAY

Water-base clay is sand so fine that, once it is wet, the particles stick together so tightly that water cannot seep through. Buy clay in ten, twenty, or fifty-pound bags at pottery supply houses. The use of clay in making pottery is taught in so many places that there is no need for me to describe it here. A good place to look for notices about lessons is the bulletin board in your local co-op grocery store. If the pottery store sells different colors of clay, ask them about the properties of each. Because we will not be baking the clay, almost any type will do. If you dig clay yourself from the banks of a river, try to get fine grained clay that is free of pebbles.

The making of a life-size clay head is no different from the making of a wax head except that the clay is too heavy to carry in one hand, and it is too heavy to hold its shape under its own weight. Support the clay on a stand high enough to hold it at a comfortable working level. Build a solid clay head around a supporting post outfitted with string-and-wood supports (butterflies) that will prevent the clay from drooping.

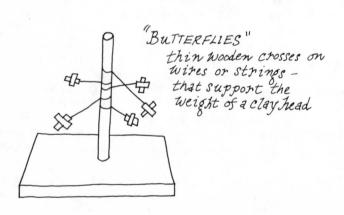

"BUTTERFLIES"
thin wooden crosses on wires or strings — that support the weight of a clay head

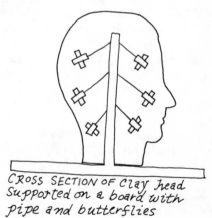

CROSS SECTION OF clay head supported on a board with pipe and butterflies

Keep the clay moist at all times by dipping your hands in water from time to time while working it. New clay can usually be added to a wet clay surface by simply pressing it on and is more efficient than wax in this respect. Make the clay bust by building up the features with clay—do not be afraid to make them large.

When you leave the clay for more than a couple of minutes, protect it from drying by covering it first with a wet cloth and then with a sheet of plastic. This method will be effective both for works in progress, and for your clay supply (which should be stored in a plastic garbage can). Properly moistened, the clay will stay workable indefinitely. If a clay piece begins to dry, it can not be worked further and is useless for casting in plaster. Let it dry, and get it baked in a kiln.

PLASTER

Plaster is white, powdery calcium sulphate which, when mixed in proper proportions with water, will form a thick paste that will harden to stone on standing. Mix plaster in a glass bowl because it is inevitable that some of the unused plaster will harden in the bowl, and plaster will not stick to glass. Remove the excess plaster from the walls of the glass bowl by pouring water over them and giving the plaster a push with your hand. Buy plaster in the local hardware store: get *plaster of Paris*.

Prepare plaster by first filling the bowl about half full of water. Then shake some plaster powder into the bowl, allowing the powder to settle into the water before adding more powder. Do not stir the water. Eventually the plaster will stand in a mound above the surface of the water: now stir the water-plaster mixture. After the mixture becomes uniform it should have the consistency of heavy cream. It is ready to use. If the glass bowl is clean, and if the plaster is not disturbed, the mixture in the bowl may stay liquid for up to twenty minutes. As time passes the plaster will slowly grow more and more viscous as the hardening process begins. When the mixture begins to grow viscous it can be made to harden almost instantly by applying it with a spoon or trowel to some porous surface, such as dry plaster, that will absorb the water out of it. The near-instant hardening effect can also be achieved by merely placing the plaster on a vertical surface because the water will run to the bottom of the plaster mass, causing the top portion to dry and harden. As a result of these properties, plaster makes an outstanding patch for ceilings or walls.

Because it is a liquid and will conform to the shape of any surface that it is placed against, plaster also makes an outstanding mold-making material for copying the wax or clay head. The objective of making a cast is to exchange the fragile wax or clay for durable plaster, and we will do this with a plaster mold.

A few points about strategy are indispensable here.

The strategy of casting ahead in plaster calls for making a plaster mold around the wax or clay original, removing the original, and replacing it with more plaster.

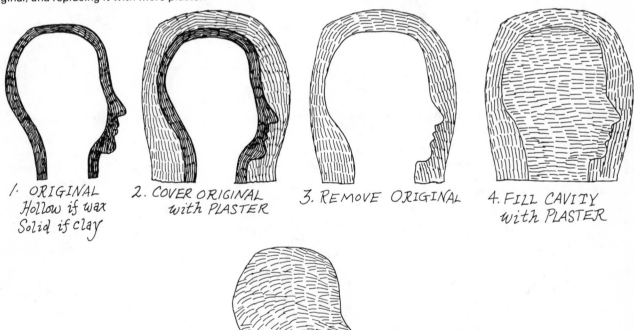

1. ORIGINAL Hollow if wax Solid if clay

2. COVER ORIGINAL with PLASTER

3. REMOVE ORIGINAL

4. FILL CAVITY with PLASTER

5. CUT AWAY MOLD- Leaving exact plaster duplicate of wax or clay original.

In order to guarantee that the steps can be carried out successfully, certain precautions must be taken at the beginning.

Step three, the removal of the original from the mold, can be completed only if the original and the mold do not stick to each other. In a clay original this is no problem because the clay can be washed away with water. When casting a wax original, make sure that the original and the mold will not stick together by covering the wax with a layer of vaseline or tincture of green soap as a releasing agent. Take care not to allow the releasing agent to gather too thickly in any of the fine details of the original, as this will obscure them in the cast.

As can be seen in stage four, the border between the plaster of the mold and the plaster of the head is very hard to see, especially in the three-dimensional object. You will be chipping the mold away from the finished head with a knife, and there is a danger of carving into the plaster of the head. To reduce this danger, mix food dye into the first layer of plaster that you place around the original piece. Then, when you cut the mold away, the border between the mold and the cast piece will show up as a border between the dyed and the white plaster.

In addition, step three, the removal of the original from the mold, will be essentially impossible unless you have direct access to the inside of the original and mold. Obtaining this access requires that the mold be able to split in two halves. You will probably want to divide the head into a front and a back half to avoid leaving scars in the face. This dividing of the mold can be accomplished in either of two ways: the two parts of the mold can be set in place simultaneously with a thin partition between them, or they can be set separately, the first one being built up against a dam, and the second being built up against the first.

For both methods the objective is to create a separable mold that can be disassembled for removing the material of the original from the plaster of the mold, and reassembled to receive the casting material.

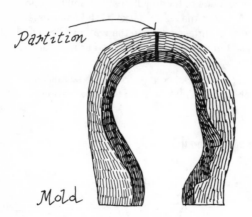
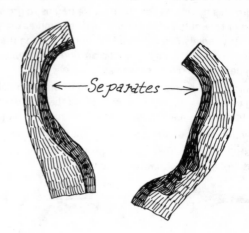

THIN PARTITION METHOD

The thin partition method is to be preferred for casting of originals made of soft, and therefore easily distorted, materials such as wax and clay.

Make the thin partition from little rectangles of shim metal. Shim metal is thin brass sheet (between .005 and .01 inches thick) usually used between two pieces bolted together, to separate them some distance. Cut up the shim metal into pieces about 1-1/2" x 2", or for larger pieces, 2" x 3". Slice the pieces of shim metal into the clay or wax so that their position marks the boundary between the halves of the plaster mold.

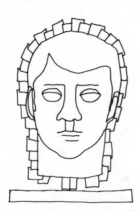
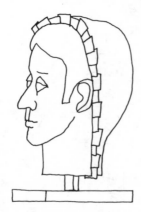
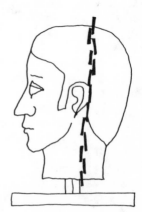

Three views of clay head, prepared with a shim metal divider, ready to receive wet plaster for mold.

Whether the original piece is clay or wax, the shim metal dividers should be covered with a releasing agent such as petroleum jelly, tincture of green soap, or silicone grease. If the original piece is wax, the shim metal dividers must penetrate the piece almost, but not quite, to the point of cutting it in two. Then, when the time comes for separating the halves of the mold, the wax piece inside cannot hold them together permanently.

Because wet plaster is runny, the plaster mold cannot be built around the clay or wax original in one layer. Instead, the mold will have to be built up in several layers, of which the first will be the thinnest (because the first layer must stick to slippery clay or wax, while subsequent layers must stick to already hard, and therefore absorbent, plaster). With a reminder that the first layer of the mold must be colored with vegetable dye, we are ready to apply the first layer of the plaster mold. Mix up a bowl of plaster and dye it.

APPLYING PLASTER

Apply the plaster with a large spoon.

When the plaster is still newly mixed and runny, it will not stick to the clay or wax. Try to get a patch of hardened plaster to form on top of the piece, and get as much plaster as possible to stick to the sides. As the plaster begins to thicken it will stick to the wax or clay, and you will be able to enlarge the patch of hardened plaster at the top. As this patch enlarges to cover the sides of the piece, apply the plaster by hand rather than with the spoon. With your fingers flip the plaster under the undercuts, covering the entire surface of the original with a layer of the dyed plaster. After some minutes the plaster will become very thick and you will be able to direct it very accurately by hand. When the plaster becomes so thick that it cracks when pushed, let it stand until it has hardened. If you want to wash the unused plaster from the bowl by running water over it in a sink, use enough water to make sure that the plaster will not collect and harden in the water pipes. Mix up a new batch of plaster (no dye necessary this time) and apply it to the hardened plaster of the mold. The plastering will proceed much more easily from now on because the old plaster will absorb water from the new.

As the mold is building, the plaster will gather most thickly around the shim metal divider. If the divider is to be effective, and, in fact, if its location is not to become lost, you must scrape away any plaster covering it so that the finished mold shows a thin line at its surface, the upper edges of the shim metal pieces.

Make the mold thick for strength. A mold the size of a hand should be at least one-half inch thick; a mold the size of a head should be at least an inch-and-a-half thick. A mold enclosing two or three cubic feet of space should be at least five inches thick, and reinforced in the outer layers with long threads of wood shavings.

When the mold reaches the required thickness everywhere, let the plaster cure. Plaster grows hot as it cures, and you will know it has reached full strength when it cools down again after heating.

When the plaster is thoroughly cured (cooled down after heating), pry the halves of the mold apart (thus ruining the clay or wax original) by alternately pressing inside the opening of the mold at the neck and pulling out the shim metal pieces with pliers. Damage them as little as possible while pulling them, because they are expensive. Scoop out of the inside of the mold all the material you can without injuring the plaster. After the two halves of the mold have come apart entirely, scoop out the material of the original piece and save it for re-use, picking out the plaster chips first. Wash out the inside of the mold to remove clay that sticks there. Pull away the last bits of wax, remove all the shim metal dividers. Now prepare the mold to receive plaster for casting the finished piece.

Line the mold with a releasing agent such as petroleum jelly, high-vacuum silicone grease, or tincture of green soap to prevent the plaster of the mold from sticking to the plaster of the cast. Reassemble the mold. Slight irregularities in the shape of the surfaces that meet will guarantee that the two halves of the mold will fit together perfectly. Bind the halves of the mold together tightly with rubber bands cut from old truck inner tubes. Invert the mold so that the hole is the highest part, and pour in fresh plaster. If the casting requires more than one batch of wet plaster, make sure that the first batch covers the entire inside of the mold so that no seams show up in the finished cast. If you want the casting to stand on an armature, suspend the armature from above (from a pipe in the ceiling, for example) and let it hang in the plaster as it cures.

After the plaster heats and cools again the cast is completed and ready for the removal of the mold.

Chip the mold away with a partly-sharp knife such as the one you made from a file. When you strike the dyed plaster you

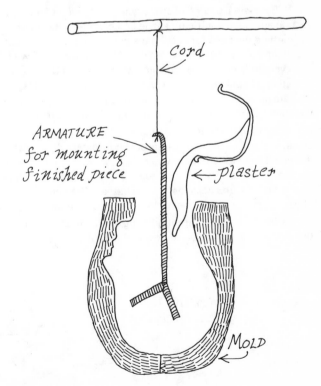

cord

ARMATURE for mounting finished piece

plaster

MOLD

will know you are approaching the surface of the plaster head. Proceed carefully, to avoid nicking it, and the dyed layer will crumble and pop away in little chips from the white layer beneath it, eventually freeing the finished plaster head from the mold.

PLASTICENE

Hand-sculpted original pieces can be made from plasticene, and oil-based modeling clay, as well as from wax or water-base clay. Plasticene has the advantage that it is nearly as pliant as water-base clay, but it never dries out, and it takes a smooth surface more easily than does wax. The best plasticene I ever used was given to me by a friend who bought it in Paris. It was coarse-grained compared to other clay I have seen, and had the quality of keeping its body at hand temperature, so that if a scoop is taken out of one side of a ball of it, the whole opposite side does not expand, obscuring any shape that it previously had.

COARSE-GRAIN PLASTICENE

Scoop

Pressure is not transmitted to opposite side of the piece— THE MATERIAL RETAINS ITS SHAPE

FINE-GRAIN PLASTICENE

Scoop

Material explodes out under pressure - LOSING ITS SHAPE

I have used plasticene for modeling the originals for tongues which I later cast into limp vinyl plastic and used in a working model of the human vocal tract. Plasticene can be an extremely sensitive medium, but only plaster molds can be successfully made from it, as the oil of the clay retards curing of the rubber and plastic mold-making materials we will use later.

Polish a plasticene surface almost (not quite) to a mirror shine by stroking it gently with a finger. Wax can be brought nearly to mirror shine by stroking it gently with a fine cloth dampened with a solvent that dissolves wax, such as acetone, or methyl-ethyl ketone.

LOST WAX CASTING

By a few changes of strategy the technique of enclosing (investing) a sculpted piece in plaster can be enriched for casting almost any intricate shape in metal or plastic, by the lost wax process. The lost wax process is directly comparable to the method we used for casting the plaster head, except that we remove the wax original from the mold not by disassembling the mold, but by heating the mold and boiling the wax away. The wax is boiled away, the hot metal is poured into the mold (and air is vented from it) through vents which are cast directly into the mold by attaching thin rods of wax to the wax original before investing it in plaster. The thin wax rods are called sprues, and they should be attached to the original in places where air bubbles are likely to collect. The sprue which will form the channel for pouring the metal should be the largest, while the sprues which will form the channel for venting air can be smaller.

Most of the time, in casting jewelry, sculpture, or machine parts, the mold must be destroyed in order to remove the cast piece. In these cases use special casting plaster which is soluble in water after it hardens. Plunge the mold into the water after the metal has hardened but while the mold is still hot. This special casting plaster is so porous that air will escape from it when the metal enters, even though no air escape channels have been built. This plaster can be bought from sculptors' and jewelers' supply houses, and perhaps from foundries. The home gadgeteer will probably be able to cast only lead metal, but with the help of your dentist you can cast gold, silver, and platinum jewelry or small sculptures.

Dentists use a centrifugal sling for casting fillings in which the lost wax mold is placed at the end of a rotating arm, and the melted metal allowed to flow into the mold under centrifugal force.

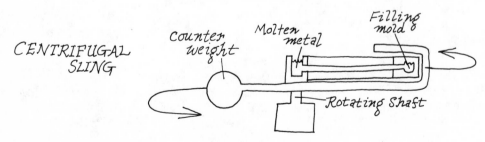

CENTRIFUGAL SLING

Counter weight

Molten metal

Filling mold

Rotating Shaft

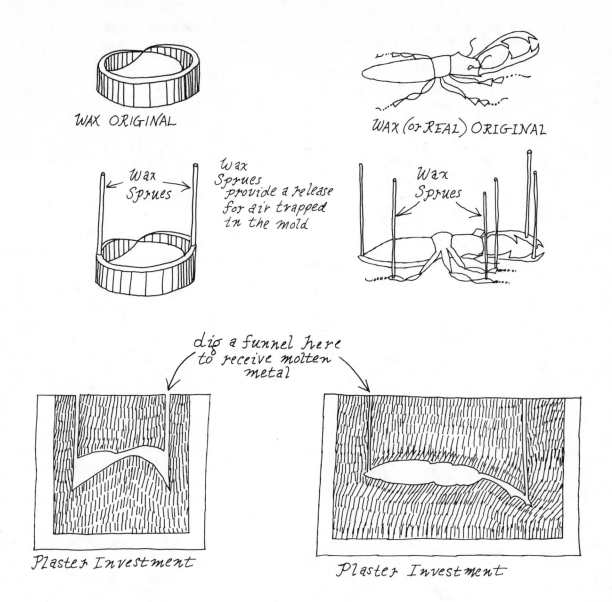

WAX ORIGINAL

WAX (or REAL) ORIGINAL

Wax Sprues

Wax Sprues provide a release for air trapped in the mold

Wax Sprues

dig a funnel here to receive molten metal

Plaster Investment

Plaster Investment

If you have access to an oxy-acetylene torch you can make a centrifugal casting device adequate for small pieces such as jewelry. The device is an arm on a rotating shaft that is wound up on a spring. The mold has a built-in reservoir to hold the metal. Heat the metal with the torch and, when the metal flows, release the arm so that the centrifugal force will drive the metal into the mold.

Casting even a small lead piece at home is a job that will push a kitchen to its limit. Heat the mold at 400 to 500 degrees for six to eight hours to drive out all the wax and the water from the plaster.

If even a small amount of water remains in the plaster when the hot metal is poured in, the water will boil; the steam will shoot a fountain of liquid metal out the vents in the mold, and several feet into the air.

After all the water is driven from the mold, remove the mold from the oven, place it on a cement or asbestos block, and pour in the molten metal. Allow the mold to cool for several hours before opening it. Even when a mold cools on the outside it can still be hot on the inside, so allow it enough time to let the metal harden.

Allowing a mold adequate time to cool is trying on the nerves, because the casting of a piece is the culmination of perhaps hundreds of hours of work in the planning and preparation of the wax, and in the making of the mold. When the wax is melted away and the metal poured, the sculptor feels that the work is out of his hands (it is) and he is impatient to see the finished piece. Opening the mold is like opening a present. Make sure the present turns out in good condition by giving it enough time to cool.

A plaster investment is such a sensitive casting medium that if the sculptor's fingerprints were present in the wax original they will be duplicated in the metal casting. Thus it is worthwhile to devote any amount of care and time to the working of the wax. Wax is more easily worked than metal, and since the finest details in the wax will be reproduced in the metal, it is worth working the fine details into the more easily-worked material.

If you do not want to make a centrifugal casting device, or if you are casting a piece too large for your centrifugal caster, force metal into the mold under steam pressure. Forcing the metal into the mold helps to drive out air bubbles that leave voids in the finished cast. For steam-pressure casting, tack several layers of cloth to a plywood board that is just larger than the top of the mold. Make sure the surface of the mold is flat. Pour water into the cloth lining on the plywood board, and after pouring the metal into the mold, press the wet cover down on top of the mold, covering ALL air vents. The water will boil and the steam will drive the metal down hard into the crevices of the mold. All the air vents must be covered because if one of them is not covered, the steam pressure on the other vents will squirt the liquid metal out the one uncovered vent.

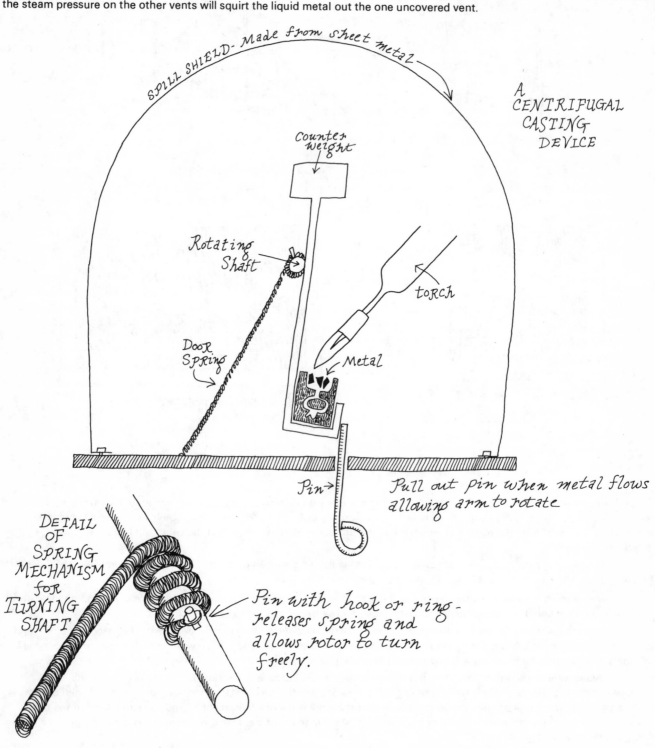

SPILL SHIELD- Made from sheet metal

A CENTRIFUGAL CASTING DEVICE

Counter weight

Rotating Shaft

torch

Door Spring

Metal

Pin→

Pull out pin when metal flows allowing arm to rotate

DETAIL OF SPRING MECHANISM for TURNING SHAFT

Pin with hook or ring- releases spring and allows rotor to turn freely.

MULTIPLE DUPLICATES

You can produce any number of duplicates of an original piece by making a mold that will not be destroyed when the casting is removed. Such a mold is usually flexible rubber backed up by plaster. Plastic or lead can be cast directly into such a mold, while bronze is cast from these molds indirectly by casting wax in them, and casting the bronze from the wax.

Latex: buy latex for mold making in jars in artists' supply houses. Brush it on as a liquid, and let it dry in the air. The mold needs to be fairly thick—build up the rubber in layers. Latex is a little fragile, and only a limited number of casts can be made from a latex mold. In addition, only wax can be cast in a latex mold. Still, latex is cheap and just about as sensitive as other mediums. Use it for limited numbers of wax duplicates for bronze casting.

For larger numbers of wax duplicates, or for direct castings in plastic (epoxy or polyvinyl chloride PVC or polyester) or lead, use a good room-temperature vulcanizing RTV thixotropic (butter-on) rubber such as Dow Corning RTV-C. This is a red silicone rubber that comes as a liquid in a can and cures to a flexible (but not elastic) condition in the presence of a catalyst. After being mixed with the catalyst, RTV-C stays runny for about half an hour, and then begins to set up, so you have about a half hour to work with it.

Materials that cure, such as RTV-C, plaster, and concrete have a way of curing slowly so that you feel they are still runny and you have plenty of time to work them—and then suddenly they are nearly set up and you have to rush. When working any material that cures, plan your moves before you mix up the material, and then execute your moves quickly. Use the extra time just before the material is too stiff to work to make sure everything is perfect. Buy Dow-Corning products from local artist supply houses or industrial supply houses. RTV rubbers cost about $7.00 for twenty-five cubic inches.

When mold-making rubbers are blended with their catalysts, some air will inevitably become trapped in the mix, making the material uneven and weak. Remove the air by placing the freshly made rubber-catalyst mixture into a large vacuum chamber, such as a desiccating jar made from a pickling jar, and applying a vacuum of about twenty-five to twenty-seven inches of mercury. The bubbles will expand, the rubber will froth, and the bubbles will break, leaving de-aired rubber. Be sure to mix up the rubber and catalyst in a cup having a volume about three times that of the catalyzed rubber at atmospheric pressure, so that when the rubber froths under vacuum it does not overflow the cup.

RTV-C is so thick that it cannot easily be de-aired, so be careful when mixing it. See the instruction sheet that comes with it.

G.E. silicone seal, sold as a bathtub calking compound, can be used as a mold-making medium, although it has a way of trapping bubbles at the surface of the piece being copied. Silicone seal comes in small tubes and is useful if you plan to make just one small mold. I have found that white silicone seal has better spreading qualities than clear, (and black and silver will only be used when color is important). Apply silicone seal direct from the tube onto the piece being copied, and spread it with a finger or, if necessary, a rubber paddle. As already mentioned, silicone seal needs no catalyst (it cures in the air), and the uncured rubber reeks of acetic acid (vinegar). It takes about twenty-four hours to cure.

The method for making a rubber mold is essentially the same as that for making a plaster mold, except that the rubber mold can be peeled away from the wax or plaster original without damage to either, thus providing the opportunity for producing multiple copies.

The strategy for making the rubber mold is this: set the piece to be copied in front of you and inspect it for planes. These planes do not need to be flat, they can be curved, but they need to be more or less the equivalent of a surface that could be covered with a single sheet of pliable plastic wrap. Eventually the rubber mold will be applied on these planes, with the result that the rubber can be lifted away from the original in flexed, but not folded, sheets. The idea is simple enough, but because no two pieces are alike, planning each mold can be a strenuous exercise in visual imagery. Even fluted edges, such as the feathers at the margins of a bird's wings, must be assigned to one plane or another for making a rubber mold.

Rubber molds are best built around an original made from a strong material such as wax or metal. After you have conceived in your mind's eye the positions of the curved planes that compose the surface of the piece to be copied, decide which one you want to work first, and build a dam around it, so that only that plane is exposed. Make the dam from wax if the original piece is bronze, and from wax or shim metal if the original piece is wax. Close all the imaginary partitions, and build the dam out by extending the imaginary plane so that the actual surface exposed is the dam and the curved plane of the piece. Anchor the dam to the back side of the piece.

Coat the piece and the dam with a releasing agent, and apply mold-making rubber to the exposed surface so that it completely covers the piece, and so that it extends about half-way out toward the edge of the dam. Build up the mold-making rubber sufficiently thick to hide all basic features of the original piece. If the original piece is plaster, you may want to shellac it before coating it with a releasing agent.

In order to provide a backing that will enable the mold-making rubber to keep its shape after it has been removed from the piece and the dam, pour a plaster back over the rubber and out to the edge of the dam. Cut off the plaster back flush with the edge of the dam at right angles to the surface of the dam so that the backing has thickness and strength at its edges.

The mold is now complete on one side. When the plaster has cooled, turn the mold over and remove the dam.

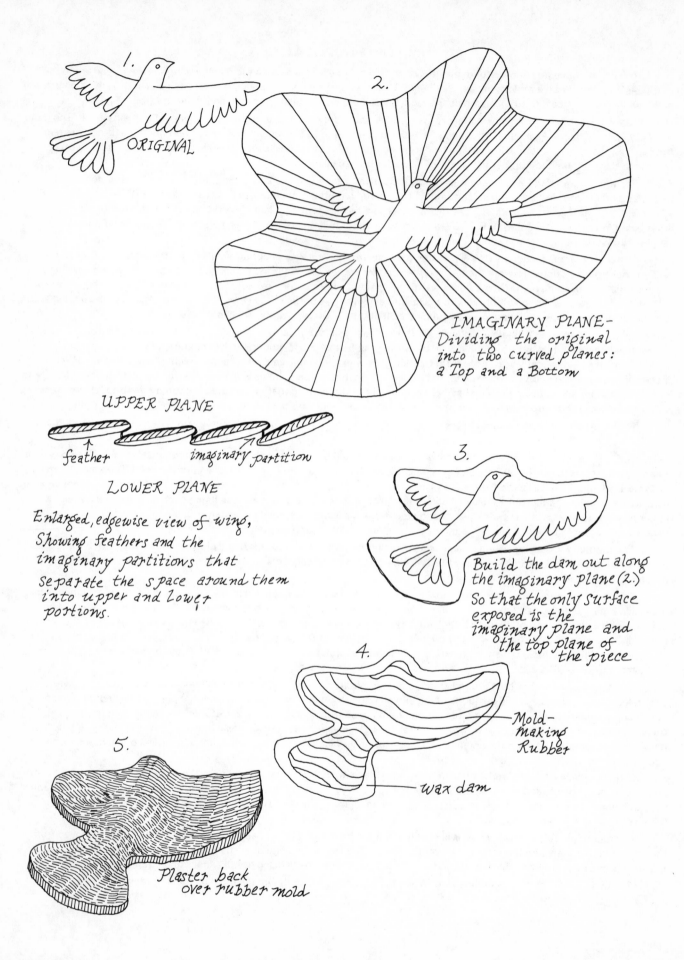

1.

ORIGINAL

2.

IMAGINARY PLANE–
Dividing the original
into two curved planes:
a Top and a Bottom

UPPER PLANE

feather   imaginary partition

LOWER PLANE

Enlarged, edgewise view of wing,
Showing feathers and the
imaginary partitions that
separate the space around them
into upper and lower
portions.

3.

Build the dam out along
the imaginary plane (2.)
So that the only surface
exposed is the
imaginary plane and
the top plane of
the piece

4.

Mold-
Making
Rubber

Wax dam

5.

Plaster back
over rubber mold

The back of the mold, consisting of the rubber and its plaster backing, forms the dam for the second part of the mold. Coat it with a releasing agent (tincture of green soap, petroleum jelly, or high-vacuum silicone grease) and apply the second half of the mold. Apply the rubber out to the edge of the original rubber, and after that cures apply plaster backing out to the edge of the original plaster. With the knife made from a file, carve down the edge of the new plaster flush with the edge of the old plaster.

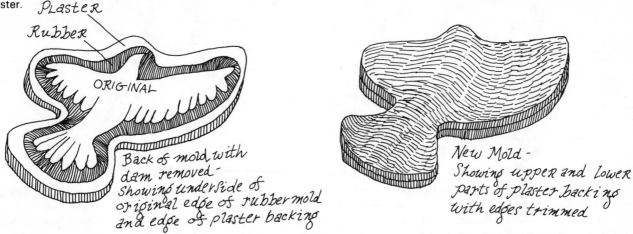

Plaster
Rubber
ORIGINAL
Back of mold with dam removed — showing underside of original edge of rubber mold and edge of plaster backing

New Mold — showing upper and lower parts of plaster backing with edges trimmed

The mold now consists of three concentric layers: the plaster, the rubber, and the original piece.

Carefully pry apart the plaster backings and open the mold. Separate the rubber sheets and remove the original piece. The mold is complete except for the channel for pouring in the hot wax or catalyzed plastic. If the mold is small enough to pick up and shake by hand you will probably want to distribute the casting material by shaking the mold, rather than by using air vents, so you will probably want to cut only a channel for introducing the mold-making material. Cut the opening into the channel in a funnel shape.

Clean out all parts of the mold and it is ready for use.

Prepare the mold for casting by sticking the rubber to the plaster with green soap or stiff high-vacuum silicone grease. Coat the inside surfaces of the mold with releasing agent and assemble the mold, strapping it together, as we did earlier, with large rubber bands.

Prepare the mold-making material. If the material is to be polyvinyl chloride, polyester, or lead, no releasing agent is necessary. Use releasing agent for wax and plaster. Polyvinyl chloride PVC, and polyester plastic resin come as a liquid in a can. They harden to a beautiful, clear, hard plastic and can be dyed various colors. Their use is simple: follow the instructions on the can and pour the catalyzed plastic into the channel in the mold, turning the mold and shaking the liquid plastic into the places where air bubbles are likely to become trapped. Fill the mold to the top of the funnel and set it aside until the plastic cures.

The procedure for wax or other melted materials is the same as that for plastic, except that care must be taken to avoid getting hot wax (or worse, lead) on the hands. Hot wax only hurts. I have had molten lead on my hands; it is an utterly horrible experience and potentially crippling.

After the plastic cures or the wax cools, open the mold and remove the copy of your original. The sharp edges of the original may have become rounded and softened a little when the material contracted as it cooled, and these may need some touching up with the waxing iron or other tool. The casting is now complete.

Often, in the casting of a complex shape, a mold more sophisticated than the above two-piece mold becomes necessary. Because no two pieces are the same, it is impossible to outline rules for building a mold for copying every piece you might build. The procedures for the two-piece mold must be extended in such a way that the many-piece mold can be taken apart and put back together. The arrangements of the rubber mold and the plaster backing may be different because the rubber is flexible, while the plaster is not. Arrange the rubber backing so that it peels off the original in planes, and use as few planes and seams as possible while still allowing the rubber mold to come apart and release the original and the copies.

To make the plaster backing in such a way that it will come apart, make it so that it does not go around any corners, and so that it does not fill any cavities.

For example, illustrations A and B show a badly-conceived mold and a well-conceived mold, respectively. In these pictures I have used this code:

ORIGINAL Piece

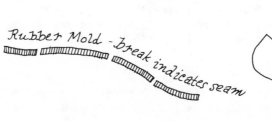

Rubber Mold — break indicates seam

Plaster Backing — line indicates seam

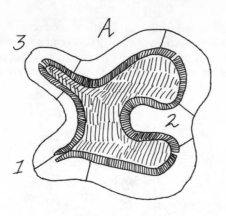

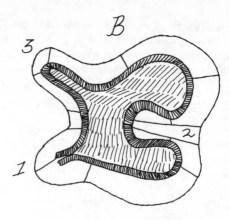

Badly-conceived Mold   Well-conceived Mold

The rubber backing in A is badly planned because it is in more pieces than necessary, and will be unnecessarily difficult to assemble. In contrast the rubber mold of B has one seam at (1), and the mold can be peeled away from the original in a continuous sheet. In mold A the piece at (2) will be impossible to remove from the undercut, while the piece at (3) will probably grip the prominence there. In contrast piece B has a triangle at (2) which can be slid out of place, releasing the other pieces. The same strategy allows piece B to be disassembled at place (3). Piece B, then, can be disassembled. To make sure that the mold can be reassembled requires that a few precautions be taken during the original construction. Recall that as each new piece is added to the plaster backing of the mold, part of the dam marking off the shape of that piece is the walls of previous pieces. Before applying the releasing agent to the plaster, cut a trough in the edge of each piece, so that the section poured next to it will have a bump that precisely fits the trough.

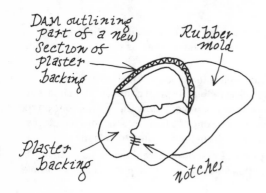

Set up for casting a new section for a plaster backing.

Note the wax or clay dam, and the notches for fitting the pieces together, later.

Later these bumps and troughs will fit together like a lock and key, acting as guides in reassembling the mold. In addition, ball point pen marks in the plaster can help in reconstructing the mold. (Note the three little stripes on the seam in the illustration.)

ARMATURES

An armature is a frame, usually made of heavy wire or concrete reinforcing rod, that stands inside a piece to lend it strength. Build life-size clay sculptures around a reinforcing rod armature. (The making of such pieces requires considerable planning.) Install an armature inside a casting by attaching thin wires to it and suspending it inside the mold before pouring the casting, making sure that the armature does not touch the walls of the mold anywhere. Lead the thin suspending wires out between the blocks of plaster on the outside of the mold, and snip off the wires at the surface of the casting after removing it from the mold.

The French make bronze sculptures by making a clay and wire armature just smaller than the desired piece, and then finishing the piece in wax. They then cut off the wax in small plates and cast these separately, thereby avoiding having to cast any very large pieces. After the pieces are cast they are brazed back together again.

DIRECT MOLDS

The painter Jim House says, "Negative space is the place where many an otherwise good sculptor has been buried."

Occasionally you may want to build an object the shape of which is not so important as the shape of the cavity it encloses, or you may want to incorporate a direct casting of some cavity into the mold for a larger piece, and in these cases you will almost certainly need to construct the mold directly from wax (or plaster), without building an original piece. The strategy for this resembles that for carving a piece out of a solid block of material: To make a direct mold, envision the cavity you want, floating between your hands, then pick up wax and build the cavity. To build the part of the mold that holds the casting material that will surround the cavity, envision the outside of this material, and build a mold around it. The procedure is a strenuous exercise in visual conception.

EPOXY

Because catalyzed epoxies are thicker than honey they are often difficult to cast in complex molds. I once had to swing a mold around my head on a rope in order to force some thick epoxy down into it. The thickness of epoxies makes them handy for covering negative molds that have an open back. By coating an object with thick epoxy, and turning the object around and around the way you turn a spoon around to keep honey on it, you can coat the object with a glassy, form-fitting coat of indestructible epoxy. Float little wax cutouts in the surface while doing this, and after the plastic has hardened, scrape them out to leave shaped troughs in the surface, or fill these with a different color epoxy to give the effect of colored designs at the surface.

The clinging nature of epoxy is such that I was once able to use it to reconstruct a jade cup that had been dropped and broken. Part of the cup was crushed almost to sand, but the epoxy held the pieces so perfectly that now the casual eye would not guess that the cup had ever been broken.

Some expoxies which are rigid at room temperature become slightly flexible when heated to about 150°F, so that stands or arms made of this material can be adjusted when heated. I used to heat epoxy models of neck bones in the micro-wave sandwich heating oven at my school cafeteria, to the horror of students who heated their sandwiches there.

LINER MOLDS

When you want to make a casting that will be so complex inside that removing the mold-making medium from the finished casting will be difficult, or inspection of the interior will be difficult, you can make the interior directly. This method works especially well with room temperature mold materials, such as epoxy. Lightly paint a sheet of coarse cloth with enough expoxy to make it stiff, but not enough to make it rigid, and form the cloth into the shape of the interior you want. The procedure may require several stages of construction (and a lot of practice). Cut the cloth, wrap it and join it until you have the cavity you want, then build in wax a negative mold around it, and pour expoxy between the liner and the mold. The result will be a finished plastic piece of known inner shape, even if the inside cannot be inspected after the casting is completed.

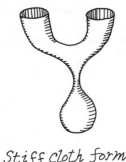

Stiff cloth form

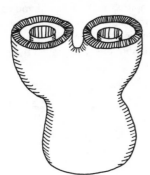

form surrounded by wax mold

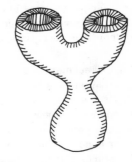

finished epoxy casting

SLURRIES

Sometimes you may want to thicken epoxy or polyester so that it can be worked on vertical surfaces, or to load the expensive plastic with a cheaper filler to get more volume for the money. Do this by making a slurry with the liquid plastic. A slurry is a mixture of a solid and a liquid: for example, slush is a mixture of water and ice. The "instant" stained glass window adhesive is a slurry of epoxy and sand, where the sand is used to increase the volume of the epoxy without increasing the cost.

The home gadgeteer will probably want to mix the solid into the plastic after the plastic is catalyzed because the plastic-solid mixture is very thick. The choice of a solid is critical in designing a slurry. For example, epoxy sticks to rock, so an epoxy-sand slurry will be at least as strong as the epoxy without the sand. I have used a sand-epoxy slurry to build up a liner for the inside of a wooden box, so that the bottom of the box would come down to a dimple, so that a monkey taking a raisin out of the box would not have to search for the raisin in the corners. When the epoxy cures, the surface is smooth and glassy, and no sand grains protrude to make it rough.

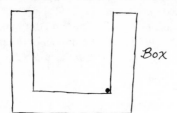
Box

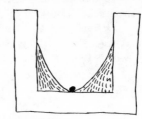
Box with epoxy-sand slurry lining bottom

Polyester makes an effective slurry with titanium dioxide powder.

Up to a limit, some rubbers make an effective slurry with talcum powder, but because they do not really stick to the talcum, the talcum weakens them.

FIBER REINFORCING

The presence of fibers in a uniform material will strengthen the material considerably. This is why we placed some long, thin wood shavings in the large plaster mold: the shavings will strengthen the plaster, as will hair. Soaking glass cloth in liquid polyester will yield fiberglass for pressing into the inside of a mold to give it strength.

Accuracy, Comparison, Measurement, Dies, Jigs, Mass-Production, and Inspection

Historically it is inevitable that the more accurate device was made on the less accurate device, and the hand gadgeteer can coax considerable accuracy out of the tools he buys in the store.

For example we have used the file to cut a perfectly straight edge on a metal sheet, so that for $1.75, the file gives you more than just a gadget that takes off metal: It gives you a straight edge that puts straight edges on other things. Subtle use of ordinary tools will yield parts that fit each other perfectly, and near-perfect multiple copies of parts for repetitive devices.

Measurement and Comparison

Measurement is the procedure of *comparing* two objects or events along some dimension for the purpose of determining whether they are the same or different along that dimension. Thus the most direct measure is empirical measure (direct comparison). For example, line up two pieces of metal and compare their lengths. If you cannot detect a difference between them, they have the same length. Let two runners run a race, starting at the same time. If you cannot detect any difference between their positions as they cross the finish line, they ran the race in the same time. Place two objects on a balance scale. If you cannot detect any difference in the position of the scale before and after you placed the objects on it, the objects have the same weight.

In contrast, indirect measures are useful because they allow us to compare two objects or events without actually juxtaposing them: compare the object or events to a standard (e.g., a centimeter, a minute, or a kilogram) and determine how many of the standard units represent the dimension being measured. The resulting number, which does not need to be a whole number, can then be compared to other objects without ever bringing the objects near to each other. A further step in abstraction leads to plans and diagrams drawn in reduced or expanded scale.

Because indirect measure is extremely useful, for example, in ordering boards cut at the lumberyard, one does well to learn to use it skillfully by learning to take all measurements according to some routine. Thus, when using a ruler, always position your eye directly above the mark you are using. When marking with a pencil or pen, position the writing instrument so

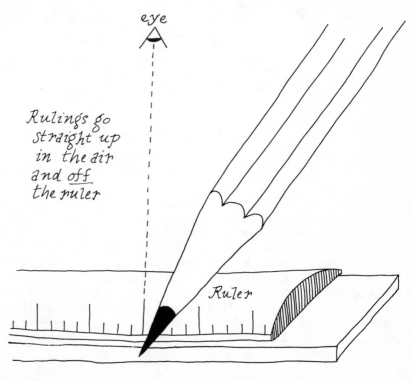
eye

Rulings go straight up in the air and off the ruler

Ruler

that the mark will fall directly below the mark on the ruler, ensuring that any two marks you make on paper using marks on a ruler as your standard of distance, will be exactly as far apart as the chosen marks on the ruler.

As you did with the saw, position the pencil accurately by rolling your thumb against it and pressing it sideways along the ruler. Used skillfully, the ruler can tell you, for example, whether a drawer will fit on its slides, without your ever testing it to find out.

Learn to use the micrometer and the vernier caliper. These are especially useful in determining the thickness of very thin sheets of material, or in determining the dimensions of larger objects to a high degree of accuracy so that, for example, parts such as pistons and cylinders can be fitted together. The use of the micrometer is self-explanatory: clamp it gently but firmly on the material to be measured and, without removing it, read on the scale the separation of the jaws. The coarse reading (on the barrel) is millimeters, and the fine reading (on the turning thimble) is 1/1000th or 1/100th of a millimeter depending on the instrument. Micrometers calibrated in inches use different fractions. Inspect your micrometer to determine its units.

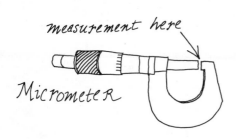

measurement here

Micrometer

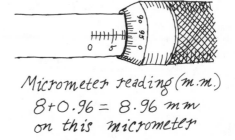

Micrometer reading (m.m.)
8+0.96 = 8.96 mm
on this micrometer

The vernier caliper measures outside diameters (as does the micrometer), as well as inside diameters and depths.

The upper scale (the unit scale) is ruled in some conventional units such as millimeters or 1/6ths of an inch. In this example the lower scale (the vernier) is divided into ten steps in the space occupied by nine units of the upper scale, so that each step of the lower scale is one-tenth unit shorter than the units of the upper scale. As a result, if two lines from the upper and lower scales line up, their neighbors on each side will be one-tenth unit short of lining up. If you move the scales one-tenth unit, one of the neighbor pairs of lines will line up. The arrows in the large drawing point to the lines that line up, showing one-tenth unit difference with each step, and the scales move past each other in one-tenth unit increments. Note the motion of the far left mark of the vernier scale: it moves through the first unit of the upper scale in one-tenth unit increments, showing that the lower scale has moved past the upper scale in one-tenth unit increments. The procedure can be repeated indefinitely with a longer unit scale thus providing a device for measuring even large objects with considerable accuracy.

Inspect your vernier caliper to determine its units.

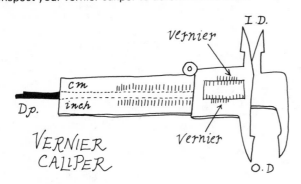

Vernier
I.D.
cm
Dp.
inch
VERNIER CALIPER
Vernier
O.D

Dp. = Depth
Cm = Centimeters
inch = inches
I.D. = inside diameter
O.D. = outside diameter

In this chapter more than in any of the others in this book the procedures outlined are only specific examples of general techniques. The examples as they stand can be useful to you only if you want to do exactly what the examples describe. In fact, you should try the procedures as they stand in order to cultivate a feel for how to execute them. But after you have mastered the procedures, if you will adapt them appropriately to your own projects they will save you hours and days of difficult measuring, adjusting, and thinking, thus empowering you to complete projects you could not have undertaken without them. The central idea of this chapter is that the most powerful procedure is a systematic procedure: the techniques presented are examples to get you started.

In spite of the great usefulness of indirect measure in formulating and communicating plans, and in predicting precise quantities so that large objects such as the Eiffel Tower can be built without waste, the proof of the pudding is that pieces must fit together—this is a matter of direct comparison, the subject of the rest of this chapter. We already used direct comparison in the daylight test, and we will use it again and again in making pieces fit or match, and in performing inspections.

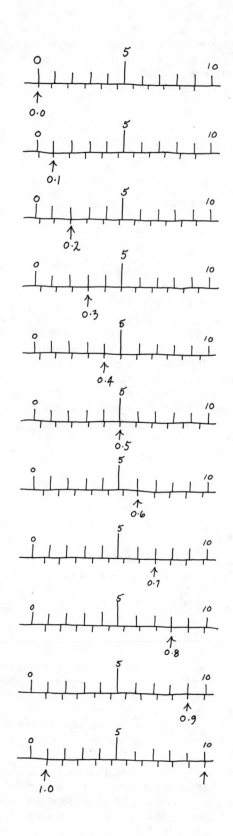

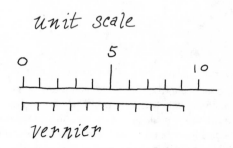

unit scale

vernier

Hanging a door without the use of a ruler is a demonstration in the power of direct (empirical) measurement. Inspect the door frame and the hinges. Decide in which position to mount the hinges so that the door will open in the desired direction, and so that the hinge pins will fit down into the hinges from the top. Holding a pencil in two fingers and resting a third finger against the edge of the door, draw a line parallel to the door edge. The line will serve as a guide for making the door hinges parallel to the edge of the door and in line with each other.

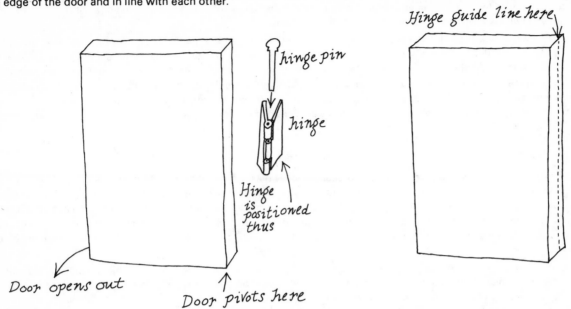

Decide where on the edge of the door you want the hinges to be, hold them approximately in place, and mark their positions with the pencil.

Now line up the top hinge exactly where you want it to be. The eye is very sensitive to even slight deviations from parallel in two lines which are close together, so that you will be able to line up the hinge parallel to the edge of the door by lining it up with your pencil line—even if the edge of the hinge does not exactly touch the pencil line. If the pencil line and the hinge are too far apart, draw a new pencil line. If necessary, tilt your line of sight, as in the above drawings, to bring the edge of the hinge into visual alignment with the pencil line, to obtain a better perspective for judging whether they are parallel. After the hinge is positioned parallel to the edge of the door, outline its position with a pencil.

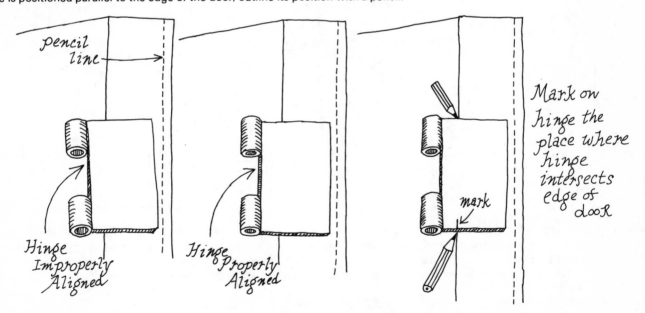

If the second door hinge is identical in construction with the first, position it by copying the position of the first hinge. Before moving the first hinge, make marks on the edge of the hinge at the places where it intersects the edge of the door. (Do this on both sides.) Now place the first hinge where the second hinge will be and align it using the marks on its edge. With the pencil, draw the outline of the hinge on the side of the door. Both hinge positions are now outlined on the edge of the door and can be cut out to receive the hinges by the procedure described in the section on chisels. Sink the hinges into the edge of the door until their surfaces are absolutely flush with the surface of the wood.

Screw both hinges into the door. (See the section on screws. If the door is old and the screw holes rip out, slide tooth-picks into the holes to give the screws something to grip.) Assemble the upper hinge and set the door in position in its frame, shimming it off the door sill with some paper or bits of wood. Unfold the hinge and press the free half against the door frame in the place where you will install it and mark its outline on the door frame.

Take away the door, disassemble the hinge, and install the second half of the hinge into the door frame. Assemble the bottom hinge and hang the door from the upper hinge. Press the bottom hinge against the place where it will fit in the door frame and outline it with pencil. Remove the door, install the lower hinge and replace the door. If the line marking the position of the lower hinge in the door frame was drawn carefully, the hinges should match perfectly. If they are off by a small amount, adjust one of the hinges by tapping it gently with a hammer. Simple strategies of direct measurement make possible very precise positioning of mechanical parts without the opportunities for error introduced by the extra steps involved in indirect measures.

Plate Glass

Earlier I mentioned that the gadgeteer's standard of accuracy is plate glass. Obtain the largest sheet of plate glass that you can manipulate easily, and satisfy yourself that it is flat by looking at reflections in it. Reflections of windows, chandeliers, or light bulbs will do. Stand as far away from the plate glass as possible and move your head from side to side as you watch the reflection through one eye. The lines of the reflection you are watching will not be bent and distorted as the reflection moves across the glass. Try the same experiment with a piece of window glass and the lines of the reflection will wobble, indicating that the glass surface is wobbly.

Because the plate glass is flat it serves as a standard for comparing other objects. Place the objects on the plate glass and they must begin on the same plane (the plane of the glass). If they end on the same plane they must be identical. Use this method of comparison to cut two brass slugs or rods to the same length.

Begin by cutting off the rods to approximately the same length using a hacksaw, and cut off the ends of the rods so that they are perpendicular to the direction of the rod. Adjust and true the end of the rod by holding the rod between the thumb and forefinger of one hand and pressing the end of the rod against a file held in the other. If the rod is long and thin, place your fingers near to the file and let the rod hang under its own weight. After removing large, obvious nicks or flashings with the file, move the rod slowly across the file while rotating the rod between your fingers. Rotating the rod will have the effect of making the end of the rod come out radially symmetrical. If you press it hard against the file and let it hang under its own weight the end will turn out flat and perpendicular to the direction of the rod.

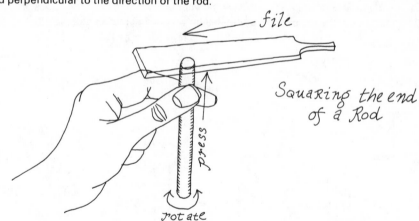

Squaring the end of a Rod

Square one end of the second rod and stand the two rods side by side on the plate glass. If one is visibly longer than the other, file it down. Square the remaining two ends of the rods and again stand them on the plate glass. Run your thumb over the tops of the two rods as they stand side by side. You will be able to detect differences in length smaller than you can measure reliably with the micrometer. Gently "kiss" the longer rod with a fine file to adjust its length.

Flat Surfaces

In addition to cutting straight edges, the file can be used for cutting flat surfaces into objects. Press the object against the file so that the pressure on the surface is distributed uniformly on the file. To ensure even pressure over the surface being filed, move the file or the piece in one direction only. Establish a rhythmic motion. After two or three strokes the arm and hand muscles will fall into a routine, and the constant use of this routine will free your attention to concentrate on applying even pressure.

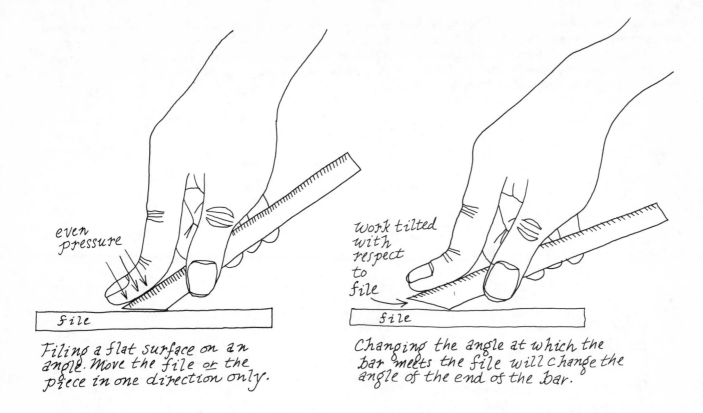

even
pressure

file

Filing a flat surface on an
angle. Move the file or the
piece in one direction only.

Work tilted
with
respect
to
file

file

Changing the angle at which the
bar meets the file will change the
angle of the end of the bar.

By applying controlled, *uneven* pressure to the end of the piece, it is possible to change or adjust the angle at which it meets the bar. Find the position which gives even pressure and then rock the piece forward or backward by a degree or so. Filing in this position will remove the material nearest the file first, thus changing the angle of the end of the piece.

By combining the technique of comparing lines to see if they are parallel (used in aligning hinges) with the technique of filing angled ends onto bars, we can accurately miter bars to fit at any angle we choose. For example we can cut three sections of brass pipe to form a near-perfect equilateral triangle.

Begin by cutting three brass pipes to exactly the same length, using the sheet of plate glass as a standard. Then determine the angles to which you need to cut the ends of the pipes.

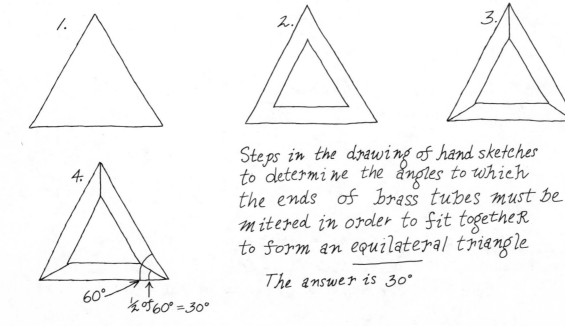

1.

2.

3.

4.

60°

½ of 60° = 30°

Steps in the drawing of hand sketches
to determine the angles to which
the ends of brass tubes must be
mitered in order to fit together
to form an equilateral triangle

The answer is 30°

For a standard 30° angle, use either the 30° angle from a 30-60-90 plastic triangle, or use a 30° angle constructed with compass and straightedge. The procedures in the figures below show how to construct a 60° angle, and how to bisect any angle. If we are willing to accept a straight angle (180°) as an angle, the two procedures together will give several angles having whole numbers of degrees: 180, 90, 45; 60, 30, 15. Combine the construction for the 60° angle with the construction for bisecting an angle to obtain the 30° angle.

PROCEDURE FOR OBTAINING a 60° ANGLE

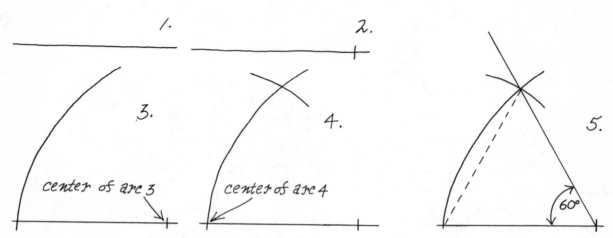

Arcs 3 and 4 have equal radii, so that the procedure works by producing an equalateral triangle. Construction requires only a compass and a straightedge.

STEPS IN BISECTING ANY ANGLE

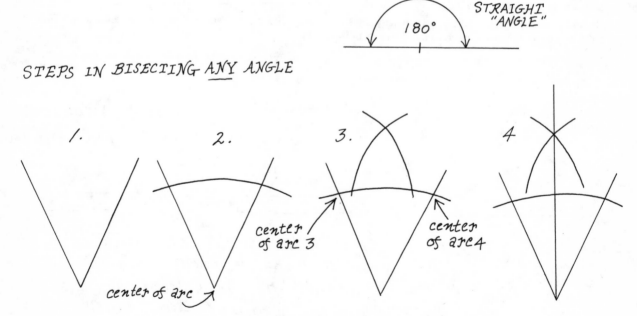

The procedure works by dividing the angle into two symmetrical portions, using compass and straightedge. If the starting angle is a straight "angle" (180°) the result will be a right angle (90°).

Construct a 30° angle, and file the end of one tube as close to it as possible by eye. Obtain greater accuracy by lining up the pipe with the 30° angle, and comparing the two by the procedure used in lining up the door hinge with a line. Because the cut end of the pipe may not be long enough to compare to the angle on the paper (depending on the size of the pipe) extend it by holding it against the file.

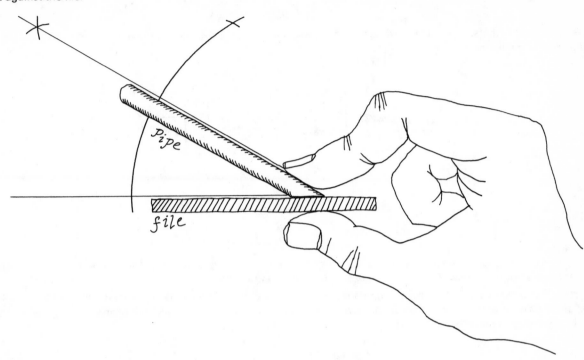

Cut the six ends of the pipes to the closest tolerance possible, keeping the mitered ends of each pipe in facing planes. Be careful, when filing the ends of the pipes, not to cut one pipe shorter than the others.

When the pipes are ready, prop them together on tile blocks and silver-solder them together. Wet the end-faces with flux and arrange the pieces as shown.

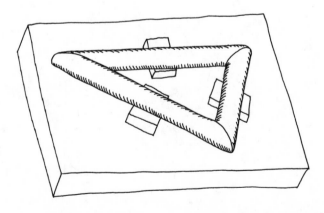

Place slivers of solder on the seams and melt the solder with the blowtorch by heating the piece from the side and slightly below.

MULTIPLE PIECES

Aligning the end planes of the brass pipesfor the pipe triangle is the first of a collection of procedures which coordinate the positions of parts with respect to each other.

Brackets—Hinges

When brackets are used for holding any object to a bar or rail, the direction of the brackets must be in line with the direction of the bar or rail.

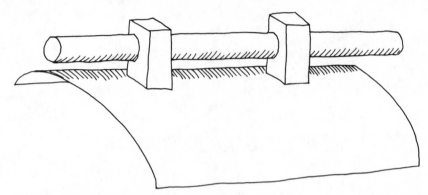

In order to guarantee that the brackets will fit on the bar, slide them onto the bar and leave them there while attaching them to the housing below. Then they are absolutely certain to fit the bar.

The same rule goes for hinges, too: hinges on the same door must be on the same line or the door won't open. For example, when installing the hinges on the cover of a guitar case, string them on a length of straight piano wire or taut cord while positioning them.

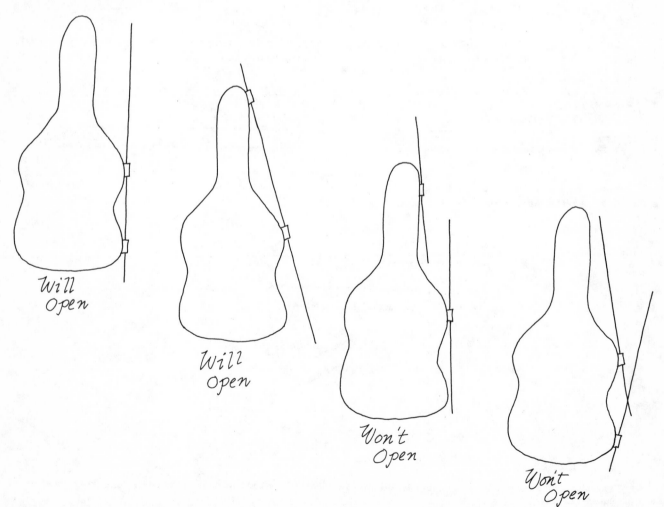

Symmetry About a Line

When drawing up plans, achieve symmetry about a line by cutting or tracing on a folded sheet of paper. For example I drew the guitar case for the example above (and would draw the plans for a real guitar case) by tracing on a folded sheet of paper, and unfolding the paper.

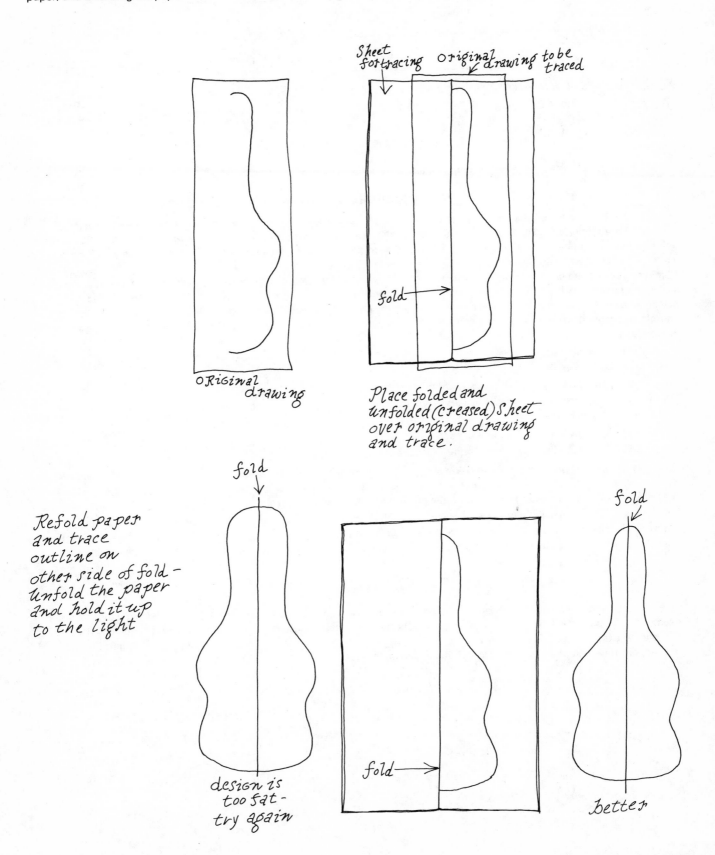

oRiGinal drawing

Sheet for tracing *original drawing to be traced*

fold

Place folded and unfolded (creased) sheet over original drawing and trace.

fold

Refold paper and trace outline on other side of fold — Unfold the paper and hold it up to the light

design is too fat - try again

fold

fold

better

Straightness

An old trick for determining whether a line is straight is to sight along it, thus concentrating the whole line into a short visual distance and allowing you to compare each portion of the line to its neighbors.

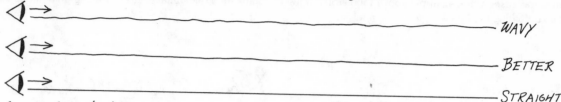

— WAVY

— BETTER

— STRAIGHT

Sight along a line to determine whether it is straight. This simple but astonishingly sensitive technique works by concentrating the entire line into a small visual angle, allowing you to compare the position of each part of the line to the positions of its neighbors. Tip this page and try it.

This method works for any edge, long or short, and can also be used for determining whether an unpolished surface is flat.

MASS-PRODUCTION

In this book, mass-production is the use of identical techniques to achieve similar results on more than one piece of material. The mitering of the ends of the brass pipes for the pipe triangle was an example of mass-production (similar results on different pieces of material), and the process deserves closer attention here. Use of a routine is indispensable when multiple identical pieces must be produced: Each piece is produced in the same way as all the others, so that the motions used in forming one piece are used in forming all the pieces. Because each separate motion is a skill which can be forgotten, the best strategy for using a skill once it is acquired is to use it continuously until it is no longer needed. You will be surprised how quickly you will forget, for example, the most effective hand postures for filing the angled surfaces at the ends of the pipes. Therefore complete an operation on every pipe before beginning the next operation on any of the pipes, approaching the work in orderly steps:

1) Saw all the pipes.
2) Square all the ends.
3) True the lengths of all the pipes.
4) Miter one end of every pipe. (Do this first to get plenty of practice mitering when the orientation of the planes is not critical.)
5) Miter by eye the other end of each pipe.
6) Adjust the second ends to required accuracy.

By using these steps you will avoid wasting the temporary skills you teach yourself in performing a complex action that is not used every day. In addition, once you have reduced an operation to a routine, you no longer have to think to perform the operation skillfully. Eliminating of thinking from a procedure helps eleminate mistakes.

Often, in the making of difficult multiple pieces such as the mitered brass tubes, the builder will notice that one piece is visibly worse than the others. This is not a rare occurrence, but the most common occurrence, especially if five or more pieces are being made. To avoid having to keep the worst piece, make one or more pieces more than you actually need, and throw away the worst pieces.

AVERAGING

To produce pieces that have identical shapes, you can "average" pieces that are flat and can be stacked together. For example, after using the fold-and-trace technique to obtain a satisfactory outline for the shape of a guitar you can adjust the contours to exactly the same shape by averaging them together. Stack the four wood quarters (top right, top left; bottom right, bottom left) together, and sand the edges off flush with each other.

Guitar boards

*Stack the pieces.
Sand the edges flush.
Shuffle them to make
sure they are identical.*

STENCILS

For transferring a pattern or plan directly onto a piece of material, it is sometimes possible to glue the paper drawing to the surface, or to cut out the drawing and rub a pencil across the edge of the paper to mark the material.

If a piece is to be duplicated many times, so that the pattern must be drawn many times, the piece of paper with the plan drawn on it will wear out. To avoid this, glue the paper plan to a piece of sheet copper, which is very easy to cut, and cut out the copper to precisely the shape you want. In many cases it is even possible to install the sheet copper piece directly into the device you are building to test it. Then use the copper piece as a durable stencil to outline a plan onto as many pieces of material as desired.

Indirect Stencil

A stencil does not have to be used directly. For example Bruce Rule suggests the following procedure for cutting the edge of a wood panel to fit the inside wall of a bus. Place the wood panel beside the contour to be fit, and trace the contour onto the panel by running the point of the compass up the wall while the pencil follows a similar path up the wood panel. Cut out the panel along the traced outline and it will fit flush against the wall.

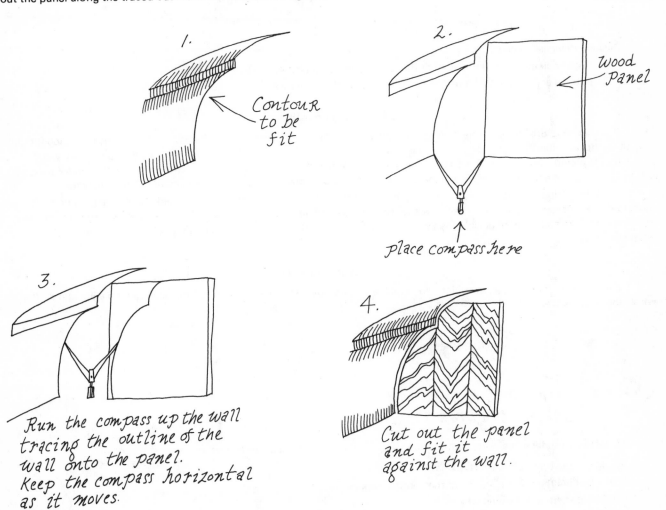

1. Contour to be fit

2. Wood Panel
   place compass here

3. Run the compass up the wall tracing the outline of the wall onto the panel. Keep the compass horizontal as it moves.

4. Cut out the panel and fit it against the wall.

DIES

When material is cut directly around the outline of a durable pattern, the pattern is being used as a die. For example if the material being cut is vinyl plastic sheet, cut it with a sharp knife directly around the copper pattern. This technique helps avoid mistakes in long, repetitive, and therefore tedious jobs. I once used this technique in cutting out rectangular rings for a miniature vinyl bellows.

Another commonly-used die is one for the accurate placement of drill holes. If you need to drill several accurately-placed holes in a number of pieces of material, begin by carefully drilling the holes into one piece of material, preferably a material more durable than that of your finished pieces. Place the holes with the greatest accuracy possible. Then clamp down the die to the pieces you intend to drill, and drill at each place indicated. The placement of each hole will guide you in placing the holes, and the size of each hole will remind you what size bit to use for each hole.

Simultaneous Drilling

Sometimes when extreme similarity in drill-hole placement is required, as when lengths of wood for a table top are to be threaded together on metal rods, the only way to achieve satisfactory drill-hole placement is to tape the lengths of wood together in a stack, and to drill each hole through all of them at once. *All* accurate drilling is done on a drill press.

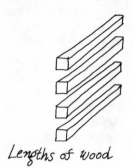

Lengths of wood

tape them together tightly

drill each hole through all four pieces at once

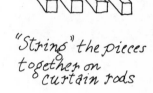

"String" the pieces together on curtain rods

JIGS

Jigs are devices which either:

a) Hold objects under a tool so that the object can be accurately worked, or
b) hold pieces or parts of a device together so that they can be accurately joined.

Drilling on a Jig

If you need to drill, for example, holes into a large number of steel pipes (for winches) the most practical method for getting all the holes in identical positions on the pipes is to build a cradle (a jig) that can receive the pieces of pipe in only one way—and to clamp the cradle on the table of the drill press. When the cradle is properly positioned on the drill press table, you will be able to place each length of pipe in the cradle and drill it correctly without any possibility of making mistakes.

The eliminating of mistakes, especially in jobs where the same operation must be repeated many times, is one of the most important uses of dies and jigs, because any repetitive job will lead to boredom and then to mistakes—and simple, easy jobs will lead to mistakes more quickly than will more complex (and therefore more interesting) jobs. Use dies and jigs whenever possible.

Soldering on a Jig

If you intend, for example, to solder two machine screws down to a brass plate—do the soldering on a jig, and do the whole job in steps.

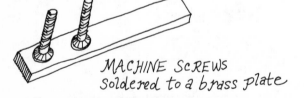

MACHINE SCREWS
Soldered to a brass plate

1) Make a model piece using copper sheet—make the model as near-perfect as possible.
2) Make the brass plates in steps.
   a) Outline the brass plates from the copper original.
   b) Cut them out the long way.
   c) Cut them to length by cutting off the ends.
   d) Trim off all flashings.
   e) Sand a clean spot on each piece at the approximate places where the bolts will be soldered.
   f) Line up the brass pieces on a sheet of asbestos.
   g) Apply acid flux and two chips of solder to each piece.
   h) Go down the row with the blowtorch, tinning each spot where a bolt will be soldered.
3) Trim off any flashing from each bolt to be used, then tin the head of each bolt.

Some steps are left out of the above procedure, but the spirit of the technique is clear. The result of the above procedure is that all pieces are finished and ready to be assembled, with no further steps needed. Assemble the pieces by soldering them together in a jig. The jig will be a device that holds the pieces together and positions them accurately for soldering.

Build the jig around the copper sheet model you made at the beginning. The specific design of the jig does not matter; anything that works will do. What matters is that the parts can be placed in the jig, a drop of flux applied between the bolts and the brass plate, and the blowtorch flame applied until the solder flows. When the solder hardens, drop the completed piece in a can of water and assemble the next piece. Using this procedure it would be almost impossible to make a mistake.

The diagrams below illustrate the use of a jig for performing the assembly described above.

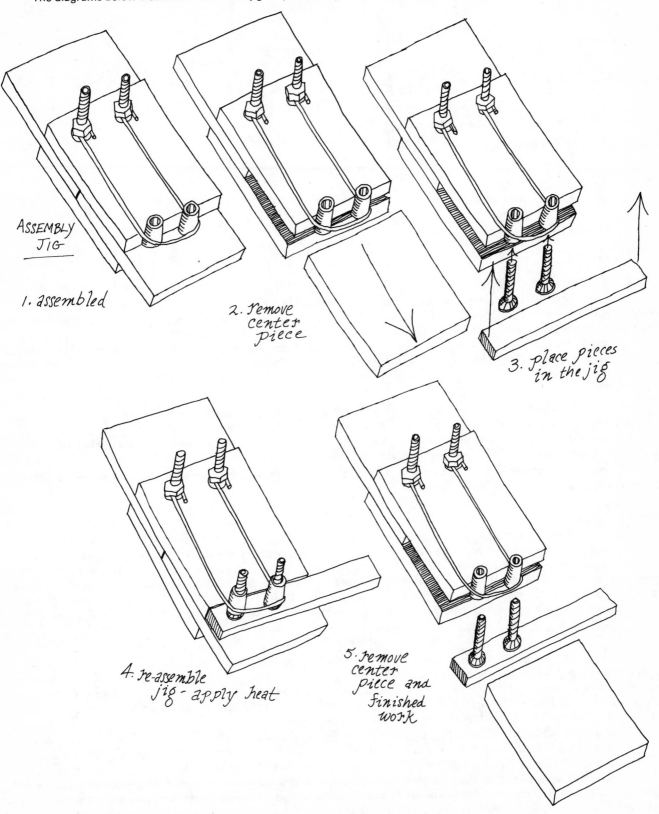

ASSEMBLY
JIG

1. assembled

2. remove center piece

3. place pieces in the jig

4. re-assemble jig - apply heat

5. remove center piece and finished work

When the pieces are completed, inspect them for defects by using the same strategy used for determining whether a line is straight: line the pieces up and sight along their features. Because the same features of all the pieces ought to stand in the same position on each piece, if one feature is out of place it will stand out against the rest. Line up the pieces on the sheet of plate glass and inspect them.

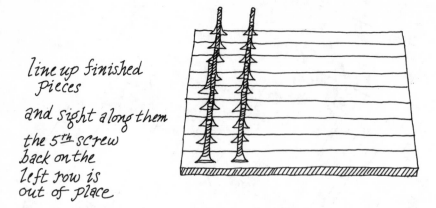

line up finished pieces

and sight along them the 5th screw back on the left row is out of place

The examples given above are only specific cases intended to illustrate general principles of effective mass-production. Because it is impossible to prepare the reader specifically for every job that may come up, I have presented principles with illustrative examples, with the intent that the reader will adapt the principles to his own uses. When I undertake a new project, I cannot know all the specific techniques that will be needed to complete it; I must adapt the principles to the specific case, and I hope that, with a command of principles, the reader will be able to do the same.

Note on Hands

If you work steadily on projects for several weeks you will feel your hands growing stronger, and at the same time more skillful. Strength is helpful to skill because when the hands are strong they do not need to be used at the limit of their strength, and they will have power left over to use for control. A sculptur like Praxiteles who worked marble and wax (wax for bronze casting) must have had hands like steel to control subtle effects in tough materials.

When squeezing tools (especially pliers) use the middle and ring fingers for strength, while relaxing the index and little fingers. Guide the hand with the index finger.

Note on Eyes

Clear vision for close-up objects is one of the gadgeteer's most powerful tools, and as a person grows older his ability to focus his eyes on close-up objects becomes worse and worse. I have noticed the process in myself. I have been able to decrease the distance of nearest focus for my eyes by doing a simple exercise: Find a place with a view of some distant object; then hold up some second object, such as your finger, as close to your eyes as they will focus. Change your focus from the near object to the far and back, repeating the exercise until it becomes easy. It takes about a minute. Practiced for a minute or less every day, the exercise may make the tissues of the ageing eye more supple, decreasing their distance of nearest focus.

How to Invent

There is little new under the sun: inventions are novel recombinations or changes of already existing things. If you are aware of what needs to be invented, and if you try out in your imagination ways to do it, eventually you will come across a solution. There is no magic in the process, and executing a solution satisfactorily often takes a hundred times more effort than the conceiving of it. Try the solution in your visual imagination (and afterward on paper) to see if it works. The best preparation for inventing is a thorough acquaintance with inventions that already exist.

Below is a short list of devices and descriptions of them. Increase your knowledge of devices and materials by looking at the stock in hardware stores, surplus stores, junk yards, garbage, lumberyards, scientific supply houses, and factories. Ask your dentist for his cast-off tools. Figure out how things work (such as those French "cricket" no-refill cigarette lighters). Look in catalogs. Talk to people about their experience with tools, materials, and processes. Notice interesting new curiosities, and talk about them. The best way to invent is to be deeply involved in some project. You will almost automatically think of new ways to do things—or of new uses for old things—or of new things to do. This holds true in anything you do: Combine and recombine.

DEVICES

Set Screw

This clever little device, most commonly used for fastening the control knobs of radios in place, is one of the gadgeteer's most useful tricks for making objects secure, while leaving them detachable and adjustable.

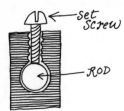

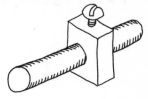

The set screw clamps the rod into the hole in the block, so that any device attached to the block is held rigidly but can be released by loosening the screw.

Toothed Wheel

Car, bicycle, printing press, motorcycle, can opener, and clock all run on toothed wheels. Toothed wheels have two basic features:

1) The teeth of one wheel mesh with the teeth of the next, so that if one of the wheels turns, the other *has* to turn.

2) If two meshed, toothed wheels have different numbers of teeth, the larger wheel will turn more slowly (in rpm's) than the smaller. If the axles of the two wheels are the same diameter, the force on the axle of the larger wheel will be greater than the force on the axle of the smaller wheel. See the illustration.

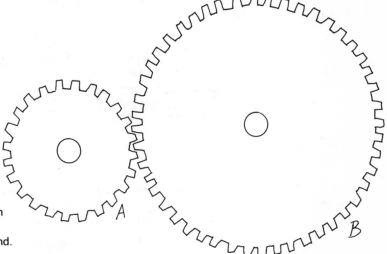

If wheel A turns clockwise, wheel B will turn counter-clockwise. Wheel B has twice as many teeth as wheel A, so for every revolution of B, A will perform two revolutions. If the force on the axle of B is one pound, the force on the axle of A will be one-half pound.

Sprocket Chain

The relationships that hold between toothed wheels meshed together also hold for toothed wheels meshed by a chain, except that when the wheels mesh by a chain, they both turn in the same direction.

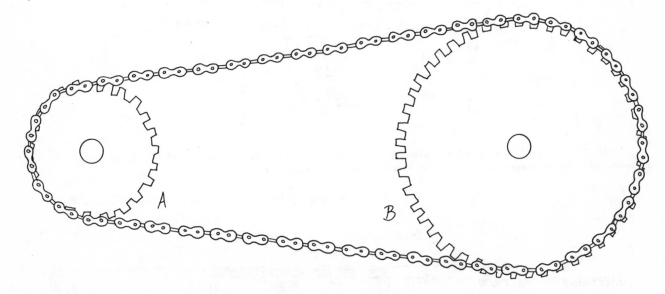

Rack and Pinion

The rack and pinion is the equivalent of two meshed, toothed gears, with one of the gears straightened out. Usually the round gear (the pinion) is turned by a knob or wheel, causing the rack to move back and forth (i.e., the rack and pinion converts circular motion to linear motion). The focus of many microscopes and instruments is a rack and pinion in a suitable sliding mount. If you use a rack and pinion, you will need to make or buy a pivot for the pinion rod, and a slide for the rack.

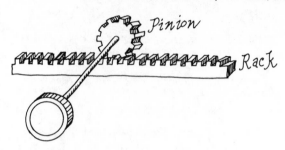

Shim

For producing subtle adjustments in the position of objects which are bolted down, slide a thin sheet of material (e.g., metal foil) between the pieces bolted together. For example, in the rack and pinion, use shims to adjust the height of the rack to hold it against the pinion.

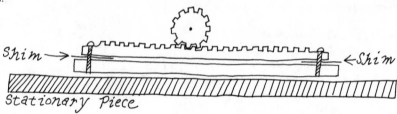

Clutch

A clutch is a linkage that connects a motor to the device that the motor is intended to turn. The clutch can be engaged or disengaged at the operator's will, allowing him to start and stop the machinery without stopping the engine. A clutch used for this purpose commonly is made from two heat-resistant disks which face each other.

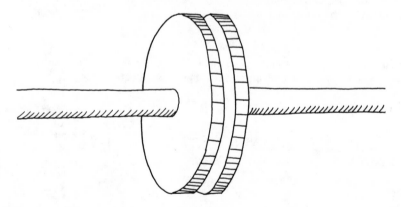

Latch

A latch is a moveable peg that fits in a hole, temporarily holding a pivoted arm (e.g., a door) in place. Some latches have a sloping side, and are loaded with a spring, so that they can be pushed shut.

Electromagnet

An electromagnet is a piece of soft iron which cannot be permanently magnetized, and in which a temporary magnetism is induced by passing current through an electric coil wrapped around it.

Electromagnets can be used for picking up magnetizable objects and dropping them at will. The electromagnet also forms the heart of the solenoid and the electric motor.

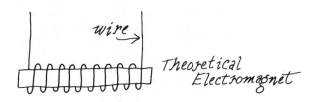

Siphon

A siphon is a vertical or sloping liquid-filled tube having its upper end immersed in a vessel of liquid. As long as one end of the tube is in the liquid and the other end of the tube is below the level of the liquid surface, the siphon will draw liquid out of the vessel, as shown in the illustration. If both ends of the siphon are immersed in vessels of liquid, the liquid levels in the two vessels will reach equilibrium.

Use the siphon (a hose) to empty a swimming pool or a vessel that is too full to touch.

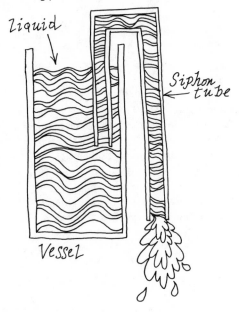

Hydraulic Press

The hydraulic press consists of two pistons connected to the same fluid-filled container. Two water-filled syringes connected by a water-filled plastic tube will do as an example.

If the plunger of one syringe is pushed in, water pressure will push the plunger of the other syringe out, so that with a long tube the hydraulic press can be used for long-distance transmittance of motion.

Notice that one of the syringes is smaller than the other so that the volume of water in it is smaller than the volume of water in the larger syringe. If the small syringe is pushed in until it is empty, this will push out on the large syringe for only a relatively short distance. This motion over a large distance (in the small syringe) inducing motion over a relatively short distance (in the large syringe) gives a kind of leverage; and if the leverage is great enough (i.e., if the small syringe is very small and the large syringe is very large) it is not too difficult to obtain 20,000 psi (pounds per square inch of pressure) from a hand-operated hydraulic press.

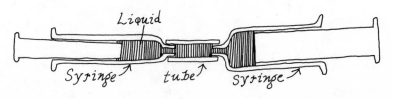

STILL

A still is a container for separating a liquid from a solid, or from another liquid of different boiling temperature. Any container that has a warmer spot and a cooler spot will act as a still: The heat at the warmer spot will cause liquid to evaporate from there faster than it evaporates from the cooler spot, so that the vapor will condense at the cooler spot. If the temperature of a liquid mixture in a still is held at the boiling temperature of the lowest-boiling liquid in the mixture, this liquid will boil away rapidly, while the other(s) evaporate relatively slowly. The low-boiling liquid can then be collected at a cool spot in the still, and in a relatively purified form.

If a little water gets into your wrist watch, the warmer spot next to your wrist and the cooler spot at the crystal will form a still that will keep the water condensed on the crystal and away from the gears until you can get the watch to a watchmaker for repairs.

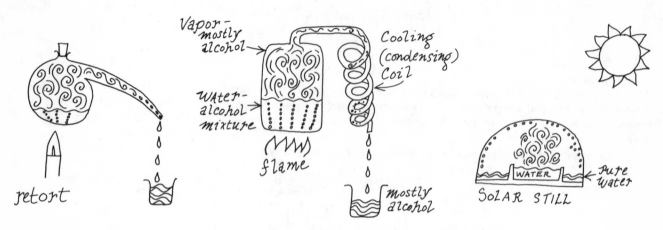

retort

Vapor - mostly alcohol

Water - alcohol mixture

flame

Cooling (condensing) Coil

mostly alcohol

SOLAR STILL

WATER

pure water

STROBE

A strobe is a device which gives intermittent views of objects in motion. A strobe cam be either a flashing light which gives intermittent "seeing" in a dark place, or it can be a shutter which opens and closes repetitively to give intermittent glimpses of an object. For example, a strobe attached to a camera will "stop" on film the motion of a pole vaulter, so that his precise position at different moments during his jump can be studied.

A strobe which opens and closes at regular intervals can be used for studying a repetitive event, such as a wheel turning or a pulsar pulsing. If the strobe opens and closes with the same period as the rotation of the wheel, the views of the wheel will all show it in the same position, and the wheel will appear to stop or stand still. If the strobe opens and closes with a period slightly faster or slower than the wheel, the wheel will appear to turn, respectively, backward or forward, but slowly. In this way the strobe allows us to observe details of structure and motion in objects that are moving so rapidly that they could not easily be observed by any other means. By knowing the period of the strobe one can time repetitive events.

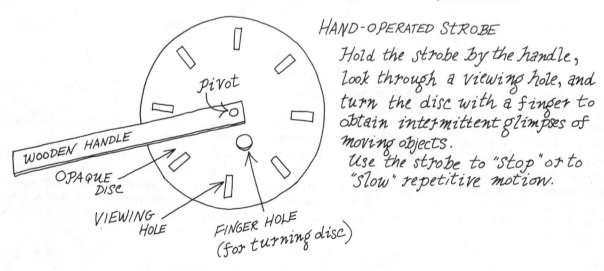

Pivot

WOODEN HANDLE

OPAQUE DISC

VIEWING HOLE

FINGER HOLE (for turning disc)

HAND-OPERATED STROBE

Hold the strobe by the handle, look through a viewing hole, and turn the disc with a finger to obtain intermittent glimpses of moving objects.

Use the strobe to "stop" or to "slow" repetitive motion.

CONCLUSION

The Sensuous Gadgeteer has been directed at your imagination in the hope that, when you know what is already known, you will be able to think of new things (that you would never have been able to think of otherwise) by recombining processes and extending materials to satisfy each new demand you make of them. If the presentation is out of order in some respects (e.g., the information about soldering is presented in widely separated parts of the book) hope that a more important order has been preserved by keeping the instructions for projects intact and coherent. The index organizes the subject matter into categories. When I undertake any project I do not have a command of the procedures that will be required for completing it; I have to invent them as I go along. Often the knowledge of a procedure is more difficult to come by than the skill to put it into practice. For example once, when I was trying to carve plastic models of the bonelets that control the wings of bumblebees in flight, I sat for four hours trying to figure out how to do it. After realizing that the technique is to envision the completed object suspended inside the block of material I was able to complete the carving in less than an hour. The technique is an ancient one but I didn't know about it at the time and had to rediscover it.

I recommend the following method for devising techniques to execute your plans in materials. Envision in your mind's eye the completed object that you want. If the object is too complex for that, envision some manageable portion of it and, also in your mind's eye, test it to see if it will function: if you have designed a machine, set it in motion to see if it works; if you have designed a sculpture, follow the eye of the beholder to see if it will travel to the right places. In other words use your imagination to give yourself the advantage of having a completed prototype in front of you without the work and expense of having to build it. If the design doesn't work, change it in your mind's eye and test it again there. When you think you have what you want, draw a picture of what is in your mind's eye, and examine the picture.

After you have the design you want, find materials that can carry it through. Use your imagination, in the way described here, in order to force the materials to fit the design. Actually manipulate the materials in your mind, shaping them and assembling them and going through every motion, and you will notice even the subtlest aspects of technique that you will need. You will catch impossible designs and processes before attempting them, and will be able to substitute better ones. Cultivate visual imagination in three dimensions.

The use of the hands, eyes, and imagination is a legitimately sensuous experience which engenders an attitude of mind and a wisdom all its own. If I have been able to share these with the reader, then *The Sensuous Gadgeteer* is a success.

ABOUT THE AUTHOR

A second-generation gadgeteer whose father holds numerous patents, Bill Abler has made two reflex cameras, a device for dissecting micro-organisms, three working models of the human vocal tract, and works of art and scientific apparatus of various kinds. After working in several factories and a sculpture studio he obtained a Ph.D. degree in linguistics from the University of Pennsylvania, and is now a postdoctoral fellow at Stanford University doing research into the organization of language in the brain and the origins of language. Plans for the future include design and construction of an improved bicycle seat, and the human-muscle-powered flying machine.

BIBLIOGRAPHY

PART ONE: gadgeteers and gadgeteering in Western history, thinking, and culture.

The Works of Archimedes
with the method of Archimedes
edited by T. L. Heath
clxxxvi+377pp.
#60009-2 $3.50
Dover Publications, Inc.
180 Varick Street
New York, N.Y. 10014

Contains a biography of Archimedes, the greatest mathematician of antiquity, father of the art of engineering, and a lifelong gadgeteer.

Autobiography of Benvenuto Cellini
by Benvenuto Cellini
translated by John A. Symonds
Doubleday, 1960 $1.25

Sculptor, goldsmith, homicide, and one of the makers of the Italian Renaissance. The care, time and love he devoted to his work ought to inspire every artistically-minded gadgeteer.

The Ancient Engineers
L. Sprague deCamp
M.I.T. Press, 1970

Mathematics for the Millions
Lancelot Hogben
Pocket Books, N.Y.
697pp., 95¢

Hogben's book, which shows the role of mathematics in Western thought and history, was the inspiration for *The Sensuous Gadgeteer,* includes arithmetic, plane and solid geometry, trigonometry, algebra, calculus, and statistics.

These articles are from *Scientific American*, a monthly magazine that every scientifically-minded gadgeteer will enjoy. All articles are short and clear. No extensive knowledge of science is needed for reading *Scientific American*, but if you read it you will soon acquire an extensive knowledge of science. The articles listed here deal directly with gadgeteers and gadgeteering concepts. Look up back issues in your local college library or other large library.

"Galileo"
I. Bernard Cohen
August, 1949
p.40

This Renaissance gadgeteer built the first astronomical telescope and discovered the motion of the earth around the sun. The Catholic Church imprisoned him for his findings.

"D'Arcy Thompson"
John Tyler Bonner
August, 1952
p.60

Thompson was the author of *On Growth and Form.*

"The Shape of Things"
Cyril Stanley Smith
January, 1954
p.58

"The Origins of the Lathe"
Robert S. Woodbury
April, 1963
p.132

"Leibnitz"
Frederick C. Kreiling
May, 1968
p.94

Mathematician, historian, philosopher, gadgeteer, ambassador. I acquired the word "gadgeteer" from Kreiling's article.

"Polishing"
Ernest Rabinowicz
June, 1968
p.91

"Leonardo on Bearings and Gears"
Ladislao Reti
February, 1971
p.100

Although Reti claims that Leonardo was no gadgeteer he is the patron saint of every artist, engineer and inventor.

"Bicycle Technology"
S. S. Wilson
March, 1973
p.81

Every detail of what Wilson would agree is the world's most humane gadget was a hard-won invention with vast consequences in industry and in man's concept of distance, speed, and transportation.

One of the regular departments of *Scientific American* is called "The Amateur Scientist," and it describes projects that the scientifically-minded gadgeteer can do at home. For subscriptions write to:

Scientific American
P.O. Box 5919
New York, N.Y. 10017

published monthly: $1.00 at the newstand
subscriptions:
U.S.A.: 1 year $10 /2 years $18 /3 years $25
all other countries:
1 year $12.50 /2 years $23 /3 years $32

PART TWO: a comprehensive but definitely not complete list of books which contain specific information about various gadgeteering skills.

The Critical Path Method
A.T. Armstrong-Wright
Longman Group, Ltd., London, 1969
from Humanities Press, Inc.
303 Park Ave. South
New York, N.Y. 10010
113pp.
also from Whole Earth Truck Store
  (see below)

The most theoretical book on this list. When working on a manifold project in which two aspects of the project could be worked on simultaneously without conflicting, save time by working on them simultaneously. It was the critical path method that launched the US atomic submarines ahead of schedule.

Creative Casting
Sharr Choate
Crown Publishers, Inc.
New York, 1966
196pp., bibliography
$7.95

Basic Drawing
Raphael Ellender
Doubleday 1964
127pp., $2.95

Transforming curved surfaces into complexes of plane surfaces so that they can be drawn: perspective.

Modelling and Sculpture
Edouard Lantieri
Dover, N.Y., 1965
3 volumes, $2.75 each

Use of molds, armatures, use of clay: planning a piece.

Direct Metal Sculpture
Dona Moilach and Donald Seiden
Crown Publishers Inc., N.Y., 1966
illustrated, index, glossary,
195pp., $7.95

Expensive but detailed treatment of techniques for working directly with metal. Applicability of techniques is not confined to sculpture.

Woodcarving
Walter Sack
Van Nostrand, Reinhold
New York, 1973
96pp., $2.95

How to deal with the wood grain: advice on tools, projects.

Cutting and Setting Stones
Herbert Scarfe
Watson-Guptill Publications,
New York, 1972
96pp., illustrated, bibliography
$8.95

Another expensive but complete book. Tells everything you want to know except how to make your own equipment when you can't buy it.

Designing and Making Handwrought Jewelry
Joseph E. Shoenfelt
McGraw-Hill paperbacks,
New York, 1960
158pp., $1.95

Sources of supply, lists of tools, bibliography, appendices. One of the best books, it deals mostly with metals, and the techniques are applicable outside the province of jewelry.

*The Scientific American Book of Projects
  For The Amateur Scientist*
C.L. Stong, illustrated by C.L. Stong
Simon and Schuster, 1970
584pp., $3.95

Incomparable for the scientifically-minded gadgeteer who wants to get started on projects but isn't sure where to begin.

PART THREE: catalogs.

Brookstone Company
Peterborough,
New Hampshire 03458

One of the best offerings of tools I have seen. Brookstone does not seek national attention, and too many requests for their free catalog could cost them more than they can afford. If you send for their catalog, buy something from it.

Edmund Scientific Co.
300 Edscorp Bldg.,
Barrington, N.J. 08007

Optics, army surplus, and space age novelties.

Greiger's, Inc.
900 S. Arroyo Pkwy.,
Pasadena,
California 91109

Rockhounding, gem cutting, lapidary and jewelry, books on centrifugal casting, casting equipment. As closely as I have been able to determine this catalog is free for the asking within the continental United States.

National Camera
2000 West Union Ave.,
Dept. JAC
Engelwood,
Colorado 80110

Another outstanding offering of hand tools and technical tools.

The Last Whole Earth Catalog
Portola Institute

The best catalog there ever was. Get it and read it.

Some of their items are still available from
Whole Earth Truck Store
558 Santa Cruz Ave.
Menlo Park,
California 94025

INDEX

Abrasives, 6, 28
Absolute, 53
Accuracy, 18, 90
Adhesives, glues, 64
Aluminum, 45
Al_2O_3, 6, 28, 31
Angles, 95
Anvil, 12, 47
Armatures, 88
Averaging, 100

Back saw, 24
Ball peen hammer, 11, 27, 53
Band saw, 24
Bees' wax, 77
Bolt cutter, 25
Borrowing, 4
Brackets, hinges, 98
Brass, 56, 57, 75, 95
Bronze, 56, 72
Bunsen burner, 55, 56

Carborundum, 13, 30, 32, 41
Carving, 10, 60
Casting, 46,61,62,63,73-89
C-clamp, 16
Cedar, 9
Center punch, 15
Centrifugal casting, 82-84
Chisels, 12, 13
Chromic oxide, 29, 32
Claw hammer, 5
Clay, 78-82
Clutch, 106
Comparison, 90
Completion, level of, 10
Coping saw, 23, 37
Copper, 47, 48, 53, 54
Copper alloys, 56 see also brass, bronze
Copper sheet, 48
Corrugation, 48, 49
Cradle, 102
Creases in foil, 46
Crosscut saw, 21-23
Cut-off wheel, 41, 42

Daylight test, 18, 60, 72
Devices, list of, 105-107
Diamond, 42, 43
Dies, 20, 101
Direct measure, 93, 94
Direct molds, 88, 89
Domes, 49, 50
Drawings, 2-4
Drills and bits, 14,15,48,58,59,102
Drill press, 16, 102

Ebony, 14
Electricity, 16
Electromagnet, 107
Emery, 29
Enamel, 53-56
Epoxy, 65, 89
Etching glass, 47
Excellence, 1
Eyes, note on, 104

Fiber reinforcing (fiberglass), 90
Files, 17,18,27,45,90,94
Fingernail, blood blister under, 5
Flat, 30, 94
Flux, 51, 53, 70

Garnet, 29
Gems, 31-33, 52
Glass cutter, 42
Glass grinding, 30-33
Glueing, 59, 60, 63-65
Gouge, 12, 13
Grain, wood, 10
Grinder, 13, 33, 34
Grinding wheel, 33, 34

Hack saw, 11, 58
Hammer, see ball peen -, claw -
Hammer head, replacing of, 12
Hands, note on, 104
Hardwood, 9, 10
Head model, 77-82
Heat conduction,44, 45, 59,61,66,72,108
Heat sink, 66
Hinges, 13, 93, 94, 98
Hollow grinding, 8
Hydraulic press, 107
Hydrofluoric acid (HF), 47

Impact wrench, 34
Indirect stencil, 101
Invent, how to, 104
Iron, 57
Irregular cuts, 17, 24

Jigs, 102, 103
Jig saw, 24

Kerf saw, 25
Knives, 6-8
Knives, making, 34-41

Latch, 106
Latex, 85
Lead, 45-47
Leather, 39, 40
Light conduction, 61
Lignum vitae, 10
Liner molds, 89
Lost wax casting, 82

Mahogany, 10
Malleability, 43, 44
Mallets, 14
Maple, 9
Mass production, 100
Materials, 28
Measurement and comparison, 90-92
Metals, 43-48
Metal fatigue, 44
Metal sheet, see sheet metal
Micrometer, 91
Mitering, 24, 95
Molds and casting, 73-89
Multiple duplicates, 85-88, 98
Mylar, 64

Nails, 5
Nuts and bolts, 20, 21

Oak, 9

Paper,folding to obtain symmetric pattern,99
Parallel, 93, 95
Pine, 9
Pipe, bending, 27
Plane, 14
Plans, 2
Plaster, 79-82
Plasticene, 82
Plastics, 57-60
Plate glass, 94
Plexiglas, 57-60
Pliers and vise grips, 25-27
Plywood, 9
Polishing,11,29,31,32,51,53,63,82
Polyester, 89, 90
Polyethylene, 64
Power drill, 16
Pressure casting of plexiglas, 62

Quartz, 29, 30

Rack and pinion, 106
Rasps, 17, 18
Reamer, 17
Ring, copper, 50-53
Rip saw, 22, 23
Rivets, 11, 12
Rosewood, 9

Rouge, jeweler's, 29
Rubber, 65
Ruler, 90, 91

Sabre saw, 25
Safety,4,10,15,18,30,33,42,46,47,57,58,61,87
Sand, 29, 30
Sand casting, 73-76
Sandpaper, 29
Sapphire, see Al_2O_3
Saws, see back -, band -, coping -, crosscut -,
     hack -, jig -, kerf -, rip -, sabre -, table -,
     tungsten carbide wire -
Saws, wood, 21-25
Scraper, wood, 43
Screwdrivers and screws,19,20,34,58,59,102,105
Seating metal in plastic, 58, 59
Set screw, 105
Sharpening, 6-8
Sharpening chisels and gouges, 13
Sharpening drill bits, 16
Sheet metal, 18,25,48,102,103
Sheet metal surfaces, 69
Shim, 80, 81, 106
Silicon carbide, 30
Silicone rubber, 47, 65, 85
Silver, gold, see copper
Silver solder, 27, 51, 70-73
Siphon, 107
Slurries, 89, 90
Softwood, 9
Soldering,26,27,50,52,66-73,97,102,103
Soldering, electrical, 66-68
Soldering, structural, 68-70
Solder, hidden, 52, 70, 71, 97
Sprocket chain, 105
Sprue, 82
Square hole, 24,37
Stained glass, 47
Steel, 57
Stencils, 101
Still, 108
Stopcock, 55
Straightness, 100
Strobe, 108
Styrene, 61
Symmetry about a line, 99

Teak, 9, 10
Teflon, 64
Temper, 13, 14, 34, 41
Thin partition mold, 80, 81
Tungsten carbide, 42
Tin oxide, 29
Tin snips, 25
Tools, general introduction, 4
Toothed wheel, 105
Torches,burners,lamps,51,54-56,59,69,70,97,103
Tropical woods, 9, 10
Tungsten carbide, 11
Tungsten carbide wire saw, 11

Vernier caliper, 91
Vinyl, 63
Vise, 27, 43, 48, 51
Vise grips, 27

Walnut, 9
Wax, 47, 77, 78, 82-84
Wax iron, 47, 78
Weight, 45
Welding plastics, 60,-wax, 78
Wheel dresser, 33
Wire bending, 25, 26
Wire cutting, 25
Wire joining, 26, 27, 67, 68
Wood and woods, 8, 11
Wood saws, 21-25
Wood surfaces, finishing, 10, 11
Wrenches, 20,21

Notes

Notes

Notes

Notes